AATMA NIRBHAR BHARAT (SELF-RELIANT INDIA)

Challenges and Opportunities

AATMA NIRBHAR BHARAT
(SELF-RELIANT INDIA)
Challenges and Opportunities

Brigadier (Dr.) Rajeev Bhutani

Foreword by

Lieutenant General Vinod Bhatia, PVSM, AVSM, SM
Former DGMO, Director, CENJOWS

CENTRE FOR JOINT WARFARE STUDIES (CENJOWS)

PENTAGON PRESS LLP

AATMA NIRBHAR BHARAT (SELF-RELIANT INDIA)
Challenges and Opportunities

Brigadier (Dr.) Rajeev Bhutani
E-mail: rajeev.deepa19@gmail.com

ISBN 978-93-90095-13-1

First Published in 2020

Published by
PENTAGON PRESS LLP
206, Peacock Lane, Shahpur Jat,
New Delhi-110049
Phones: 011-64706243, 26491568
Telefax: 011-26490600
email: rajan@pentagonpress.in
website: www.pentagonpress.in

Cover conceptualized by Dr.-Ing. Akanksha Bhutani
Printed at Aegean Offset Printers, Greater Noida, U.P.

Dedicated to

The Gallant Soldiers of Indian Army who made the Supreme Sacrifice in the Galwan Valley while defending the national frontiers.

CONTENTS

PART II
IMPACT OF CORONAVIRUS AND CHALLENGES AND OPPORTUNITIES FOR INDIA

Foreword

It is indeed an honour to be asked by Brigadier (Dr.) Rajeev Bhutani (Retd) to write the Foreword for his third book, *Aatma Nirbhar Bharat (Self-Reliant India): Challenges & Opportunities*. Brigadier Rajeev Bhutani is a well-regarded and respected researcher and author, known for his excellent research work. The book, result of an extensive and detailed research could not have come at a better time, as it aligns with India's focused approach for self-reliance, an imperative for India to achieve its national aim of ' Transforming to a Modern, Prosperous and Secure nation' ensuring the well-being of 1.35 billion Indians. The timing is even more relevant as the book analyses India's growing global leadership role in an emerging 'Post-COVID-19 World Order'.

COVID-19 has undoubtedly been the biggest disruptor in centuries. The pandemic caused by the made in China 'Corona Virus' has changed the behaviour of individuals, families, society, people, regions and nations. The pandemic has impacted all walks of life, in an interconnected world. The world has changed, taking a major economic hit, with millions out of work. While the world still battles the Pandemic not so successfully, seeking an elusive vaccine, it is time to look at an insecure and uncertain future, and more importantly a self-reliant India's role, opportunities and challenges in a post pandemic world. The author details the emerging geopolitical environment starting with the end of World War II, the Sino-Soviet split and the Sino-US rapprochement, China's peaceful rise, Mao's

Three Worlds, Deng's Three Goals for China's Great Power Status, Hu Jintao's concept of a "Harmonious World", to Xi Jinping's "New Era" precede Obama's Pivot to Asia' policy shift. The Sino-Indian equation is analyzed very well, specially so the present situation along the Line of Actual control, China's aggressive behaviour and arrogance and more importantly India's response.

An Expansionist China seeks a Bi-Polar world challenging the US as the sole superpower. The arrogance and aggressive behaviour of China are a constant threat to peace in the world and the region. The COVID-19 or the made in China Corona Virus has impacted the emerging world order. Chinese forces are not only demonstrating an unprecedented aggressiveness along the India-China LAC, but also in the South China Sea, Taiwan, Korea, East China Sea, Vietnam, Philippines, Indonesia, and Malaysia. India will need to discern China's intent and the larger strategic signals emanating from Beijing, in the geopolitical domain.

In the emerging world order the author argues on the dynamic balance of economic alliances between the West and the East, emergence of a China-centric world economic order vis-à-vis a weakening of China's economic footprint post COVID-19. In the contextual framework of a likely world order the author then analyses the many challenges and opportunities for India, in the economic, diplomatic and security and technological domains. The author rightly adds a sixth 'I' Implementation, to the five 'I's—Intent, Inclusion, Investment, Infrastructure and Innovation as the mantra for a self-reliant India or *Aatma Nirbhar Bharat* as envisioned by Prime Minister Modi.

The book is well laid out and is easy to read and comprehend. It is so very apt that the author has dedicated the book to Colonel Santosh Babu and the 19 gallant soldiers who made the supreme sacrifice defending the territorial integrity of the nation, in the highest traditions of the Indian armed forces.

Lt Gen Vinod Bhatia, PVSM, AVSM, SM (Retd)
Former DGMO, Director CENJOWS

Preface

When the nationwide lockdown was announced on March 24, 2020, by Prime Minister Narendra Modi to control the spread of coronavirus in India, it appeared as if the lives of people would come to a standstill. But the human mind is very flexible, when faced with difficulties; it can accept challenges and create opportunities to overcome the same. Indian people stood up to the challenge and gathered the momentum to keep the national machinery running. It is the process of 'digitization', which was the focus in PM Modi's first tenure that came to the rescue of people, whether it was working from home or delivery of daily essentials.

At the Centre for Joint Warfare Studies (CENJOWS), we have to think ahead so that solutions for the futuristic emerging situations can be offered. Immediately with the onset of lockdown, Lieutenant General Vinod Bhatia, PVSM, AVSM, SM (Retd), Director CENJOWS brought everyone on the virtual platform and organized the whole functioning of the think-tank in digital mode. The number of articles, which started appearing on the CENJOWS website, were much greater in number than before the lockdown period and the trend continues.

Visualizing that post-COVID-19 world will be something different, with nations seeking new alignments or strategic partnerships, the Director tasked me to work on "Challenges and Opportunities for India in the post-COVID-19 New Emerging World Order". A very challenging subject because the novel coronavirus having emerged from the central city of Wuhan, China, in December 2019, spread like wildfire and had the whole world in its deadly grip in the form of a pandemic in less than three months. While the world leaders are still struggling to contain the pandemic, the global economy took a downturn, involving every country of the world. Prediction of a Post-COVID-19 new emerging world order with accuracy, may go awfully wrong because much will depend upon how the major powers of the world emerge after the pandemic is over. At best, one can guesstimate various economic scenarios or options available and how best the national interests of India can be maintained in any of the scenarios.

I completed my work based on the above thought process in around 20,000 words by May 17, and forwarded it to the Director for his perusal. Not only did he appreciate my effort but encouraged me to write a comprehensive book. When I embarked upon writing the book, events took a rapid turn—Prime Minister Modi launched the "Aatma Nirbhar Bharat Abhiyan" or "Self-Reliant India Mission" with the release of Rs 20 lakh crore economic package on 12 May and on the other hand China commenced an aggressive build up of its troops all along the Line of Actual Control (LAC) against India, culminating in to a premeditated and surreptitious assault by Chinese soldiers. They used clubs studded with barbed wire, and iron rods on our unsuspecting soldiers, who had gone to check on the agreed-upon disengagement in the Galwan Valley, Eastern Ladakh, on the evening of June 15. Twenty Indian soldiers including Colonel Santosh Babu, the Commanding Officer gave a befitting reply to the PLA soldiers reportedly causing some 43 fatalities, and that too without resorting to use of their personal arms, before making supreme sacrifice at the altar of the nation. Forty-five years of peace maintained between the two nations since 1975 was shattered by this dastardly act of Chinese soldiers. The much sought after disengagement and de-escalation between the two countries is hanging in balance with troops readying themselves for a long haul. Simultaneously, China commenced aggressive naval manoeuvres in South China Sea and East China Sea threatening small nations of Southeast Asia and Japan, compelling the United States to deploy its three nuclear-powered carriers there. With the onslaught of COVID-19 pandemic unrelenting, the country touched a million infections on July 16, posted its second million in exactly 21 days thereafter on 7 August and crossed four million on 04 September—taking in overall 187 days to reach this figure. On the economic front, earlier, the International Monetary Fund had given a rosy estimate of 1.9 percent economic growth for India in 2020-21 but now it expects the country's economy to shrink by 4.5 percent in the same period.

Taking into account the above developments, I have carried out my analysis in two parts: *Geopolitical overview to evolve India's response to external belligerent environment*; and *Emergence of 'Aatma Nirbhar Bharat' or 'Self-Reliant India'* to assert India's role in the fields of economy, public health and diplomacy, making true Prime Minister Modi's motto of *'Vocal for Local to make it Global'*.

With my biology background and being a postgraduate in Organic Chemistry, I could easily comprehend the biological composition of coronavirus as also about the development of vaccines and pharmaceuticals. During the lockdown as also afterwards, electronic media was of great help, keeping one updated on everything related to the COVID-19 pandemic—its impact on public health, economy and society. I am extremely thankful to 'Hindustan Times', particularly its expert columnists, viz. R Sukumar, Sanchita Sharma, Jamie Mullick, Saubhadra Chatterji, Rhythma Kaul, Rajeev Jayaswal and Roshan Kishore for providing well-researched and updated knowledge in their columns. I am grateful to Mr. Mukesh Kumar Jha, the librarian with the Institute for Defence Studies and Analyses (IDSA), New Delhi, who has been extremely prompt and resourceful in arranging and providing me the desired reference material in no time. I am very thankful to Colonel Sanjiv Shukla, Secretary CENJOWS, for providing his valuable support in my endeavour.

Consequent to the aggressive troops build up by China on the LAC, Lt Gen Vinod Bhatia, being the former DGMO, became extremely busy in TV discussions, debates and webinars with people seeking his expert opinion. However, being a workaholic and voracious reader, he could find time to go through my book and commended me for my work—my heartfelt gratitude to him.

My daughters Dr.-Ing. Akanksha (Electronics engineer and presently Postdoctoral Research Associate in Germany) and Srishti (Civil Engineer and presently Graduate Research Assistant in the United States) are the invaluable sources of my strength as they inspire me to keep writing and provide value addition to my work.

My wife Deepa has been a constant source of support in all my professional and academic endeavours and it is because of her encouragement, and that too during these tough times with no help available in the house, I could take up the challenge of writing my third book and complete it in time, to be of crucial importance. Most importantly, it is the youngest member of our family 'Gullu' who deserves the credit for giving his silent blessings and imbibing patience in me through his aura.

Brigadier (Dr.) Rajeev Bhutani

1

Introduction

"Making India self-reliant is the only way to ensure that the 21st century belongs to India."

—Prime Minister Narendra Modi

When Mr. Narendra Modi took over as Prime Minister in May 2014, he created a vision of building "New India"—with economic prosperity, security and well-being of the countrymen being its primary components. Various policy initiatives and schemes like Digital India, Clean India, Skill India, Start up India, Make in India, etc., were launched to further the main aim. Though confident of achieving the laid down objectives in first five years, these missions had a mixed level of success. Hence, subsequent to BJP's resounding victory in assembly elections in Uttar Pradesh and Uttarakhand in March 2017, Prime Minister Modi resorted to a mid-course correction, when he said that the election results were a foundation for a "New India" and exhorted people to take a pledge to build it by 2022. He said, "If we are successful, no one can stop India from becoming a world power".[1]

Having commenced his second innings with a greater mandate, Prime Minister Modi declared that his government's budget for 2019-20 laid down a road map for nearly doubling the size of the Indian economy to USD 5 trillion in five years by raising per capita income, boosting consumption and increasing productivity.[2] However, the globalized world had something else in store for the mankind. As the world stepped into 2020, the novel coronavirus emerged in the Wuhan City of China and spread to every nook and corner of the world and was a deadly blow not only for the public health systems but also for the economies worldwide. India also could not remain untouched from this world crisis, i.e., the pandemic caused by Novel Coronavirus, named as Coronavirus Disease 2019 (COVID-19).

Currently, 213 countries and territories around the world are fighting a war with an enemy, which is not visible to the naked eyes. As of 9 September, there have been 909,180 fatalities from around 28 million cases of the disease registered globally. The United States, the world's largest economy and also its most powerful country, has been laid low by the pandemic, with around 6.55 million cases and around 195,318 deaths. From 602 positive cases and 12 deaths on 25th March, India has thus far seen 4.49 million cases and reached the death toll of 75,328 on 9 September, making it the third hardest hit nation after the United States and Brazil where 195,318 and 128,653 fatalities respectively have taken place.[3] However, India's case fatality rate (CFR)—the proportion of deaths to the total recorded infections—at 1.7 percent is lower than the global average of 3.2 percent, indicating that the nation has controlled the number of deaths better than other nations with similar or higher caseload.[4]

The world leaders are grappling to contain the virus with no solution in sight as to when the nations will come out of this crisis. For the medical fraternity it is a race against time, with containment the only option before a viable medicine or vaccine is found or invented and made available on a large scale. How far into the future, will this pandemic prolong or will it re-emerge as a second wave or third wave, nobody can predict. In fact, some countries of Europe are stated to be already passing through the second wave of the pandemic. In a short span of hundred days from the time the virus was officially reported by China in December 2019, it had engulfed the whole world—halting industries, bringing flights, trains and public transport to a standstill, closing educational and training institutes and forcing the postponement of sporting events and concerts. Even the Tokyo Summer Olympics have been postponed by a year. Most experts are of the opinion that at this stage it is extremely difficult to exactly estimate the ultimate economic damage likely to be caused by this pandemic.

In end July, the US, France, Italy and Spain reported precipitous contractions for their coronavirus-battered economies, with pandemic wiping out years of growth in a matter of weeks as lockdowns closed shops, factories and restaurants and could mark the beginning of a period of recession. Quarterly data for European countries released on July 31, comes exactly seven months after the world first came to know about the emergence of a mysterious virus in Wuhan. In the April-June quarter, France's economy contracted by 13.8 percent, Spain by 18.5 percent and Italy by 12.4 percent. Germany, Europe's largest economy, reported a 10.1 percent drop in GDP during the April-June period. Europe as a whole saw GDP fall by 12.1 percent in the Eurozone. The effect of COVID-19 on the US economy was even more pronounced than in Europe, as it posted a second-quarter loss of 9.5 percent compared with the same period a year ago. If that trajectory is carried through the entire year, its economy would collapse by nearly a third (32.9 percent).[5] According to IMF, the global economy is expected to contract by around 4.9 percent this year (as against –3 percent of its April 2020 Forecast)[6]. The Indian economists estimated their economy to shrink by 5 percent in 2020-21 but foreign agencies like Fitch have brought it down to 11 percent in FY 2020.

The much awaited GDP data for Indian economy in the first quarter of 2020-21 (April-June) has been declared by the National Statistical Office (NSO) on 31st August. The Indian GDP has declined by a record 23.9 percent in April-June quarter, reflecting the economic cost of the nationwide lockdown imposed from 25 March to 31 May 2020 to fight the spread of Coronavirus. However, Krishnamurthy Subramanian, the chief economic adviser, claimed that "India is experiencing a V-shaped recovery after the unlocks have been announced...and we should expect better performance in subsequent quarters."[7]

However, every elite ranging from journalists to analysts, economists to strategists and academics to policy makers appear to be competing with each other in making projections about the future world order. International and national think tanks, management and analytics firms like Forbes, KPMG, etc., with their professional teams, are churning out material about the emerging 'new world order' with astonishing speed. Everyone agrees that we are on the cusp of a new world order while some disagree by saying that the world will go back to the way it was before, once the pandemic is over. Or again there is old talk about the 'Balance of world power' in which it has to be seen whether the scale will tilt towards China or the United States will recover to reassert its power. In 'A forecast of the post-COVID new world order', V.R. Ferose, Head of SAP Engineering Academy (California), rightly states, "The challenge when it comes to predictions is that if you get it right, you're called a genius, and if you get it wrong, an idiot."[8] Rightly so, making prognosis in international arena is hazardous because behavioural change by a country or an unexpected event can occur with bewildering speed thereby setting the nations on new and altogether different courses.

What sort of new world order will emerge post-COVID-19, is very difficult to predict. Further the transitory period from pre- to post-COVID-19 itself appears to be quite prolonged and difficult times lie ahead. There is an age-old army commando saying, "When the Going gets tough, the Tough gets going." Thus, in spite of unprecedented challenges, the strong national leaders will seek opportunities for their country in the time of adversity. In his address to the nation on May 12, Prime Minister Narendra Modi said, ***"Coronavirus outbreak has provided an opportunity for India to become self-reliant."***[9]

While the whole world was grappling to contain the onslaught of Coronavirus, China came out relatively unscathed from its fury and thought it as an opportunity to assert its hegemony in the Indo-Pacific region. China contemplated that the United States would not physically challenge its military manoeuvres, as being an election year; the US leadership was under stress due to decision dilemma between public health versus economy when the Coronavirus was marching uncontrolled. The United States' allies in Western Europe were also in the grip of the pandemic. Commencing in April, China started bullying the small nations of Southeast Asia in South China Sea through aggressive manoeuvres by its coast guard and naval ships. In May, China sent the aircraft carrier Liaoning and its strike group on its first round-trip mission through the Miyako Strait—between the islands of Okinawa and Miyako as Japan nervously looked on.[10] Simultaneously, China started building up its troops all along the Line of Actual Control against India. In Eastern Ladakh, the disengagement measures were agreed upon between Indian and Chinese military commanders on June 6. However, China shattered the 45-year long peace on the evening of June 15, when its soldiers launched a premeditated and brutal assault, using clubs studded with barbed wire, and iron rods in the Galwan Valley on Colonel Santosh Babu and his patrol who had gone to check on the agreed-upon disengagement. Twenty Indian soldiers, including Colonel Babu made the supreme sacrifice at the altar of the nation. But they gave a befitting reply to the PLA soldiers reportedly causing some 43 fatalities, before laying down their lives and that too without resorting to use of their personal arms. China's treachery has inflamed Indian public opinion, and caused intense anger among Indian policymakers and the country's elite. The nation is in no mood to appease China and Anti-China demonstrations have broken-out in many cities, calling for a boycott of Chinese goods, including mobile phones and clothes.

In this time of geopolitical uncertainty, India is facing complex challenges as seen never before: internally, to maintain public health and control the spread of pandemic as also rejuvenate the economy; and externally to defend her sovereignty and territorial integrity on land and sea both. While against the external foe, India has to be prepared militarily and without sacrificing her national interests, align or partner with friendly countries so that disengagement and de-escalation can be achieved with China. War prevention and war avoidance should be the aim of both countries so that they can achieve prosperity for their people. Internally, India has to optimize her sources for the upkeep of public health and economy both. Delivering his speech from the ramparts of the Red Fort to mark India's 74th Independence Day, Prime Minister Narendra Modi focused on two key issues, Coronavirus and China (though without naming them) being the greatest concerns in the minds of Indian people. He expounded ***"A strong, confident and 'aatma-nirbhar' (self-reliant) India is essential not just for itself, but for the sake of larger global good."***[11]

To determine 'Challenges and Opportunities' for Self-Reliant India, the subject has to be dealt with in two dimensions or levels: external or geopolitical level and internal or socio-economic level. It is intended to tackle the subject, the way an Appreciation is written in the Armed Forces, i.e. first define the problem and then find the best possible solution to it. Interestingly, following the norms of an Appreciation writing, its authors do not have to make predictions because firstly one follows a well-considered approach to produce best possible options on the basis of which an enacting plan is to be formulated, and secondly it can be reviewed after a pre-determined period. Hence, it is proposed to study the subject in two parts that are as follows:

Part I. Geopolitical Overview: To analyze the emerging geopolitical environment and India's Response.

Part II. Impact of Coronavirus and Challenges and Opportunities for India.

- The Novel Coronavirus—Its peculiarity and how does it differ from the previous ones; Cause of the Spread—When, where, why and how did it occur and lead to a pandemic.
- The Multitudinous Effects of the COVID-19 Pandemic—on the economy, society, international environment and so on.
- Emerging New World Order (Post-COVID-19)—likely scenarios.
- Challenges and Opportunities for India.
- Self-Reliant India.

PART I

Geopolitical Overview

2

Emerging Geopolitical Environment

The geopolitical rivalry that started between the two original superpowers, i.e. the United States of America and the Soviet Union from the end of World War II and was most commonly called as the Cold War supposedly ended in 1989–1991 with the collapse of the Soviet empire. Initially, the United States led the capitalist or democratic forces of the Western Europe collectively organized as North Atlantic Treaty Organization (NATO) while the Soviet Union commanded the Eastern Bloc countries and was named Warsaw Pact. However, seeds of the Cold War were sown much earlier with Lenin's seizure of power in Russia in November 1917. Since then began "the protracted war of the communist enterprise for a monopoly of world power".[1] Communist conquest of China in October 1949 provided fillip to their struggle against the Western world. Fortunately for the West, the Sino-Soviet split paved the way for Sino-American rapprochement with the 1972 Nixon visit to China.

Causes of Sino-Soviet Split

Mao Zedong was committed to leaning towards the Soviet Union even before the end of the civil war, albeit for various reasons. The Soviet Union had devoted an enormous amount of its national treasure towards the Chinese economic development, amounting to almost 7 percent of the economy at certain points during the 1950s.[2]

Having grown up in a world where China was weak and suffered humiliation at the hands of foreign powers, Mao and other Chinese Communist Party (CCP) officials were determined to restore China's 'Middle Kingdom' status and centrality in world politics. Under Mao, China followed a social competition strategy based on continuous revolution at home and support for revolutionary movements in the Third World.[3]

In the early 1960s, competition for ideological leadership emerged between Beijing and Moscow. The Soviet Union naturally saw itself as the leader of the movement, as it had the most powerful and longest established socialist regime. The Chinese regarded their revolution as indigenous, and saw the developing world as key to the long-term success of the socialist bloc. The two countries fought this battle in a series of pamphlets and conventions, often through proxies in the Communist world. This struggle helped drive personal tension between the leadership of the two countries. In the case of Mao, this amounted to a claim of communist purity, while Khrushchev developed a reputation for flexibility and practicality. Given the centrality of ideology to the legitimacy of both regimes, the competition took a serious turn. Eventually, Soviet suspicion of China would result in a deterioration of the military and economic relationship, which caused an even greater degree of Chinese hostility. China's relations with the Soviet Union became increasingly conflictual—firstly, Soviet refusal to support China against India in 1962[4] and secondly, culminating in armed clashes in March and August of 1969 along the Ussuri River. With Soviet troops massed along the Chinese border and Soviet officials hinting at a pre-emptive strike against China's nuclear facilities amounted to the last straw.[5] The two states could not agree to coexist as leaders of the same ideological bloc. Ideological affinity could not bridge gulfs between geostrategic interests. Mao had come to view the Soviet Union as the leading threat to China's security, and was therefore receptive to conciliatory signals from US President Richard Nixon and National Security Adviser Henry Kissinger of a Sino-American rapprochement.

Sino-US Rapprochement

Indications for a political thaw between the United States and the People's Republic of China (PRC) started appearing in the late 1960s. It was the congruence of national interests, which brought them closer. While the United States wanted a way out of an escalating Vietnam War, Sino-Soviet tension contributed to the Chinese leadership's desire for a rapprochement with the United States. Nixon established a secret channel to the PRC's leadership through Pakistani President Yahya Khan. Besides, removing restrictions on Americans from travelling to Mainland China by Nixon, both sides resorted to informal "Ping Pong Diplomacy"—allowing their table tennis players to play in each other's country. Henry Kissinger, the National Security Adviser, travelled to Beijing twice during 1971 to prepare the ground for normalization of relations. Shortly after Kissinger's visit to China in October 1971 to draft the so-called Shanghai communiqué in preparation for Nixon's visit in February 1972, the UN General Assembly voted to admit China to the UN as a permanent member of the Security Council and to expel Taiwan[6]—a 'great victory' for Chinese foreign policy and a 'significant enhancement' of the PRC's international status.

Mao's 'Three Worlds'

Without emulating the social and cultural values of the United States and other Western nations, China intended to attain a central role in international politics by other means—through moral superiority and aligning with the Third World. Believably, the 'Three Worlds' theory was Mao's idea, which Deng Xiaoping presented in a 1974 speech before the UN General Assembly, "The United States and the Soviet Union make up the First World. The developing countries in Asia, Africa, Latin America and other regions make up the Third World. The developed countries between the two make up the Second World". He said that the two superpowers were vainly seeking world hegemony. In contrast to the United States and the Soviet Union, which tried to bully and control other states, i.e. developed and developing countries respectively, he emphasized, "China is not a superpower, nor will she ever seek to be one." Deng criticized both the superpowers for exploiting other countries economically, plundering their wealth and grabbing their strategic raw material and resources. He advocated "Self-reliance" that in no way meant "self-seclusion" and rejection of foreign aid. Rather it is considered beneficial and necessary for the development of the national economy that countries should carry on economic and technical exchanges on the basis of respect for state sovereignty, equality and mutual benefit, and the exchange of needed goods to make up for each other's deficiencies.[7] That provided an ideological transition towards the later 'reform and opening' policy of Deng Xiaoping.

Deng's 'Three Goals' for China's Great Power Status

Deng set three goals as China's agenda during the 1980s—anti-hegemony, national unification, and economic development or modernization—and all of these have remained central aims for enhancing China's status. Opposing the US hegemony would restore China's international position, unification is mainly about Taiwan, Tibet and Xinjiang, and success on these issues is closely linked to the cultivation of China's capabilities and status as a great power,[8] and economic development was an important task because 'the role we play in international affairs is determined by the extent of our economic growth'—not the spread of communist revolution or the acquisition of military power.[9] As part of Deng's opening up policy, China offered incentives for foreign investment, allowed more trade, and encouraged students to study overseas—a departure from Mao's policy of self-reliance.

Deng sought to improve China's status through economic development, which entailed cooperation and integration into the global economy. He had hoped to absorb Western science, technology and managerial skills without importing foreign cultures and values. Deng's vision for transformation was 'Socialist construction with Chinese characteristics.' China became more active in international organizations, such as the World Bank and the International Monetary Fund (IMF). Deng followed a different path towards achieving great power status. In the past, states had to possess superior military capabilities to gain admittance to the great power club. Japan, for example, despite its post-war economic growth rate and position as the world's second largest economy, was not considered a great power after 1945.[10] Deng, however, downgraded the importance of military modernization and cut defence spending to allow more investment in domestic development. The 'independent foreign policy' was announced in 1982 at the 12th National Congress of the CCP, when General Secretary Hu Yaobang declared that "in the 33 years since the founding of our People's Republic, we have shown the world by deeds that China never attaches itself to any big power or group of powers, and never yields to pressure from any big power."[11] Instead of forming a united front against the Soviet Union, therefore, China would align with neither superpower.

The strategy of maintaining equidistance between the two superpowers could not, however, be sustained after the disintegration of the Soviet Union. In 1992, a time of domestic economic crisis and international isolation following its handling of the 1989 Tiananmen Square Incident, Deng said, 'we will only become a big political power if we keep a low profile and work hard for some years; we will then have more weight in international affairs.' Later, Deng's thinking on foreign policy evolved into the 'twenty-four character' principle: *'lengjing guancha, wenzhu zhenjiao, chenzhuo yingfu, juebu dangtou, taoguang yanghui, yousui zuowei'* (observe calmly, secure our position, cope with affairs calmly, never seek leadership, hide brightness and cherish obscurity, get some things done), sometimes translated as 'keeping a low profile' (*taoguang yanghui*).[12] This cautious strategy was to become the Chinese foreign policy slogan in the immediate post-Cold War era, but did not rule out China's search for status by other means.

Post-Cold War: Peaceful Rise/Development

Initially, Chinese analysts had assessed that the end of the Cold War would result in a gradual trend towards multipolarity as the United States' power was declining due to domestic economic problems and growing differences with its allies. The United States, therefore, would eventually be challenged by the emerging powers like Russia, Japan, and China. However, China's dilemma was that it was an outsider in relation to the dominant liberal Western powers and it could not compete on its model of socialism. Hence, Chinese leaders showed ingenuity in enhancing China's status by devising concepts like – responsible power, new security concept, peaceful rise, peaceful development, harmonious world and so on.

Responsible Power. Deng's successors abandoned his cautious policy in Asia by advancing China's sovereignty interests in the South China Sea and Taiwan. In February 1995, the Philippine government discovered China-built platforms on Mischief Reef, an islet in the Philippines claim area.[13] From July 1995 until the spring of 1996, China deployed ground, air, and naval forces near Taiwan and conducted military exercises, including the launching of test missiles in the Taiwan Strait, in efforts to dissuade Taiwan voters from electing pro-independence candidate Lee Teng-hui, as also to deter the United States from taking any further steps towards accepting Taiwanese independence. The Clinton administration positioned two aircraft carrier battle groups in waters off Taiwan.[14] China realized that time has not yet arrived to challenge the American military supremacy. Further, the United States upgraded its alliances with Japan and Australia. On the other hand, China's growing power in East Asia, its actions in the South China Sea and the Taiwan Strait contributed to the perceptions of a **'China threat'** among smaller states in the region.[15] Ensconced in the belief that the status hierarchy was stable for the immediate future and with a view to neutralize the 'China threat' theory, in 1997, Beijing adopted the identity of 'responsible major power.' Chinese President Jiang Zemin used the term **'responsible power'** (***fuzeren de daguo***) in a speech before the Russian State Duma in April 1997.[16] Though the connotation of 'responsible power' was not immediately known but soon Beijing got an opportunity to demonstrate its responsibility in the 1997–98 Asian financial crisis, when it gained prestige by refraining from devaluing its currency and provided financial assistance to struggling states such as Indonesia and Thailand. Earlier PRC had regarded multilateral organizations with suspicion, as tools of the United States but in the mid-1990s China began to take a more proactive role in Asian-related economic and security organizations, such as the Association for Southeast Asian Nations (ASEAN) Regional Forum (ARF) and the organization for

Asia-Pacific Economic Cooperation (APEC).[17] In essence, the 'responsible power' concept implied a more proactive and less passive Chinese foreign policy than Deng's warning to 'keep a low profile.'[18]

New Security Concept. In 1996, China's Foreign Minister Qian Qichen publicly proposed the New Security Concept (NSC) at the ASEAN Regional Forum. The NSC was primarily directed at China's relations with its Asian neighbours. Arguing that the Cold War mentality of competing and antagonistic blocs is outdated, with the generation of NSC (xin anquan guan), China promoted a policy of increasing its security through diplomatic and economic interaction. The concept was further elaborated in December 1998 in China's first Defense White Paper. According to a Ministry of Foreign Affairs Position Paper on the NSC, the objective of the NSC is "to rise above one-sided security and seek common security through mutually beneficial cooperation". Basically, the NSC posits that nation-states can put aside selfish security interests and can seek common ground with other nation-states. Its focus is enhancing trust through dialogue and promoting security through cooperation.[19] According to Western thinkers, the NSC illustrated China's more proactive stance in international affairs and its aspirations to be treated as a world power. It was a Chinese reaction to policies and actions by the US that Beijing perceived as threatening.[20] A good example of the NSC is the Shanghai Cooperation Organization (SCO), which China established in 2001 (with Russia, Kazakhstan, Kyrgyzstan, Tajikistan and Uzbekistan as other members at that time) to combat terrorism, Islamic extremism, and separatism. Consistent with the NSC, the SCO was not directed against any particular state, and dealt with non-traditional security threats. This was the first instance of China taking the leadership role in establishing a multilateral security organization and that too naming it after a Chinese city.[21]

Peaceful Rise/Peaceful Development. Another description of China's foreign policy doctrine was 'Peaceful Rise.' The term was first used in a speech given by Zheng Bijian, the former Vice Principal of the CCP's Central Party School and President of the China Reform Forum during the 2003 Boao Forum for Asia. Zheng is considered as the originator of China's Peaceful Rise (*Zhongguo heping jueqi*) doctrine. In brief, the term 'Peaceful Rise' was used primarily to reassure China's neighbours that China's economic and military development would not threaten peace and stability in the region, and other nations would benefit from China's rise.[22] Peaceful rise could be viewed as propaganda aimed at reassuring foreign publics about China's fast economic growth and convincing them that unlike past states, China could achieve great power status without military competition or territorial expansion—through peaceful economic development, largely because globalization would enable China to acquire the resources and technology it needed through trade.[23] Various analysts were sceptical about the concept of 'Peaceful Rise' as it had never before occurred and it was not feasible. Peaceful rise was soon picked up by President and General Secretary Hu Jintao and Premier Wen Jiabao. The term 'peaceful rise' had a brief vogue during 2003–2004 and was then replaced by the bland phrase 'Peaceful Development' on the grounds that 'rise' sounded too provocative.[24] The term 'Peaceful Development' replaced that of peaceful rise in Hu Jintao's April 2004 speech to the Boao Forum. In its very benign promise, the White Paper, China's National Defense in 2004, elucidates that the pursuit of comprehensive national power is for **'Peaceful Development.'**[25]

Zheng Bijian had elucidated that China would require 45 years *"before it can be called a modernized, medium-level developed country."* Zheng had divided this period into three stages. In the first (from 2000 to 2010), China would seek to double its GDP. In the second (from 2010 to 2020), Beijing would aim to repeat this feat, bringing per capita incomes to approximately $3000 (per annum). Over the following thirty years (from 2020 to 2050), *"China will continue to advance until it becomes a prosperous, democratic and civilized socialist country."* He stated that by that time, *"China will have shaken off underdevelopment and will be on par with the middle rung of advanced nations. It can then claim to have succeeded in achieving a '**peaceful rise**.'*[26] But China rose inexorably along the developmental track and what Zheng had anticipated to happen by 2020, was already accomplished in half of its time. According to the World Bank's statistical record, China's GDP in year 2000 was $1198.5 billion and by 2010, its GDP at $5878.6 billion[27] was almost five times. As far as per capita income was concerned, China had attained the figure of $3414 by the year 2008.[28]

Harmonious World. "Harmonious World" ***(hexie shijie)***, heralded as China's official foreign policy strategy by President Hu Jintao in September 2005, in fact was an extension of the concept of "Harmonious Society" ***(hexie shehui)*** introduced in 2004 to tackle China's growing domestic issues that had arisen due to the country's rapid development, or had been inherited from its past.[29] Concept of Harmony is a traditional Chinese concept expounded by Chinese philosopher Confucius (551 B.C. to 479 B.C.), who said that the Universe exits only because it is in a status of harmony.[30] Mao had attempted to eradicate Confucianism, believing that it was detrimental to China's development. This reworking of Confucian values exemplified the clever tactics of reframing negative characteristic as positive.

When related to traditional Chinese values, there was a greater emphasis on developing 'soft power.' Hu Jintao said in a 2006 speech to the CCP's influential Foreign Affairs Leading Small Group, "the enhancement of China's international status and international influence must be reflected in both hard power, including the economy, science and technology, and national defense power, and in soft power, such as culture.' Hu made advancement of China's soft power an official objective in his work report to the 17th CCP Congress in October 2007, wherein he declared that *China must 'enhance the country's cultural soft power* (*wenhua ruanshili*).'[31]

Chinese strategists realized that a country could not be recognized as a great power unless its values, norms, and way of life had appeal for others and the traditional Chinese Confucian values, such as harmony both within society and between humanity and nature, could have substantial attraction for the rest of the world by virtue of their contrast with the Western materialism, science, and individualism.[32] In fact, the Chinese government began establishing Confucian Institutes around the world to promote the teaching of Chinese language and civilization in 2004.[33]

Whilst 'common peace and prosperity' were professed to be the end goal of the 'harmonious world' policy, the means, or route taken, were not pacifistic, but in fact forcefully asserted to ensure stability and unity. This perspective was further supported by the release of a 2010 book *China Dream: The Great Power Thinking and Strategic Positioning of China in the Post-American Age*, by Lui Mingfu, Senior Colonel of PLA and a Chinese professor. The success of his bestselling book within China demonstrated that his views also resonated with the interests of domestic audience. In his book, Lui argued from a realist perspective that China must ensure that its 'economic rise' is matched by a 'military rise,' as a "'peaceful world' and 'harmonious world' can only be realized in the context of an international balance of power."[34]

Doubts were raised in the West about the continuation of China's peaceful rise policy from 2009 to 2010, when China asserted its sovereignty interests more forcefully. In March 2009, five Chinese naval vessels harassed a US naval surveillance ship, the Impeccable, within China's Exclusive Economic Zone (EEZ). A few months later, China submitted to the UN Commission on the Limits of the Continental Shelf a map with a nine-dash 'U'-shaped line encompassing 80 percent of disputed waters in the South China Sea. China reacted more stridently to the Obama administration's announcement in early 2010 of an arms sale to Taiwan and a presidential meeting with the Dalai Lama at the White House.[35] In September, China engaged in a contentious dispute with Japan over the arrest of a Chinese fishing captain who had rammed two Japanese coastguard vessels near the Diaoyu/Senkaku islands, which are claimed by China and currently administered by Japan. Using the implicit threat of economic coercion, China induced Japan to release the captain.[36] Similarly, China displayed limited willingness to restrain its North Korean ally for its escalated hostility toward South Korea in March-November 2010. Some Western analysts opined that China's actions represented no significant change from previous behaviour. While Chinese analysts contend that China has merely responded to the provocations of others, and that being more outspoken about its 'core interests' is entirely appropriate in view of the increase in the country's power and influence.[37]

The recent incidents raised questions as to just how peaceful China's 'harmonious world' might be, particularly if China felt other international powers were being 'disharmonious, the same way as it used the 'harmonious society' concept domestically in sorting out dissidents and activists. Further, the disparities between the Chinese leadership's practices and understanding of 'harmony' domestically and internationally provide enough reasons to explore its strategic ambiguity.[38]

China's Three Foreign Policy Strategies

According to Chinese foreign policy scholars, China has three possible foreign policy strategies: Aggressive nationalism, Utilitarian realism, and Cooperative internationalism.[39] Which foreign policy strategy, China will practice at a particular time; it will be guided by internal as well as external factors.

- **Aggressive Nationalism**. Whenever, China's leaders feel pressure due to strong nationalistic feeling, especially from middle-class or among the young, they might adopt aggressive nationalism. In the past, few instances that sparked popular nationalism in China were: May 1999 accidental bombing of the Chinese embassy in Belgrade; April 2001 collision of an American EP-3 surveillance plane and a Chinese jet fighter over the South China Sea; and the election of Chen Shui-bian as president of the Republic of China on Taiwan.
- **Utilitarian Realism.** China has been preparing itself to face US hegemony one day in the future. According to this strategy, China needs to be aggressive in catching up with a militarily declining United States. However, in 2000, the Chinese assessments of US military might, would have found that the United States enjoyed military superiority in almost every field but that the US is likely to fall behind in military intervention capability after 2010. China's utilitarian realist foreign policy requires that China should do everything to catch up with the US economy first and then follow it up with massive military investment.
- **Cooperative Internationalism**. This policy option requires China to become a full member of the international economy. This strategy says that China is growing economically and

> militarily but is not aggressively expansionist. It calls for creating win-win situations in resolving international differences, rather than engaging in zero-sum games reminiscent of the Cold War. *China's NSC is modelled on this third foreign policy strategy.* China has reaped tremendous economic benefit from integration in the international economic system.[40]

China had a revolutionary national identity in the Mao era and under him China's territorial ambitions had been expansionist. Firstly, it more than doubled its size by annexing Tibet and Xinjiang; later it invaded India in 1962 and captured 43,000 square kilometres of land in Aksai Chin, which was initially part of Ladakh and connects Xinjiang to Tibet. Further, it also annexed Shaksgam Valley, through an illegal deal with Pakistan. In the 1980s, China under Deng Xiaoping adopted a policy of 'Opening and Reform' (kaifang), keeping a low profile. Deng's successors abandoned his cautious policy in Asia and between Chinese presidents Jiang Zemin and Hu Jintao, Chinese foreign policy alternated between all the above three strategies. The New Security Concept and China's 'Peaceful Rise' illustrated China's future aspirations. China's future aspirations were embedded in its 'Peaceful rise.' It was evident that as China's economy strengthened, it would likely challenge and attempt to replace the United States as the dominant regional power, i.e. displace the United States as the dominant power in Asia, so driving a wedge between the United States and its Asian allies and supplanting American access to markets and raw materials.

Obama's 'Pivot To Asia'

Asia's rapid growth and economic dynamism had greatly expanded the region's economic and strategic weight and its Sino-centric focus was detrimental to US interests. Shift in the balance of economic power became clearly visible in the 'Indo-Pacific' region. This was clearly visualized by the US strategic thinkers. By a significant margin, almost every Asian country had China rather than the United States as its largest trading partner, and China's share continued to grow. For example, in case of Japan, trade with China reached a little over 20 percent of the total, while the United States accounted for just 12.5 percent. The same was true in case of South Korea and Indonesia.[41]

Further, senior Obama administration officials believed that the war on terror and U.S. military commitments in Iraq and Afghanistan had produced an imbalanced global footprint. The United States was committed too heavily in the Middle East and this wasn't the case for the US in the Asia-Pacific. Therefore, the strategic ***"Rebalance to Asia"*** was announced in November 2011 that involved the transfer of resources and strategic attention from the Middle East and Europe to Asia. This strategy was also termed as ***"Pivot to Asia."*** For the US military, this came in the form of the January 2012 defence strategic guidance signed by President Barack Obama, which declared, "We will of necessity rebalance toward the Asia-Pacific region."[42] By putting Asia at the centre of its security strategy, the Obama administration inadvertently made the entire strategy appear to Beijing like an effort to contain China militarily. Simultaneously, the Air-Sea Battle doctrine was developed to counter China's growing military capabilities and was officially declared as such. The signal received in Beijing was that the US had hostile intentions towards China and was trying to contain it militarily. The result was that the entire pivot was seen by Beijing as part of a broader effort to encircle China. A greater economic response in the US strategy to take advantage of an opportunity was missing. Even trade deals were being presented as a way to counter the threat from China.[43]

Another grave error was that American neglect of Europe was followed by Russian adventurism in Ukraine, an increased threat to the Baltic States, and the erosion of democracy in Poland and Hungary. Further, when America pulled back from the Middle East, the Syrian Civil War displaced 11 million people and caused a refugee crisis, Islamic State moved into Iraq, and America's relationships with its Gulf allies frayed as Iranian influence expanded throughout the region.[44]

The pivot did not contain the rise of China. Instead, China became more aggressive, pressing its claims in the South China Sea and to the Senkaku Islands. China also continued to close the gap in military capabilities with the U.S. Its economy continued to grow, as did its share of global GDP.

"New Era" of Xi Jinping

Ever since he became Communist Party leader in 2012 and completed his ascent by becoming President of China on 14 March 2013, Xi Jinping ushered in an era of increased assertiveness and authoritarianism. He manoeuvred behind the scenes with a ruthless ambition to dominate China's enigmatic elite politics and assured himself a life term for having abolished from the Constitution the two-term limit for President on March 11, 2018. His sole ambition appears to be to make China a superpower and that too when he is leading the country (unless destiny has something else in store for him and the country). In a clear sign of Mr. Xi's influence, the Communist Party incorporated his philosophy called "Xi Jinping Thought on Socialism with Chinese Characteristics for the New Era" in the preamble of its constitution.[45]

Shortly after taking office in 2012, Xi had promised the public to eradicate corruption. Xi launched an anti-corruption campaign of unprecedented scale led by his closest associate, Wang Qishan. The effort was dubbed the *"tigers and flies"* campaign since it promised to entrap corrupt officials whether they were mere low-level "flies" or high-ranking "tigers." From 2012–17, more than 900,000 party members had been disciplined and 42,000 expelled and prosecuted in criminal courts. Among those had been 170 high-level "tigers," including dozens of high-ranking military officers, 18 sitting or former members of the 150-person Central Committee, and even former members of the Standing Committee.[46] Xi slowly but successfully consolidated his power by not only exercising power in the party and the military but also made himself head of several 'leading Groups' and 'commissions' that are secretive party agencies but in fact they have the final say on everything from economic reforms to state security to cyberspace affairs. While previously Premier Li Keqiang controlled economic and financial affairs, the state of the current political structure witnessed Xi Jinping exercising leadership in almost all sectors.[47] Even though as the Chairman, Central Military Commission, he was already in charge of the armed forces, Xi appointed himself the Commander-in-Chief of the new Joint Forces Battle Command of the PLA.[48]

Xi Jinping practiced all the three foreign policy strategies like a consummate political chess player.

First and foremost, Xi Jinping ***established himself as a world leader*** in his first term—having travelled extensively to over 50 countries, paid visits to the headquarters of different regional and global organizations and delivered multiple speeches overseas, beside hosting and presiding over a number of international seminars, conferences and summit meetings within the country.

Soon after assuming power in 2013, ***Xi launched his trillion-dollar flagship project 'One Belt and One Road' (OBOR) or Yidai Yilu,*** later called the Belt and Road Initiative (BRI). In Xi's grand geopolitical vision, OBOR comprised a network of high-speed rail, motorways, oil and gas pipelines, ports, transmission lines and fibre optic cables connecting Asia, Europe, Africa, the Middle East and the Americas with China at the geo-economic centre of the connectivity. In fact, Xi's visualization was more than an infrastructure-development plan; besides boosting economic development, stimulating growth, and creating new markets for Chinese firms through unfettered trade in manufactured goods, it was more importantly aiming to enhance Chinese influence in more than 70 countries. Further, with growth slowing at home, China needed other markets for its homemade steel and cement, as well as construction contracts for its companies and workers.[49] OBOR has become the centrepiece of Xi Jinping's foreign policy and it has been enshrined in the Party's constitution during the 19th National Congress of the Communist Party of China (CPC).[50]

Pakistan is the main entrance for China to enter the Indian Ocean, the Arabian Sea and the Persian Gulf and other regions. Its special geographical position could be an important fulcrum to connect the "Silk Road Economic Belt" with "21st Century Maritime Silk Road". Therefore, ***China-Pakistan Economic Corridor (CPEC)*** became the "flagship project" of "OBOR". CPEC is a 3,000-kilometer corridor from Kashgar in Western China to Gwadar in the Baluchistan province of

Pakistan. Besides serving as a deep-water cargo port and naval base, it will also serve as a key base to secure greater Gulf energy resources for China. The Gwadar port will also facilitate trade between China and the Central Asian and Middle Eastern nations. Historically, India is at the most important meeting point of the North Silk Route, the South Silk Route and Maritime Silk Road, hence China wanted India's participation in the 'OBOR.' India has continuously opposed the CPEC as it passes through the disputed territory of Gilgit-Baltistan in the Pakistan Occupied Kashmir, challenging its sovereignty and territorial integrity. Further, with increased infrastructure investments and presence in Chittagong port (Bangladesh), Hambantota port (Sri Lanka), Port Sudan (Sudan), Maldives, Somalia and Djibouti, China has established its dominance in the Indian Ocean.[51]

China Dream. When he took office, Xi Jinping declared his over-arching ambition for China in a single phrase: "The greatest Chinese dream is the great rejuvenation of the Chinese nation." Xi has spoken of the Chinese dream and Chinese renaissance, or fu xing in Putonghua, on several occasions since then. The phrases caught the imagination of officials, the media and strategic analysts across the world. Mostly, Xi's "China Dream" has been interpreted as the same that had been set out as the goals of the Party Congress i.e., " building of a moderately prosperous society when the party celebrates its 100th birthday in 2021, and the building of a prosperous, strong, democratic, culturally advanced, harmonious and modernized socialist country when the new China marks its 100th anniversary in 2049."[52] However, Xi's "China Dream" combines prosperity and power both. As regards prosperity, Xi qualified the first Centennial Goal, "China will build a moderately prosperous society" by doubling its 2010 per capita GDP to $10,000 by 2021, when it celebrates the 100th anniversary of the Chinese Communist Party."[53]

Transformation of Chinese People's Liberation Army (PLA). Xi Jinping has reportedly opined, "To achieve the great revival of the Chinese nation, we must ensure there is unison between a prosperous country and strong military."[54] At the Third Plenum of the 18th Central Committee of the Communist Party of China (CPC) in November 2013, major reforms of the Chinese PLA were announced. These are the most significant reforms of the PLA in at least three decades and the process is scheduled for completion in 2020. Through these ambitious reforms and modernization, Xi Jinping wants to have a politically reliable and modern force capable of joint operations.[55] In his report to the 19th CPC National Congress, Xi, also general secretary of the CPC Central Committee and the nation's president, pledged to make sure that by 2020, the PLA will basically achieve its mechanization, make big strides in informatization, and gain substantial improvement in strategic capabilities. He also set a midterm goal for the Chinese military—to turn itself into a modernized power by 2035—as well as a long-term one—to become a top-tier military by 2050.[56]

South China Sea. Although Chinese foreign policy became much more pragmatic since the introduction of economic reforms in 1979, the PRC showed no inclination to compromise its claims on sovereignty over areas it regarded as historically part of Chinese territory. China's increasingly assertive behaviour in the South China Sea has been evident since the early 1990s. China continued to seize reefs and built permanent structures over there for establishing its permanence in the region, such as occupation of Da Lac reef near Vietnam in July 1994 and occupation of Philippine-claimed Mischief Reef in January 1995. The Chinese policy had been variously referred to as "creeping assertiveness" or "creeping sovereignty".[57] After China's core interests definitions having been included in 2011 White Paper 'China's Peaceful Development', a spokesperson of the Chinese Ministry of Foreign Affairs emphasized that both the East and the South China Seas are now 'core interests on a par with Taiwan and Tibet.'[58] President Xi Jinping gave a new direction to island building in the disputed South China Sea. According to an article published in the Communist Party publication, "On the South China Sea issue, [Xi] personally made decisions on building islands and consolidating the reefs, and setting up the city of Sansha". Through creation of seven man-made islands in the South China Sea, Beijing further militarised the region and altered the geography to bolster its claims. On each of the islands, China has constructed enough concrete hangers for 24 fighter jets and four or five larger planes such as bombers or early warning aircraft.[59]

The airfields and advanced surveillance and early warning radars will allow China's military to operate over virtually the entire South China Sea.

Sino-Indian Equation. China shares its land border with 14 countries and it has resolved boundary dispute with 12 of its neighbours, leaving aside India and Bhutan. In her ambition to establish regional supremacy, China wants to marginalize India by keeping the border issue alive and exploit it to her advantage. With the coming in of Xi Jinping as the paramount leader of China, border incidents followed an identical pattern but unlike the previous one, increasing in scope and intensity every time. With each standoff, China stepped up the intensity of its aggression. In **April 2013**, a three-week standoff took place at the ***Depsang plains in Eastern Ladakh*** after a Chinese platoon set up a camp near Raki Nalla. The situation was diffused after diplomatic intervention at the highest level. On **September 10, 2014**, a military standoff started at ***Chumar in Eastern Ladakh***, with around 1,000 Chinese soldiers ranged against an equal number of Indian troops; that too just a week before Chinese President Xi Jinping's three-day visit to India. It took almost 17 days when troops from both sides agreed to pull out in order to restore the pre-September 10 status quo. The standoff in the ***Doka La area of the Doklam plateau*** that took place on **June 16-18, 2017** was not only a continuation of such incidents and intrusions but appeared to be a part of greater Chinese design. On August 28, Indian and Chinese troops agreed to disengage, ending a 73-day standoff. While the disengagement was carefully projected as a peaceful resolution at the politico-diplomatic level so as not to define a winner or a loser but satellite images later showed that China has considerably beefed up its military presence in the region just to the North of the standoff site.[60]

Sometime in **mid-April 2020**, when India was struggling to contain the COVID-19 pandemic by enforcing the country-wide lockdown, China's PLA created multiple pressure points from Naku La in Sikkim to Lipulekh Pass in Uttarakhand and then to Eastern Ladakh through well-coordinated intrusions and building up of forces. Indian patrols had discovered the intrusions in early May. The places affected in **Eastern Ladakh were Galwan Valley (to include Hot Springs, Patrol**

Point (PP) 14, PP 15 and Gogra Post), Pangong Tso Lake (key strategic heights around the Lake, in the area stretching from Fingers 4 to 8) and **Depsang Plains**. There has been massive build up of Chinese forces on its side of the Line of Actual Control (LAC), comprising more than 20,000 troops supported by armour, heavy artillery, variety of air defence missiles (including ground-to-air HQ 16 and HQ 9 missiles) and combat aircraft and helicopters.[61] India has also ensured a matching deployment on its own side of the LAC. The diplomatic and political interaction had succeeded in an agreement on restoration of status quo at Galwan and Hot Springs, but had left out Pangong Tso. As a follow up to that the two corps commanders in their meeting of June 6 agreed upon disengagement starting at Galwan. Following protocol, Indian troops were sent to monitor the vacation on June 15. It was approaching dusk when the PLA troops unleashed an unprecedented pre-meditated attack on unsuspecting Indian troops with iron rods, nail-studded clubs, spikes and stones. It resulted in the death of Colonel Santosh Babu, the Commanding Officer and 19 Indian soldiers, who despite being outnumbered inflicted heavy casualties on the Chinese before making the supreme sacrifice. Officially, PLA as is their norm has not given out any causality figures but several sources give figures of around 43 Chinese who died. This violent incident has not only shattered the 45 year-long 'Peace and Tranquility' maintained along the India-China border but demolished the trust and growing relations between the two countries.

What are the reasons behind these Chinese incursions? For this one has to study the geostrategic importance of the locations, the strategic intent of the country, the timings, the likely reason or reasons behind and the forces or the capability employed to achieve the desired objectives.

Geostrategic Importance. After the arrival of Xi Jinping, China has launched intrusions (resulting in a standoff) at two locations—Eastern Ladakh, i.e. opposite Aksai Chin and Doklam Plateau.

Aksai Chin. It contains the main axis (the strategic highway, G219) connecting two most troubled regions of China – Tibet and Xinjiang and both happen to be its core interests. That is why China had captured 43,000 sq km of Indian Territory in Aksai Chin and adheres to its "claim line" of November 1959 (whereas India's LAC is of September 1962).[62] During the China-Pakistan boundary agreement of 1963, Pakistan had ceded the Trans-Karakoram tract (the so-called Shaksgam Valley) to China and thereafter started the construction of Karakoram Highway in 1967 and it was the starting point of strategic cooperation between China and Pakistan. Having been completed in 1979, Karakoram Highway (KKH), formally known as the China-Pakistan Friendship Highway is a 1,300 km road, which links Hasan Abdal (located a few kilometres beyond Islamabad, the capital of Pakistan) with Kashgar, the second most important city in Xinjiang, China. In the past KKH has been used by China to supply nuclear and missiles material to Pakistan as also for equipping the Taliban in Afghanistan during their fight against the USSR.[63] KKH is being upgraded and has now been absorbed into CPEC, which terminates at Gwadar Port. With the fructification of CPEC, the geostrategic importance of this region will be enhanced manifold as this corridor will not only reduce the distance for Chinese goods bound for the US, Europe, Africa and the entire Western world by a substantial 2,000 miles and vice versa[64] as compared to the present sea route, but will also be China's energy lifeline overcoming the 'Malacca dilemma.'

What is the importance of Galwan River Valley in this scenario? Galwan River Valley was a flashpoint in 1962 War also. The ridgeline of the Galwan Valley dominates the newly constructed 255 km Darbuk-Shyok-Daulet Beg Oldie (DBO) Road, which will provide a crucial connect between Leh and DBO (an advanced landing ground that lies quite close to the LAC with China). The Valley is also an important connecting link to the Chinese-controlled Aksai Chin. Alternatively, through the dominating ridgelines of Galwan Valley, India can threaten Aksai Chin plateau (which houses the crucial Xinjiang-Tibet highway pass).

Doklam. Doklam became famous because of the 73-days standoff that took place between Indian and Chinese troops near the Doka La pass in Doklam during June-August 2017. However, the terrain in question was the Doklam triborder area (also known as the Dolam Plateau) and in that too the point at which India, China and Bhutan meet.

Bhutan claims that the triboundary point lies at a location known as Batang-La, some four kilometres North of the Doka La pass, whereas China claims the triboundary point at Mount Gipmochi or Gyemochen, a point some two-and-a-half kilometres South of the Doka La pass.[65] Mount Gipmochi marks the terminus at the Indian border—the Jampheri Ridge, which marks start of the descent into the foothills of Southwestern Bhutan that then lead to the strategically vital Siliguri Corridor. India's concern was the proximity of this area to the vulnerable Siliguri Corridor—a geographic choke point between Northeast India and the rest of the country measuring just 23 km at its narrowest point. By bringing itself closer to the Jampheri Ridge, China will be in a position to threaten the Siliguri Corridor in a much shorter timeframe.

Naku La Pass. Through Naku La Pass, Chinese forces can threaten or block the single road axis leading to the North Sikkim, thereby cutting off Indian troops. Possibly, it should be a diversionary attack launched in support of the main offensive launched in some other theatre so as to tie down Indian troops over here.

The Strategic Intent. The strategic intent or strategic objectives of China will be dependent upon its national interest and the national interest normally remains the same, irrespective of the change in leadership unless there is change in the form of government or in governing philosophy. The last testament of Sri Aurobindo, the great Indian nationalist and world visionary, on the 'Invasion of Tibet: 11 November 1950' that had appeared as an editorial in his own paper, *Mother India* on November 11, 1950, before his passing away on December 5, 1950, read as follows:

> *"The basic significance of Mao's Tibetan adventure is to advance China's frontier right down to India and stand poised there to strike at the right moment and with right strategy, unless India precipitately declares herself on the side of the Communist bloc."*

After citing the reasons in political and military terms, the editorial elevated the discourse to a higher moral and spiritual level and concluded by stating:

> *"The hour is upon us of constituting ourselves such a spearhead and saving not only our own dear country, but also South-East Asia whose bulwark we are.* ***We must burn it into our minds that the primary motive of Mao's attack on Tibet is to threaten India as soon as possible."***

When this last testament of Sri Aurobindo was shared by Mr. Sudhir Ghosh, Gandhi's Emissary, with the President of the United States, John F Kennedy in the White House on March 28, 1963 (in the words of Mr. Ghosh) The President read the words of Sri Aurobindo's last testament several times over and said: *"Surely there must be some typing mistake here. The date must have been 1960 and not 1950. You mean to say that a man devoted to meditation and contemplation, sitting in one corner of India, said this about the intentions of Communist China...."*

Similarly, in his last letter to the Prime Minister Pandit Jawaharlal Nehru, dated November 7, 1950, Sardar Vallabh Bhai Patel, the then Home Minister before his passing away on 15 December of the same year, wrote:

> *"While our western and non-western threat to security is still as prominent as before, a new threat has developed from the north and north-east. Thus, for the first time, after centuries, India's defence has to concentrate itself on two fronts simultaneously.... In our calculations we shall now have to reckon with communist China in the north and in the north-east, a communist China which has definite ambitions and aims and which does not, in any way, seem friendly disposed towards us."*[66]

Thus, the strategic intent of PRC has been evident from the time the Communists headed by Mao Zedong have taken control of it. They captured Tibet (*Xizang*, "Western treasure house") and Xinjiang ("New Territory" in Chinese) and linked these territories through Aksai Chin. They won over Pakistan and extended their reach through it into the Indian Ocean both for economic as well as military purposes. To ensure the security of their major artery or axis, they attacked India in 1962 and continued with the similar expansionist designs, even though numbers of leaders have changed since Mao. Leaving aside the famous *"tao guang yang hui"* (TGYH) strategy of Deng Xiaoping, his successor

Jiang Zemin launched China's expansionist designs in the South China Sea in 1994–95. Thereafter, China's efforts to build ports and naval facilities throughout the Indian Ocean to protect its energy supplies—its "string of pearls strategy"—began under Hu Jintao. He turned China's attention to the South China Sea, which it viewed as America's soft underbelly. By the end of Hu's term, China effectively controlled Scarborough Shoal, had started regular patrols in the South China Sea, begun the militarization of islets, and strengthened what it called the Sansha administrative district to govern territories within the South China Sea. Hu Jintao set the stage for Xi's aggressive international diplomacy and accelerated military modernization program. Xi's policies are not a radical break from Hu's. They are built on them.[67]

Xi Jinping's aggressive nationalism commenced both on sea as well as land frontiers. Geopoliticians termed it as the **'creeping assertiveness'** or **'creeping sovereignty'** strategy of China and game theorists refer it as the **"Salami Slicing"** tactics. However, the military professionals, who are the masters of terrain and have to achieve the political ends, term it as capturing the **'Ground of Tactical Importance' (GTI),** i.e. an important piece of dominating ground from which various axes/approaches are emanating or leading to it and the capture of which will provide tactical advantage to self and deny the same to the enemy. At higher level the same ground is termed as **Vital Ground**. That is the reason that Galwan River Valley Ridgeline is important for both the nations.

Likely Reasons and Timings. When a nation goes to war or deploys its forces to threaten other nation, i.e. achieving political ends through military means, the one and the only reason is the achievement of national or strategic objectives guided by its national interest. And in Eastern Ladakh region, China's strategic objective is to ensure security of its major axis stretching from Xinjiang to Gwadar and for this capture various GTIs to provide strategic depth to own areas and deny the same to India, which could be used as launch pads. However, there have to be a host of factors—internal, external, regional and global – on which will depend the timings of such movement.

Globally, when most of the major powers of the world are struggling to control the onslaught of COVID-19 pandemic, China having recovered from the pandemic much earlier, considered itself in a better position for geopolitical manoeuvring. The United States, being in the election year, is not only tightly gripped by the coronavirus but its economy is also in deepest trouble since the Great Depression. China thought it an opportune moment to challenge its leadership in the Indo-Pacific.

The Indian economy was facing a downward trend even before the commencement of the nationwide lockdown due to the pandemic. Further, the social turmoil caused due to Citizenship Amendment Act (CAA) 2019 and the proposed National Register of Citizens was indicating as if the Indian federal structure was weakening with the Central government losing hold over states. Even Bangladesh was miffed with the CAA. India's traditional influence in its neighbourhood was withering with Nepal raising boundary issues with India. China has made deep inroads into Sri Lanka. More importantly, last year's Balakot Strike was depicted as a victory over Pakistan and it even helped Prime Minister Modi win a re-election, but it was a poor handling of media and Pakistan devised a better narrative thereby giving the opposition a chance to browbeat the government.

Consequent to COVID-19 pandemic, the entire world is re-assessing its overdependence on China's manufacturing and supply chains. India provides a suitable alternative destination for companies looking for relocation and number of companies have approached India for shifting their manufacturing bases from China. If India cannot ensure peace and tranquillity on its borders, these companies will be apprehensive in making investment and setting up their bases. Hence, one of the reasons for building up of forces on the LAC and transgressions into the Indian territory is to discourage these companies to move to an unsafe place.

Subsequent to U.S.–China Trade War and the US blaming China as the originator of Coronavirus and calling it as "Wuhan Virus", the U.S.-China relations have hit new lows. With India getting closer into the US strategic circle and as a counterbalance to China, the Chinese strategic thinkers already consider India as a "quasi-ally" of the U.S. with no scope for reversal.[68] Creating a massive force build up on India's borders is probably Chinese way of coercing India to keep away from the US and the West. But India is not a minnow but a leading power amongst the comity of nations that cannot be coerced.

However, the final decision might have been triggered by last year's opening of the vital Darbuk-Shyok-Daulet Beg Oldie (DBO) Road that runs parallel to the LAC, providing key all-weather access to the post at DBO. Another argument is that China's move was expedited not only by India's infrastructure upgrade but also by abrogation of Article 370 as applicable to J&K on August 5, 2019, and carving out two Union territories of J&K and Ladakh from the erstwhile state. While moving the resolution for the same in Lok Sabha on August 6, 2019, Union Home Minister Shri Amit Shah had asserted. "The boundaries of Jammu and Kashmir decided in our Constitution, and also in the Constitution of Jammu and Kashmir, includes PoK and Aksai Chin,"[69] and Chinese had reacted very strongly to it.

A confluence of all these factors might have stimulated China to make aggressive moves on LAC with India. Combined with this Xi's reputation has taken a beating due to mishandling of coronavirus both domestically and globally as also the continuous decline of China's economy under his leadership; both these factors perhaps compelled Xi to play the Aggressive Nationalism card.

Transformation in Warfare Methods

In the pre-Cold War period, majority of the disputes between nations were settled through conventional/regular warfare or nuclear deterrence. In the post-Cold War era, the geopolitical conflicts are increasingly being resolved by using non-military means. In fact, the character of warfare has changed with more options for pursuing strategic ends just below the threshold of traditional armed conflict. Israel-Hezbollah War of 2006 has given rise to the modern concept of **'Hybrid Warfare'**, where Hezbollah (backed by Iran) employed a host of different tactics against Israel, which included guerrilla warfare, innovative use of technology and effective information campaigning.

But in 2014 Russian actions in Crimea and Eastern Ukraine resulted in the emergence of Gray-Zone that is a continuum of 'Hybrid Warfare'. **Gray-Zone** encompasses the space between peace and war in which aggressors use hybrid tactics to shape the battlefield and achieve strategic objectives short of all-out declared conflict.

China and Russia know that they cannot compete head-on-head with the United States—economically, militarily and technologically—so they create new battlefields. They engage in Gray-Zone conflict primarily through unconventional techniques with the hope of not only achieving short-term tactical victories against the US and NATO but to challenge the regional and/or global order of alliances and influence international norms of conduct.[70]

China has been increasingly involved in unconventional operations to dilute United States' hegemony. Though China avoids direct military engagement vis-à-vis the United States and its allies but its activities targeting weaker opponents are largely meant to undermine the strength and unity of alliance structures, such as their actions against Vietnam, Philippines, other Southeast Asian states and Japan in South China Sea and East China Sea respectively. In spite of having its ambitions to develop a modernized conventional force on priority, China always prefers to use unconventional tactics that should remain between the thresholds of open war and peace.[71]

In 1999, two Chinese PLA officers, Colonels Qiao Liang and Wang Xiangsui brought out a book "Unrestricted Warfare" in which they advocated the concept of combining unconventional and covert tactics against the United States. They generally identified four alternatives to conventional warfare: one, political action to promote favourable global change in policy and international norms; two, increasing economic pressure on allies and opponents based on its burgeoning economy; three, engagement in cyber and network warfare; four, incorporation of non-state actors into conflicts.[72] Over the past decade, China's actions have largely adhered to these principles.

The other aspect of PLA's future military capability is the **'Asymmetric warfare',** i.e. to effectively **"defeat the superior with the**

inferior" through exploitation of Revolution in Military Affairs (RMA). Asymmetric approach involves identification of enemy's weaknesses or vulnerabilities, which need to be exploited. Chinese military strategists have identified a number of weaknesses in the armed forces of the United States in particular and other potential adversaries. China's development of Anti-Access (A2)/Area-Denial (AD) capabilities, such as DF-21D anti-ship ballistic missile (ASBM) dubbed "the Carrier-killer", DF-26 called the "Guam-killer" and even anti-satellite missile are meant to attack the US vulnerabilities.

In 2003, the CCP Central Committee and the CMC approved the concept of **"Three Warfares"** (*san zhong zhanfa*), a *PLA information warfare concept* aimed at preconditioning key areas of competition in its favour. The three warfares are composed of the following:

(a) ***Psychological Warfare.*** Seeking to undermine an enemy's ability to conduct combat operations through psychological operations aimed at deterring, shocking and demoralizing enemy military personnel and supporting civilian populations.

(b) ***Media Warfare.*** Aimed at influencing domestic and international public opinion to build support for China's military actions and dissuade an adversary from pursuing actions contrary to China's interests.

(c) ***Legal Warfare.*** Uses international and domestic law to claim the legal high ground or assert Chinese interests. It is intended to build international support and manage political repercussions of China's military actions.[73]

China has been endeavouring to establish its supremacy without getting in direct confrontation with the US and practicing all of the above concepts by staying within the Gray-Zone.

Xi Jinping's Three Greatest Blunders

Belt and Road Initiative (BRI). In 2013, when President Xi Jinping launched his flagship project—BRI, Chinese media heralded the BRI as a "golden opportunity" to "revitalize" the region. In fact, Xi wanted to create a "golden opportunity" for China by utilizing its surplus infrastructure building capacity in reviving the Old Silk Route as also find new markets along the Route for its export-oriented economy because in spite of its huge population, China's own household consumption is the lowest even among the BRICS countries. As of 2018, total Chinese BRI investment was estimated at over $1 trillion, more than eight-times the size of the Marshall Plan in today's dollars. Unlike the Marshall Plan, which mainly dispersed aid in the form of grants that did not have to be repaid, China provided loans often at commercial interest rates.[74] Chinese loans are given with extremely high interest rates. For example, for the Hambantota port project, Sri Lanka borrowed US$ 301 million from China with an interest rate of 6.3 percent, while the interest rates on soft loans from the World Bank and Asian Development Bank are only 0.25-3 percent. Interest rates of India's line of credit to the neighbouring countries are as low as 1 percent, or even less in some cases.[75]

But Xi's ambitions are much beyond plain economics. Far from being a "win-win" project to develop much needed infrastructure in Asian and African countries, the BRI was devised as a strategy to entrap various countries in a huge 'debt trap' by making them invest in a series of economically unviable projects and keeping national assets of countries as collateral, such as infrastructure (ports, highways) and energy resources (oil, gas, minerals). If the countries were unable to pay back the loans, then Beijing would in turn get complete access to a port or highway like Hambantota port in Sri Lanka. China is funding a high-speed rail line in Laos that will cost equivalent to half the country's GDP. Eighty-eight percent of Djibouti's GDP, which corresponds to $1.72 billion, is owned by China and it is because of investment based on development and infrastructure loan. Kenya holds the 3rd highest Chinese debt in Africa and if it defaults on loans from China's EXIM bank, it is at the risk of losing control of the Port of Mombasa.[76] Further, those countries are forced to behave like a vassal or a client state. Through BRI, China had ensured that projects are allotted to Chinese contractors and jobs are given to its own people. They create their own ghettos, do not integrate with the society and thereby alienate the local population.

A recent report by Center for Global Development, a non-profit research organization, found that eight BRI recipient countries—Djibouti, Kyrgyzstan, Laos, the Maldives, Mongolia, Montenegro, Pakistan, and Tajikistan—are at a high risk of debt distress due to BRI loans.[77] The Council on Foreign Relations, a US think tank, calculated that the combined debt of 67 countries, which are a part of the project, tracked in 2017, amounted to $135 billion. All these countries supported China's decision to impose the security law in Hong Kong.[78] Another Global Business expert Mukesh Aghi, who is the CEO and President of US-India Strategic Partnership Forum, has tracked this looming loan defaults rising to almost $520 billion in 2020.[79]

The IMF has scrutinized multiple aspects of the BRI, repeatedly warning of unsustainable debt levels, predatory lending, and the lack of project transparency.[80] Rampant corruption is driving some of these projects, for example, in Pakistan almost $2.3 billion worth of bribe was reportedly given to the leadership for the power plant projects.[81] Pakistan moved its troops to Gilgit-Baltistan along the Line of Control (LoC) and allowed the PLA to use its airbase at Skardu in June at the height of the face-off. In April only the Imran Khan Government had sought an extension on a debt repayment of $30 billion that Islamabad had taken to build the CPEC. Behind the troop movement lies the cold calculations of easing the repayment process.[82]

In 2013, when Xi rolled out BRI, China's foreign exchange reserves were approaching $4 trillion. But the world has changed since then. China's economic slowdown triggered a capital flight, draining more than $1 trillion from its foreign exchange reserves. Taking into account, the trade war's impact on China's economy in the future, China may not be able to generate sufficient foreign exchange surpluses to finance BRI on the same scale.[83] In the first half of 2019 alone, China's tariff war with the US cost as much as $35 billion to China.[84] With Chinese exports to the US having been significantly reduced, the resultant current-account deficit cannot be offset with increased exports to other markets. On the domestic front, Beijing faced a perfect storm of rising pension costs, slowing economic growth and dwindling tax revenues. With the resources getting restricted, Chinese leaders would have limited choice for allocating funds. ***And that was the scenario in 2019, much before the commencement of COVID-19 phase.***

The Coronavirus pandemic has seriously affected the projects under the BRI. Many projects under BRI are either on hold or receiving minimal works. Many of the countries from Asia and Africa that took billions of dollars in loans from China to build mega projects have been requesting Beijing for debt repayment freezes or debt cancellations. In the 1st quarter of 2020, the PRC recorded a GDP of 20.65 trillion Yuan, equivalent to 2.91 trillion U.S. dollars—a 6.9 percent reduction compared to the GDP of the previous year.[85] Thus, China has far less money to splash out on expensive infrastructure in Africa and elsewhere. President Xi is facing severe political pressure on two fronts: from poor countries wanting loans cancelled and from his citizens who did not want the money sent abroad that could be used to aid recovery at home.[86] One should not be surprised if Beijing eventually lets BRI, at least BRI 1.0, die quietly. ***Xi Jinping is trapped in his own "debt trap diplomacy".***

Aggressive Nationalism on Multiple Fronts. There is nothing new about 'Aggressive Nationalism' as China's leaders have adopted it in the past to unify people, divert their attention and reassert the legitimacy of the Communist Party's rule. However, Xi's predecessors had restricted themselves to confronting one or two nations at a time in the East China Sea or South China Sea. Besides Xi's super ambition of making China a superpower in his own lifetime while he is ruling the country, he is embroiled in a number of problems – internal as well as external. In the first quarter of 2020, China's economy shrank by 6.8 percent. China's official (registered) urban unemployment rate is 5.5 percent, or more than 25 million people. Real estimates suggest 70-80 million or more are unemployed, including migrants.[87] The initial mishandling of the virus in China has been politically expensive for the Communist Party in terms of losing public trust and confidence in the political system and party leadership.[88] With his flagship BRI coming to a screeching halt and rising international opprobrium against China's role in the outbreak of Coronavirus pandemic, Xi's reputation has been badly damaged. He has activated China's forces and efforts on multiple fronts on sea and land both. From Australia to Japan, Taiwan to Hong Kong, South China Sea to Indian Ocean – deepening confrontation with the United States and then threatening India along its entire LAC; will China be able to manage so many fronts simultaneously?

Under cover of the coronavirus pandemic, China has ramped up its aggressive expansionism both in the South China Sea as well as in the Indian Ocean Region. On April 19, 2020, China renamed 80 geographical features in the South China Sea—signalling that it was establishing sovereignty over parts of the South China Sea covered by a 9-dash line that is deemed illegal according to international law. This step was taken after Chinese ships rammed and sank a Vietnamese ship three days after Vietnam protested to the UN against China's sovereignty claims in the South China Sea. The Philippines backed Vietnam and protested against new territorial districts announced by China in large swaths of the sea. Japanese foreign minister Toshimitsu Motegi also lodged a protest against China for sending its ships into Japanese territorial waters near the Senkaku Islands in the East China Sea. In response to Chinese aircraft carrier moving near Taiwan, a US warship sailed through the Taiwan Straits for the second time in a month.[89] The Association of Southeast Asian Nations (ASEAN) leaders held their annual summit by video on June 26, 2020, with the coronavirus pandemic and the long-raging territorial disputes high on the agenda. Emboldened by the proactive US stance, Southeast Asian leaders said a 1982 UN oceans treaty should be the basis of sovereign rights and entitlements in the South China Sea, in one of their strongest remarks opposing China's claim. The ASEAN leaders took the position in a statement issued by Vietnam on behalf of the 10-nation bloc.[90]

With a view to counter China's intimidating moves against Southeast Asian states, the United States carried out a rare two-carrier (involving its nuclear-powered carriers USS Nimitz CVN 68 and USS Ronald Reagan CVN 76) freedom of navigation operations (FONOP) in the South China Sea in the first week of July. Further, the US announced a sale to Japan of 105 F-35 Joint Strike Fighter aircraft and related equipment for an estimated $23.1 billion.[91] According to Dean Cheng, a top expert on the Chinese military, for almost three years (2012–15), the US did not run any FONOPs at all, sending a clear signal to China by their absence. From 2015–16, the US conducted a handful of 'innocent passage' operations, which implicitly recognized Chinese territorial/sovereignty claims. But now, aligning with the Southeast Asian states about their rightful maritime claims based on international law and supporting the UN Tribunal ruling, the US Secretary of State Mike Pompeo left no room for any doubt in his concluding statement, "The world will not allow Beijing to treat the South China Sea as its maritime empire. America stands with our Southeast Asian allies and partners in protecting their sovereign rights to offshore resources, consistent with their rights and obligations under international law."[92] Presently, The United States Navy has positioned three aircraft carriers (third one being USS Theodore Roosevelt) and several hundred aircraft into the contested South China Sea.[93] Extra-regional nations, such as the UK and France, have also voiced their disapproval of China's actions in the disputed South China's Sea and carried out FONOP in this strategically vital area.[94] The United States and the UK are moving in concert to finish the utility of Hong Kong as a financial centre and technology hub for the PRC. China had been expecting access to certain technologies via Hong Kong that are unavailable on the mainland.[95]

Contrary to the previous occasions, this time China has indulged in simultaneous face off at three different places along the LAC with India. Not only the Chinese moves are well coordinated but are supported by deployment of adequate forces in depth. A general impression has been created that Chinese PLA is quantitatively and qualitatively far superior to the Indian Army. The PLA currently maintains approximately 2 million personnel after downsizing roughly 300,000 members in 2017. Out of this, Army has got approximately 13, 60,000 personnel and out of these 5,50,000 are two-year conscripts,[96] whose training standards and fighting experience cannot be compared with regulars. With approximately 14 lakh servicemen in the Indian Army along with another 9 lakh in reserve, the Indian Army has become the world's largest standing volunteer army, ahead of China.[97]

Belfer Center for Science and International Affairs has carried out an elaborate analysis of the strategic postures of China and India in the current scenario and it is very logical. Both the countries have matching ground deployments with Indian Air force having been better placed. Some of the relevant aspects are highlighted below.

> "As regards ground force availability, it is assessed that Indian Army has around 225,000 personnel opposite China's border areas (including about 34,000 troops in the Northern Command facing China). However, China is estimated to have a total of 200,000 – 230,000 ground forces under the Western Theater Command, and Tibet and Xinjiang Military Districts. Moreover, this apparent numerical near-equivalence with that of Indian ground forces is misleading because even in a war with India, a significant proportion of these forces will be unavailable, reserved either for Russian tasking or for countering insurrection in Xinjiang and Tibet. The new joint Western Theater Command is estimated to hold around 90,000-120,000 troops, principally divided into the 76th and 77th Group Armies, which are headquartered in the interior of Western China, in Chongqing and Baoji respectively. Because of ongoing unrest in Tibet and Xinjiang, a special PLA Army-directed Military District (MD) has been created for each of these regions. In Tibet, the region closest to Indian border areas, the PLA presence is judged to number just 40,000 troops. More numerous forces are located in the Xinjiang region north of Tibet, totaling around 70,000".[98] .

If China intends to launch an offensive against India to capture any feature of tactical importance in high altitude area, it has to create a force superiority of 1:10 to 1:12 and for that it has to draw forces primarily from Xinjiang and secondarily from the Western Theatre Command forces deeper in China's interior and that is her predicament.

The PLA Air Force (PLAAF) is at disadvantage compared to the IAF in terms of numbers as also in quality of fighter aircraft. Further, location of Chinese air bases in High Altitude restrict the carrying capacity of their fighters to half the designed payload and fuel, and necessitating the flight refuelling that is also limited. IAF aircraft are not affected by these geographical constraints. While Chinese forward air bases and airfields are vulnerable to a dedicated Indian offensive, India is better placed with a large number of airfields in the East and West. Further, PLAAF combat proficiency may be significantly weaker than often estimated. Rather than launching pre-emptive air strikes to neutralise India airfields, Chinese strategic planners believably envision early long-range missile strikes against Indian air bases in the event of conflict. However, India benefits from the greater number and redundancy of regional air bases, and the daunting number of Chinese missiles that would be required to truly incapacitate relevant IAF bases. Taking into account the precision, accuracy, circular error of probability (CEP) and possible rate of failure of ballistic missiles, a minimum of two to three missiles per target will be required to damage/ destroy it and there are five to six targets in an airfield. Further, IAF has the capability to repave the blast crater with quick-drying concrete within six hours. To keep an airfield shut for 24 hours, approximately 80 to 90 missiles will be required, even by a conservative estimate. China has a stock of 1200-1600 SRBMs/MRBMs[99] and that is not enough to neutralize the vast spread of Indian airfields. Further, majority of these missiles are deployed for Taiwan contingency. India is presently inducting runway replacement fiberglass mats and associated paving equipment, which will further reduce its runway reconstitution timeframe.[100] However, China has a wide variety of armed and reconnaissance drones. India is soon going to acquire state-of-the-art, battle tested predator drones from the US. The much-debated ammunition shortfall in the Indian Army has been taken care of.

The Belfer Center analysis concludes by stating, ***"India is in a stronger conventional position vis-à-vis China"***. India of 2020 is much different than what it was in 1962 both in terms of force capability as well as leadership. Knowing fully well that it cannot enforce its will on India through the use of force, China is trying to create a new narrative to fulfil its ambition of becoming a superpower. Chinese media, its policy makers and scholars are projecting the emergence of a **"New Cold War"** between the United States and China with a view to present the world with a *fait accompli*: China declaring itself as an established superpower and as an equivalent of the United states.[101] By activating sea and land frontiers simultaneously, China wants to display its comprehensive national power on a global geopolitical chessboard in which India is just a part of it. By asking India not to get played by the United States, China is endeavouring to convey that its real competition is with the US and not India. However, when the unarmed Indian soldiers inflicted more than double the number of casualties on Chinese soldiers as compared to their own, in the Galwan Valley, Chinese ambitions have suffered a serious setback. India has proved that it is capable of solving its bilateral problems with China on its own. India has poured cold water on China's backdoor machinations to claim superpower status by establishing regional hegemony first.

Further, no comparison can be drawn between the erstwhile US-USSR rivalry and the current Sino-US rivalry. The United States and the Soviet Union were in an altogether different league during the Cold War: first, it was a clash of two different ideologies having their own set of follower countries; second, their economies were on a different scale but they had matching nuclear deterrent capabilities, which prevented direct confrontation between them; and third, their concerns were primarily focused on Europe, and in particular on Germany. It was a conflict for Europe and over Europe, where they set up two political and military blocs—NATO and Warsaw Pact.[102] Whereas China is no match to the military and nuclear might of the United States. Its developmental model being projected through BRI is turning to be a failure. The meteoric rise of its economy is commendable but given the impact of Coronavirus pandemic, the future is unpredictable.

Mishandling of the Coronavirus. In 2019, Xi's political star was already getting dimmed due to a host of issues—slowing down of economy, the US-China trade war, Hong Kong and cross-strait relations with Taiwan—when at the end Coronavirus emerged in Wuhan and spread like wildfire, first in China and then across the whole world. Though, world may never come to know how this virus originated—accidently or deliberately, but its handling has left question marks on the leadership of Xi Jinping both domestically as well as internationally.

In the early stages of this crisis, the peculiar absence of Xi for days on end from the public limelight had hit his popularity hard. In fact, Xi did not visit Wuhan until March 10, although he sent Premier Li Keqiang in late January.[103] To manage the internal dissensions, the Communist Party followed its familiar techniques: first, suppressed the information; second, when these efforts could not succeed then resorted to propaganda effort as to how efficiently they were controlling the virus—the government has acted decisively to build hospitals in record time and locked down entire cities; allowed some non-state controlled information to flow for about two weeks and then clamped down hard on information flow with emphasis on telling positive stories only – highlighting heroic efforts of frontline workers and downplaying the sufferings of patients. The CCP's whole efforts were concentrated on bolstering the legitimacy of the party. Party officials not only deflected the blame on local authorities but exploited the nationalistic sentiment by creating narratives about a 'People's War' against disease. Projecting the uncontrollable spread of virus in the US and Europe as their shortcomings, the party is propagating that China's political and governance system is far superior. The rapid spread of COVID-19 left countless hospitals, cities, and entire countries with a dire shortage of personal protective equipment (PPE), including face masks, respirators, and rapid test kits. China sought to fill the void with large-scale exports of PPE, that too on exorbitant prices, which the US and western countries saw as a move to exploit the COVID-19 pandemic for China's own political and economic benefit.[104] Quality of Chinese-produced medical supplies and rapid test kits were found to be defective. This so-called "mask diplomacy" of China backfired in Europe, with the EU sounding an alert that China's aid was an attempt to "rise to the challenges of global leadership." Rather than a gesture of goodwill, China's "mask diplomacy" is being interpreted abroad more as a measure to rehabilitate the image of the Chinese government after it came under significant fire at the initial stage of the outbreak.

China's celebration of victory over its own COVID-19 epidemic was short-lived as the rest of the world struggles with the pandemic; blame and hostility against China, which is considered to be the cause of the crisis, intensified: First, China confronts a **'credibility challenge'** by facing accusations that it is accountable for the outbreak of COVID-19; Second, China confronts a **'diplomatic challenge'** as the Sino-US relationship is becoming increasingly strained and even hostile amid the pandemic; Third, China faces the threat of a **'financial challenge'**, with claims of financial compensation from multiple organizations, governments, and individuals across the world. The Henry Jackson Society, a British conservative think tank, claimed that the G-7 would lose at least $4 trillion because of "the Chinese government's negligence." Compensation claims filed by individuals and organizations in all the countries collectively are worth more than China's GDP over the course of 20 years and 1,000 times more than the "Gengzi compensation" China was forced to pay after the Boxer Rebellion.[105] Although these claims may have no legal value for China but they depict a harsh international environment for China. However, the most devastating aspect for Chinese economy will be the decoupling of global supply chain from China, a direct and visible impact of COVID-19.

3

India's Response

In the Indian security-cum-academic circles, it is considered as a conventional wisdom to commence the discourse with a phrase "India did not have a strategic culture." Then after animated discussions, the common pearls of strategic gospel, which flow are: India should have strategic autonomy; The United States is not a trusted ally as it will not come to our rescue in our land border confrontations, hence we should not have an alliance with the United States; India needs a national security strategy (as if the nation is functioning without it); India should believe in neighbourhood realism and win back its friendly neighbours. Till the Galwan Valley incident, China was being treated as neighbourhood adversary with whom India could have a relationship balanced between competition and cooperation. But that so called 45 years of peace and tranquillity maintained along the India-China border/LAC, for not having fired a single bullet by either side, has been demolished by the use of brutal force by China in the Galwan Valley on 15 June 2020. What George Fernandez, India's Defence Minister declared in May 1998, *"in my perception of national security, China is enemy No 1...and any person who is concerned about India's security must agree with that fact"*,[1] must reverberate in the ears of India's security planners. And not to be left behind, there is a community of persons, who were earlier part of the government but now appear as security/defence experts/speakers; they portray that all the intelligence about Chinese construction activity and build up close to the Galwan Valley was available through satellite imagery and even the conduct of PLA exercise in Aksai Chin was known but there was a failure in intelligence interpretation by intelligence agencies to provide a coherent assessment of China's real intentions. The Artificial Intelligence (AI) has so much permeated the minds of people that without knowing its limitations, it is being asked whether it was employed or not in this instance. If these experts had gauged the Chinese intentions so accurately, why could not they have informed the government well in time rather than writing or speaking after the incident.

In today's world of fast communications, media—print as well as electronic—wants to remain ahead of events. Therefore, everyone who is ready to express is treated as expert by the media without even knowing his credentials because the serving officials who are in the know cannot communicate on security matters because of obvious restrictions by the government. The Indian academics, who have no experience of armed forces, give expert opinion on comparative force capability of China and India in the present context. The Belfer Center study categorically points out about a former Indian Army commander, who wrote during the Doklam Standoff that he expected the episode to end in a barrage of Chinese missile strikes to expel Indian forces from the area and settle the dispute on Chinese terms.[2] Use of ballistic/cruise missiles in mountains against infantry troops, well dug in and tucked away in the folds of mountains—India should be too happy for China to waste its missiles in this manner.

Before evolving a comprehensive and long-term Indian response, it is necessary to deliberate upon some of the above issues.

Is China a Friendly Neighbour or Enemy? Never in the 70 years history of PRC, it has given any indication that it is India's friend. Leave aside the bitter memories of 1962 invasion; China's friendly or rather conciliatory overtures to India have been based on promoting its national interests. China considers India as an impediment to her aspirations of becoming a Superpower. Therefore, China always endeavoured to marginalize India by exploiting border tensions and cultivated India's neighbouring countries as a politico-military counter —the well-known 'Strings of Pearls' strategy. Subsequent to the historic visit of India's Prime Minister Rajiv Gandhi to China in 1988, it was the economic interest due to which it came closer to India; intentionally keeping the border issue on a backburner and trade became one of the top priorities. In 1990, bilateral trade between India and China was only USD 264 million, reached USD 2.9 billion in 2000[3] and attained a peak of USD 89.6 billion during 2017-18, with trade deficit at a whopping (–) USD 62.9 billion.[4] China not only destroyed India's local industries by dumping its cheap products but made India so much dependent upon import of ingredients and components for its pharmaceutical, electronics and other items that India cannot easily get out of China's vice grip. Modi's government did succeed in bringing down this trade deficit to (–) USD 48.66 billion in 2019-20 by reducing the imports[5] but China has got the message that they will no longer be able to exploit India to its economic advantage.

In fact, the tussle had started when India refused to join Xi Jinping's flagship project of BRI because its vital portion, the CPEC passes through Gilgit-Baltistan, thereby violating the territorial integrity and sovereignty of India. However, the lesser-known fact is that many Indian leaders have long been asking China to make the BRI corridor cross Kunming in Southwest China up to the port of Kolkata, where it could reconnect to the maritime "Silk Road" through the Bay of Bengal. Or alternatively, China and its Silk Road could enter Uttarakhand, via Kailash Manasarovar in Tibet to later reach the port of Mumbai. This is one of the real issues of contention.[6] Thus China is not interested in economic upliftment of India but BRI/CPEC is a geopolitical initiative for securing its energy route and economic lifeline through Pakistan, China's "iron and blood brother".

China has been consistently opposing India's entry in the Nuclear Suppliers Group, tried to raise the Kashmir issue repeatedly at the United Nations and openly helped Pakistan by blocking the UN Security Council from classifying terrorist group Jaish-e-Mohammad's (JeM) Chief Masood Azhar for as long as it could.

After the bloodiest clash in the Galwan Valley, despite talks between India's National Security Adviser Ajit Doval and Chinese foreign minister Wang Yi as also between the corps commanders of two countries, there has been thinning of troops at the stand-off points but the disengagement is still a work in progress. Rather, there has been build-up of PLA troops all across the LAC beyond Ladakh, at Lipulekh Pass, parts of North Sikkim and Arunachal Pradesh. India has also matched the strength of the PLA troops. De-escalation is not in sight. Chinese troop movements and mistrust has led the Indian Army to prepare to station soldiers on the icy heights of Ladakh through the winter same way as the Siachen Glacier is being defended. Emergency purchases of high-altitude clothing and snow tents from Europe, Russia and the US are being done.[7]

There is a new awareness and a wave among Indian masses to boycott Chinese goods.

China cannot be a friend. War prevention and war avoidance should be our strategy but in the words of Chinese strategic thinker Sun Tzu, "Best is to Win without Fighting."

Does India have a Strategic Culture? Contrary to the popular belief in the Western world, India is the originator of geopolitics and statecraft and it dates back to more than 5000 years ago. This was not acceptable to majority of the European colonial historians because a prevalent thought during their times was that the world itself had been created only on Sunday, October 23, 4004 BC.[8] Since the European colonists were the political masters of India and if European history didn't go back beyond 5000 years, then how could it be possible for India, their slave, to have a history more glorious and more ancient than their own? With this mindset, it was natural for them to convert India's ancient history to mythology.

It is Mahabharata's 'Shanti Parva', which is the oldest text on geopolitics and statecraft but Kautilya's *Arthashastra* (around 4th Century BC), being of later origin became more famous as India's unique contribution to statecraft and geopolitics. The text was influential until the 12th Century, when it disappeared. Until dramatically in 1904, a full-text on palm-leaf in the *grantha* script, came into the hands of Dr. Rudrapatna Shamashastry, a refined scholar of Sanskrit, the librarian and later curator of the Oriental Research Institute (ORI) (set up in 1891 by the then Maharaja of Mysore). He transcribed, edited and published not only the Sanskrit edition in 1909 but painstakingly rendered the work into English, publishing it in 1915. The manuscript is believed to be a recopy of a recopy made some 500-600 years ago and was with a pandit in Tanjore, who handed it over to the Institute not knowing what was written on it.[9] Subsequently, another original manuscript and some fragments, in a variety of scripts, as well as old commentaries of the text were discovered.

Kautilya's *Arthashastra* remained hidden, therefore his work is greatly underrepresented in the Western world. In academic circles, Kautilya is labelled as the 'Indian Machiavelli'[10] even though the *Arthashastra* was written some 1800 years before Machiavelli's *The Prince*. Moreover, it is much broader in scope and content than the *The Prince*. Thus, Indian scholars, having studied in Western-oriented institutes remain oblivious about the greatness of their own ancient strategic culture and take pride in starting their discourse from Machiavelli and Clausewitz.

Kautilya, in *Arthashastra*, had evolved the Mandala Sidhanta or Mandala Theory to create balance of power between many states based on inter-state relations. He had suggested a state to act in order to enhance its power and self-interest. In this, he has described the notion of *Raja Mandala* or Circle of States and *Shadguna* or six-fold diplomatic policy, which can amazingly encompass every aspect of modern foreign policy. Many observers are now connecting the ancient Indian strategic thought of Kautilya with contemporary Indian strategy. The Raja Mandala theory is based on assumption that two neighbouring states, which share their borders, are hostile to each other, and the enemy of hostile neighbour is a natural ally. Apart from the above six Shadgunas, Kautilya has mentioned four tactics to overcome the opposition viz. *Sama* (Conciliation), *Dama* (Gifts), *Bheda* (Dissension) and *Danda* (Force).[11]

None of the Indian scriptures, either Mahabharata or Kautilya's *Arthashastra*, talk about the policy of non-alignment or strategic autonomy. In fact, the Mahabharata War is the best example where the mighty Pandavas, who were assured of victory because Lord Krishna was on their side but still had to seek alliances and support from friendly kings/states. The force ratio of Pandvas and Kauravas was 7:11 but despite that quantitative inferiority, Pandavas were victorious because of better weapons/technology and superior leadership.

National Interest should be the Basis of Foreign Policy. India's first Prime Minister Jawahar Lal Nehru was the architect of Non-alignment policy that was new in the history of international relations. It was a utopian dream that had no relevance in realpolitik. In 1962 when China attacked and India was overwhelmed by the power of Communist China, Mr. Nehru made desperate appeal to the US President John F. Kennedy for air protection irrespective of India's non-alignment policy.[12] Though the Non-Aligned Movement (NAM), with 119 developing nations as its members, still holds its triennial meetings[13] but it has lost its sheen after the end of the Cold War. Currently, India's stated official foreign policy is to maintain 'Strategic Autonomy' and it avoids being drawn into an alliance type of relationship.[14] However, in the academic circles, India's 'Strategic Autonomy' is considered as the direct intellectual heir of non-alignment in the post-Cold War era and the two shared a core characteristic, namely, maximizing freedom of action.[15]

As it is evident from the past history; India is not alien to balance of power strategies. Its de facto alliance with the Soviet Union during the 1970s was a classic balancing act against Sino-US rapprochement and its practical utility was demonstrated to the whole world in December 1971 when President Nixon had dispatched the US Seventh Fleet's Task Force 74, led by the nuclear-powered aircraft carrier Enterprise to the Bay of Bengal with sinister designs but was neutralized due to prompt action by Soviet's nuclear-armed flotilla on the sea and movement of land forces against the Chinese.[16]

Presently, India is in a very precarious situation; Chinese PLA has deployed troops all along the LAC with Pakistan ready to collaborate with China to activate the second front; and Nepal which had always been supportive of India or at best it was neutral, its present government is inclining towards China. Chinese PLA Navy (PLAN) has extended its reach into the Indian Ocean. Can India ensure its sovereignty and territorial integrity on the basis of 'Strategic Autonomy' alone? Even the United States, being the sole superpower with an unmatched military power and technological supremacy, seeks alliances. A long-lasting alliance between two nations should be based not on the physical proximity of neighbours but on the congruence of national or strategic interests. Given the present geopolitical environment, the Trump Administration has been far more vociferous in criticizing the actions of PRC than any previous Administration since 1990, to satisfy its domestic and political requirements as also meet the wider economic, military and technological challenges. Subsequent to US-China trade war, the situation created by COVID-19 pandemic has left no option for the United States except to forge alliance with like-minded countries in economic as well as military spheres to counter the revisionist China's expansionist ambitions.

There are enough evidences available to indicate that the United States and India have converging interests in political, economic and military fields. However, since 1947 successive governments in India have created a public opinion that alliance with other nations should be a taboo. Hence alternative concepts like strategic partnership and its various grades have been devised. First of all, the current international environment demands that India and the United States should have a comprehensive deal in politico-economic-military spheres. It may be named as comprehensive global strategic partnership but it should be a de facto alliance with certain clauses to be kept as closely guarded state secrets and should not be in open public domain. Such an agreement is possible if the economic and socio-political interests of two countries are so intertwined that to protect those interests, a common security paradigm becomes a necessity. Modi government has been consistently working over the past six years to make India's economy more open and reform-oriented. Prime Minister Narendra Modi, while delivering the keynote address at India Ideas Summit organized by the US India Business Council (USIBC) on July 22, 2020, pitched India as a trustworthy and open business partner for the United States, seeking American investors in fields ranging from agriculture to healthcare to defence in a bid to boost economic recovery in the wake of the Coronavirus pandemic. PM Modi said, *"American investors often look out for the perfect timing to enter a sector or a country. To them, I would like to say: there has never been a better time to invest in India."*[17]

It is a timely initiative by the Indian government to create opportunities for the United States, Western Europe, Japan and South Korea to set up their manufacturing bases in India and reorient the global supply chain using India as its epicentre. In November 2019, the US, Japan and Australia had unveiled the **'Blue Dot'** infrastructure network, ostensibly to promote infrastructure development, but in reality as an alternative to China's BRI. The Western alternative has been in the making for some time as nations have voiced alarm at the 'debt-trap diplomacy' of China through its BRI projects and their security ramifications. Blue Dot is proposed to be funded by Japan and America's newly founded International Development Finance Corporation and Ausaid, as also by a number of global development finance windows backed by the West.[18] It may be advantageous for India to join this initiative because it will ensure close integration and better relationship with countries in its immediate as well as extended neighbuorhood, weaning them away from Chinese 'debt-trap.' In addition it will provide employment opportunities to its youth—the much talked about demographic dividend can be leveraged for economic prosperity of India.

India and the United States being the largest and the oldest democracies respectively, the liberal democratic traditions are ingrained in all of its institutions. Further, the Indian Americans are among the most highly educated racial or ethnic groups in the US, constituting an influential political force. India-US bilateral relations have matured into a "global strategic partnership", having signed a major civil nuclear cooperation agreement and are now major defence partners. India and the US conduct more bilateral exercises with each other than any other country now. Their defence relations have been strengthened with the signing of two of the three foundational agreements—Logistics Exchange Memorandum of Agreement (LEMOA) and Communications Compatibility and Security Agreement (COMCASA). LEMOA has been realized by the two navies in terms of reciprocal provision of logistics support, supplies and services and the pact would serve as a template for similar arrangements with other countries such as Russia. Valid for 10 years, COMCASA aims to provide a legal framework for the transfer of highly sensitive communication security equipment from the US to India that will streamline and facilitate interoperability between their armed forces. Third foundational agreement, Basic Exchange and Cooperation Agreement (BECA) will allow sharing geospatial intelligence.[19] Thus, the United States and India become the natural partners to contain the aggressive designs of China in the Indo-Pacific region.

Self-Reliant Economy. The 'Self-Reliant Economy' should not be misconstrued as akin to 'Swadeshi' (or Indigenous) but it truly means economy not based on resources that become unreliable during crisis situations. Coronavirus pandemic exposed the vulnerability of countries and companies that relied heavily on global supply chains originating from China. Supply chains had been severely disrupted because raw materials and components were not being produced and transportation networks have ground to a halt. The electronics, automobiles and pharmaceuticals sectors are particularly hard hit. Chinese companies applied for a record number of force majeure certificates to try to get out of contracts they couldn't fulfil without having to pay penalties.[20] A force majeure event occurs when unforeseeable circumstances, such as natural catastrophes, prevent one party from fulfilling its contractual duties, absolving them from penalties. Due to retaliatory tariffs imposed on each other in the U.S.-China trade war, companies had already started diversifying their supply chains out of China. The speed at which they do this will now accelerate. The outbreak is expected to accelerate a trend among multinationals to move to a "China plus one" or even "China + 1, 2, (or) 3 supply chain strategy".[21] The United States and West European countries are seeking "economic and strategic independence." Michael

R. Pompeo, the US Secretary of State during his press briefing on April 29, 2020, said that they were in conversation with Australia, India, Japan, New Zealand, Republic of Korea, and Vietnam about how to restructure global supply chains, keeping them running smoothly and to prevent something like this from ever happening again.[22]

Much speculation has been created about the spirit behind the Self-Reliant India campaign that it was probably a reversal of a liberal, globalized economic paradigm. Prime Minister Narendra Modi, in his speech by video link to the inaugural session of India Global Week, an event organized by a London-based group, India.Inc., on July 9, 2020, clarified, "Self-Reliant India is about merging domestic production and consumption with global supply chains. It is not about being self-contained or closed to the world. It is about self-sustaining and self-generating, and pursuing policies, which promote efficiency, equity and resilience." He proclaimed that very few countries offer the kind of opportunity India does today.[23]

Strengthen the Military. Since the modern warfare has permeated multiple domains and the rapid pace at which the technology is advancing, no military in the world can claim to be invincible. The weapons and equipment soon become obsolete, having been overtaken by new generation equipment or even by new technological invention. Therefore, military leaders will ask for more funds every year to modernize the armed forces but there being a finite budget available, the political hierarchy will not accommodate their demands fully unless there is a threat of war.

India's defence budget for 2020 amounted to USD 66.9 billion (Rs 4,71,378 crore), whereas China's budget of USD 179 billion is about 2.7 times more than that of India. The US defence budget of USD 732 billion is four times more than that of PRC. However, there is lack of transparency in China's defence expenditure, which according to defence analysts is much higher than what is announced due to the rapid expansion of Beijing's military and modern weapons. According to Stockholm International Peace Research Institute (SIPRI), China's defence spending in 2019 amounted to USD 261 billion (as against its defence budget of USD 177.61 billion).[24] In contrast, India's military spending was $71.1 billion in 2019 (3.7 times less than that of China). Though, India's military expenditure has risen significantly over the past few decades as it grew by 37 percent over the decade 2010–19 but its military burden fell from 2.7 per cent of GDP in 2010 to 2.4 percent in 2019. India's military spending has grown due to an expanding salary and pension bill of its armed forces personnel and capital expenditure for procuring warships, submarines, aircraft and helicopters.[25]

The military expenditure or defence budget of a country is directly related to the strength of its economy. The GDP of China is 4.78 times greater than that of India.[26] It means India can never have its defence budget anywhere near that of China. But unless a country's frontiers are secure, it can never be sure of its economic progress and prosperity of its people. Now with the external threat looming at two or may be two and half fronts, defence preparedness cannot be neglected. Over the number of years, modernization of defence forces has been neglected. The mountain strike corps, sanctioned seven years ago, was stalled two years back for lack of funds. With only one of its two divisions raised, it now exists in a truncated form.[27] Had the raising gone as per schedule, the mountain strike corps could have been an effective deterrent against trans-LAC incursions by China. Currently, the IAF has 30 active fighter squadrons against a sanctioned strength of 42 squadrons. Rafale aircraft deal was signed between the governments of India and France in September 2016[28] but it took four years to have the first five aircraft delivered. It is believed that even in the best-case situation of the timely induction of all planned procurements including the emergency purchase of the SU-30s and MiG-29s, the IAF will at the maximum have 32–34 fighter squadrons by 2030. China's PLAAF is estimated to have around 50 squadrons of "strong fourth-generation fighters" and 10 squadrons of modest fifth-generation J-20-class aircraft by the same time.[29] Indian Navy has reworked its plan of having 200 warships by 2027, in view of its fund crunch. The navy has a requirement of three aircraft carriers but due to fund constraints it will have two operational at all times.[30] Then, there is a need to allocate funds for procurement of high-tech equipment for cyber, space, special operations and intelligence, surveillance and reconnaissance (ISR).

The government is resorting to buy weapons—ranging from small arms to fighter aircraft, missiles and ammunition, on an emergency basis during a military crisis. It has started with Doklam standoff and continued during the Pulwama crisis. India is fast-tracking purchase of equipment worth Rs 400 billion from foreign and domestic suppliers.[31] This is mainly about signalling determination in light of the military confrontation with China as also a likelihood of second-front opening by Pakistan. These actions point to the gaps in the country's defence requirements and the planning. Inter-service rivalry is also one of the reasons, which created doubts in the minds of political bosses about the inter-se priority of weapons or equipment to be procured. Now with the appointment of Chief of the Defense Staff (CDS), the planning and procurement should be streamlined and when the funds are limited, only criteria should be winning the war with economy of resources. It may be remembered that state-of-the-art defence equipment are not available off the shelf. After identifying the need and placing order for procurement or development, it takes five to ten years for delivery.

The most important factor in winning a war is 'the man behind the equipment.' History is replete with examples where well-motivated and trained soldiers commanded by capable leaders are known to have defeated the mighty armies, better equipped and many times their size. The Indian Army thrives on its ethos of ***'Naam, Namak and Nishaan'***, i.e. its soldiers fight and sacrifice their lives for the good name (Naam) of their village/town/country, loyalty to the mother earth whose salt (Namak) they have partaken and for the National Flag/Regimental Standard (Nishaan). These are the basic ethos that are imbibed in every regimental soldier and officer and this was the motivating spirit behind the young officers and soldiers, who sacrificed their lives in capturing the dominating heights of Kargil, from the well-entrenched enemy in the most difficult high altitude terrain with treacherous weather conditions. On the evening of June 15, 2020, in the Galwan Valley, when Colonel Santosh Babu, the Commanding Officer 16 BIHAR and his party were surreptitiously attacked by Chinese soldiers with nail-studded clubs, iron rods and stones, though outnumbered, they fought so valiantly that they inflicted more than double the casualties on the enemy before laying down their lives on the altar of the nation. It is because no Indian soldier wants to go back to his village with the name of his country/village being tarnished—only his sacrificed body will go wrapped in the Tricolour. No amount of sophisticated weaponry could have achieved the deterrence what fighting spirit and valour of Indian soldiers attained by instilling fears in the mind of the enemy. Though it is too early to say because deterrence is always in the mind of the adversary.

The government has a great responsibility in maintaining the morale of the soldiers. There should not be any doubts in any one's mind that Indian Army is the first and the last line of defence of the country. The difference between border guarding during peacetime by organizations like Border Security Force (BSF) or Indo-Tibetan Border Police (ITBP) and the role of Indian Army defending the territorial integrity must be clearly understood. When the hostilities commence, these organizations are withdrawn and come under the command of Indian Army. They are neither equipped nor are they trained to perform the role of Army and are usually employed for rear areas security as the battle progresses. In a similar manner, Indian Coast Guards cannot replicate the role of Indian Navy. But politicians sow the seeds of discord by making loose statements at times, either to nurture their election constituency or for turf building to prove themselves of carrying more power among their fellow ministers. Then, this message is carried forward by the heads of these organizations to proclaim the superiority of their organizations. Every man or woman is performing his/her duties in the service of the nation and it should be respected in that form, for example the unique role of COVID warriors cannot be replaced by others. Thus, it is completely undesirable to decimate the importance of Indian armed forces soldiers and this tendency must be ruthlessly curbed if we want to maintain high morale of our soldiers.

Leverage Soft Power. According to Harvard Professor Joseph S. Nye, Jr., who first coined this term in the modern context in the late 1980s, *"soft power is the ability of a country to persuade others to do what it wants without force or coercion."* It excluded the more traditional forms of influence such as investment and aid or payment.[32] However, China gave a twist to this form of power by employing gravitational pull of its economic strength to entice developing nations of Asia, Africa and Latin America in a debt trap in exchange for their strategic resources or real estate to establish bases. Hambantota in Sri Lanka and Djibouti are the prime examples known to the whole world.

Further, no two countries in the world are as closely placed, geographically, culturally and strategically, as India and Nepal. Deep linguistic and cultural similarity, religious affinity, historical ties, geographical proximity and family connections between Nepal and India cannot be overwhelmed by trade or economic ties with China, which are likely to prove unsustainable in the long-term. Further, the Nepalese enjoy equal rights like Indian citizens. They can travel freely to each other's countries, live and work there, engage in business and own property.[33] Nepalese will never be given such privileges by China, who treats its own people like Tibetans and Uighurs as second-class citizens in its own country. But China has been able to pit the present ruling dispensation of Nepal against India through its economic influence.

Consequent to the outbreak of Coronavirus from Wuhan City of China and engulfing the whole world in the grip of COVID-19 pandemic, China is not only being held responsible for this pandemic, if for nothing else but for holding back the information by manipulating the WHO officials. Later, China exploited the pandemic for its own political and economic benefits. Chinese products were already infamous in the world as being unreliable but supplying defective PPE and test kits and price gouging from needy countries during this humanitarian crisis has badly affected the reputation and character of Chinese people in the eyes of the whole world.

On the other hand, India was extremely helpful in providing medicines and PPEs to most countries of the world in spite of its own requirements. Thus, India is on a moral high ground as it follows the principle of ***"Vasudhaiva Kutumbakam"*** a Sanskrit phrase that means, ***"the whole world is one single family"***[34] in true letter and spirit. India must use this opportunity to leverage its soft power. Every country in the world has been affected by the coronavirus and according to health experts; the viral attacks and pandemics are going to be regular phenomena due to climate change and environment degradation caused by human greed. Prevention is better than cure, hence it is advisable to develop body immunity rather than waiting for a vaccine after every virus attack. The Indian system of Ayurveda based on herbs and Yoga and, in particular, *Pranayam* (Breathing exercises) are the best means to build immunity against several diseases. These need to be promoted through conduct of international webinars in concert with different countries and institutes as also through daily TV programs in different languages. There should be scientific trial and evaluation of Ayurvedic medicines and its peer review need to be published in international medical journals and health magazines. Indian cuisines because of their elaborate cooking and pungent taste are being recommended as a preventive measure against throat infection. These are very popular in the UK and need to be popularized in other countries also. India is a land of diversified culture, where all religions have flourished. Presently, when the international tourism is at standstill and it may remain so for almost a year; this is the time when virtual tourism or sightseeing of memorable destinations in India should be promoted through dedicated TV channels. So that when the pandemic is over and normal international travel is restored, India should be the popular choice of international tourists. The upcoming Ram Temple in Ayodhya, where Prime Minister Narendra Modi did the Bhumi pujan (foundation laying ceremony) on 5th August and it was televised world over, can become a popular tourist destination but we have to create facilities to attract tourists from varied strata. A Ram circuit is being created of all the places where Lord Ram put his footprints.

Invest in Emerging Technologies and Innovate. Before the Coronavirus pandemic struck, the world had already moved into the Fourth Industrial Revolution. The global pandemic is only accelerating the pace of digital transformation. The emerging technological trends, which will define the next decade, are: Artificial intelligence (AI) and machine learning; Big Data Analytics; Blockchain technology; Cloud and Edge computing; Robots and collaborative robots (or cobots—

the latest generation of robotic systems designed to work alongside humans as robotic colleagues) and autonomous vehicles. Fifth generation of cellular network technology or 5G is going to be the backbone of our future online society and a smarter world. The 5G networks will give us not only greater speeds but also the ability to connect more and more devices within a geographical area. The Internet of Things (IoT) is another important field that refers to the increasing number of everyday devices and objects, connected to the Internet and gather and transmit data. While the first so-called common smart device was a smartphone but we now have smartwatches, TVs, air conditioners, refrigerators, and so on. Currently, there are 20 billion smart devices, but it is expected to grow to at least 200 billion connected devices soon. These smart devices are responsible for an explosion of data and are rapidly changing our world. The ability of machines to connect to and share information with each other is a key part of the IoT. Quantum computing will completely redefine what a computer is and could give us computing power that is millions or trillion times more powerful than supercomputers today. Although conventional binary computing will continue for many tasks we do on computers in the near future, but quick quantum computing is likely to have a variety of applications in fields such as AI and decoding complex structures such as genomic information.[35] This brings us to an important field of Biotechnology, i.e. Genomics (that focuses on the understanding and manipulation of DNA and genomes of living organisms) and Gene Editing. Coronavirus pandemic has sensitized the whole world about the crucial importance of this field.

In fact, the real issue in U.S.–China Trade War is not about the bilateral trade deficit. The United States alleges that China wants to replace the technological hegemony of American companies. China in 2015 launched a plan to become the world's lone technological superpower by 2025 by subsidizing its businesses and acquiring cutting-edge intellectual properties. The US companies and experts assess that China is using unfair business practices for forced technology transfer and stealing technology to displace the US as the world's tech superpower. Xi Jinping personally put his name on this policy, called "Made in China 2025," reflecting how core it is to China's future plans. But Trump took offense to the idea of China as the world's leader in technology. China has long downplayed the significance of Made in China 2025, and has simply stopped using that phrase, rather than actually allowing the US to continue leading in technology.[36]

President Trump's tough stance on China remains popular in the United States, not so much due to the bilateral trade deficit or frustration about lost business opportunities, but because of the concern that China is about to outcompete the United States for technological leadership in a number of sectors considered critical for national security (on both sides of the Pacific).[37] China has reached a stage that given its economic might and kind of investment it is making to attain technological prowess in emerging fields like AI, Robotics and cyber space that the United States will find it difficult to counter China without support from countries like India and Japan. These technological fields require collaborative and cumulative efforts by scientific brains. Hence, the United States must share the technology with India so that India can contribute in taking the technology forward to the next generation through innovation by using its expertize in software.

That's why Prime Minister Modi, during his keynote address at the India Ideas Summit on July 22, 2020, suggested that India and the US could together help the world recover. He invited US businesses to invest in technology and said that there were vast opportunities in front-line technologies such as 5G, big data analytics, quantum computing, block-chain and Internet of things.[38]

QUAD. The United States, Japan, India and Australia came together as the "Core Group" to provide urgent humanitarian assistance in the aftermath of the 2004 Indian Ocean Tsunami disaster. The US Vice President Dick Cheney endorsed the idea of quadrilateral involving the above countries. They then met formally just once as the Quadrilateral Security Dialogue in 2007. Thereafter, on the sidelines of the November 2017 East Asia Summit in Manila, the Philippines, officials from the United States, Japan, India and Australia met once again to re-establish and re-conceptualize the Quadrilateral Security Dialogue (or QUAD). China's expanding maritime strategy and the increasing assertiveness of its land reclamation and territorial claims in disputed areas in the South and East China Seas over the past decade was proclaimed as the key driver for strengthening alignment among the Quad members.[39] Since then, the group had met only five times. Initial meetings were at bureaucratic level and open reference to China as the target was avoided. After their ministerial-level meeting was held in New York on the sidelines of the United Nations General Assembly on September 26, 2019, the grouping gained momentum; their senior officials met in Bangkok on 4 November 2019 and now the agenda was "consultations on collective efforts to advance a free, open, and inclusive Indo-Pacific." The group has found renewed relevance with US Secretary of State Mike Pompeo stating, "One of the purposes of the quadrilateral is restraining China."[40]

Earlier, the US has resisted the urge to convert the QUAD into an anti-China grouping but post-COVID-19, the aggressive moves by China in South China Sea and East China Sea have motivated all these countries to form a de facto military alliance. The United States is contemplating to open its training facilities at the Anderson Air Force Base in Guam in Western Pacific Ocean for the fighter jet pilots of India, Japan and Australia—ostensibly to step up military cooperation among the four nations.[41] There is also a proposal to expand the QUAD into QUAD Plus, by bringing in other democratic nations in Indo-Pacific. Emmanuel Macron, the French President has called for Paris-Delhi-Canberra Axis amid the Asia-Pacific tensions. To compel China to disengage and de-escalate on the LAC to restore status quo ante, India must leverage its geostrategic strength in the Indian Ocean and combine it with the naval powers of QUAD Plus to dominate the Sea Lanes of Communications and choke points.

India's Own Three Warfare Strategy: Diplomatic, Media and Legal. In today's dynamic world with ever evolving techniques of war fighting, every country is devising its own strategy of winning a war without fighting. 'Non-contact Warfare' is also an emerging trend but it has different connotation for different countries. China's 'Three Warfare Strategy' falls in this category. As an old saying goes, "*if you want to defeat your enemy, beat him in his own game.*" Thus, India should define and activate its own 'Three Warfare Strategy', which should encompass diplomatic, media and legal aspects.

Diplomacy. India needs to exploit the current unprecedented global anti-Chinese sentiment by enhancing its own diplomatic footprint. All Western democracies are voicing their anger against expansionist designs of China and its wayward attitude of economic exploitation during the humanitarian crisis of COVID-19. G-10, Democracy 10 or D-10 (New Alliance proposed by Britain, incorporating India, South Korea, Australia and G-7 to break China's monopoly on 5G Technology)[42] and the International Parliamentary Alliance of the European Parliament (with more than 100 members) are the multilateral organizations on which India should focus—have its representation, attend their regular meetings—to expose China's deeds that violate international norms and behaviour. In its extended neighbourhood, India should support countries of the Southeast Asia and consistent critics of China, like Japan, Mongolia and Australia in their tussle against China.[43]

Beijing always flaunts its "One-China policy" and many countries have signed this policy—around 200 odd countries except for 15 or so—and none of these got a reciprocal arrangement from China.[44] Under this policy, China considers Taiwan as its own territory, and it has occupied Tibet as also Xinjiang as part of this policy. But China has never acknowledged the "One-India policy", which means that Pakistan-occupied Kashmir (PoK), Gilgit and Baltistan and Aksai Chin are part of Indian territory. The latter is occupied by the Chinese themselves. India has to seek reciprocity from China. If Beijing refuses to see reason, then India must pay China in the same coin, albeit gradually. During her first meeting with Wang Yi in New Delhi in June 2014, India's External Affairs Minister, Mrs. Sushma Swaraj had made it clear that China would need to adhere to a *One-India Policy* and stop supporting Pakistan on the issue of Kashmir if it wanted India to stick to its *One-China Policy.*[45] But Beijing does not reciprocate diplomatic nicety, therefore New Delhi has to take some ground action. India must establish diplomatic relations with Taiwan and Taiwanese companies need to be approached for boosting India's manufacturing sector. China should be made to realize that India has the capability of leveraging the Tibet issue by giving enhanced importance to Dalai Lama and even encouraging debates and seminars/webinars on Xinjiang by encouraging Uighur leaders to travel and speak in India. Of course, there may not be any official Indian government participation.

Media. The Social Media and 24 hours TV channels have enhanced the potential of media manifold in influencing the public opinion both at domestic and international levels. There should be coordinated efforts by a central agency nominated by the government to ensure that China's aggressive behaviour and expansionist attitude of eyeing and grabbing the neighbours' territory as also its predatory economic policies are thoroughly exposed in print, electronic and social media. The anti-China debates, discourses, discussions and videos must be beamed on different channels in such a coordinated manner that if anyone opens any TV channel at any time, he finds China being discussed.

Legal. India has yet to realize the potential of legal aspects of warfare against China. A small country like Philippines has set a precedent in challenging the Chinese exaggerated claims in South China Sea. The Philippines' arbitration award at the Hague's Arbitral Tribunal in July 2016 ruled against China's "nine-dash line" expansive claims to the sea, including within the Philippines' EEZ. Beijing rejected the ruling but it has lost its stand on legal grounds. Some ASEAN members and the US have approached the UN for the implementation of the Permanent Court of Arbitration Ruling in the dispute between the Philippines and China awarded in July 2016.[46] Since China has no intention to vacate the annexed portion of Aksai Chin and number of bilateral meetings have not been able to arrive at even on a common LAC, it is high time that India should draw a leaf from Philippines' precedent and resort to legal recourse by approaching the International Court for constituting an arbitration tribunal.

China's expansionist designs, either in sea or on land, are based on its national aim of avenging the "century of humiliation" and restoring its "Middle Kingdom" Status. Therefore, it accepts those previous treaties, which support its annexation and denies the existence of others. For instance, China tacitly accepted 'McDonald – McCartney Line' of 1899, which was proposed to the Chinese government by Sir Claude McDonald, the then British Ambassador to China because China constructed its Highway 219, linking Xinjiang to Tibet, to the East of this Line. Whereas Ardagh-Johnson Line drawn by other cartographers (1865 to 1897) based on the Treaty of Tingmosgang between Ladakh and Tibet (1684), determining the extent of Ladakh, and later reiterated by Treaty of Chushul of 1842, is not acceptable to China. When these treaties were quoted by Jawahar Lal Nehru to Zhou En Lai in their exchange of letters in 1959, the latter showed his unawareness about the existence of such treaties.[47]

India has plenty of legal luminaries, who can present India's case in International Tribunal against China's illegal occupation of our land and create enough reason for the international community to put pressure on China to vacate the annexed portions of land. Additionally, such action will motivate Tibetans and Uighurs to approach International court to restore their land.

Always Have an Alternative. In international relations, there is no permanency. Every nation has to look after its national interests. One has to keep in mind that the United States will decide its China strategy based on its own interests. Some experts are of the opinion that President Trump may still strike a deal with China before the November elections, if that helps him domestically. Though apparently all out efforts are being made by India and the US to leverage their converging strategic interests but India must always have an alternative option up her sleeves.

The erstwhile USSR (now Russia) has always been a reliable strategic partner of India. Moscow has long been the main supplier of military equipment to India—accounting for 62 percent of its total weapons imports during the last five years. In view of the ongoing troop confrontation with China in Eastern Ladakh, India has requested Russia to fast-track contracted weapon systems as well as urgently rush critical spares for its fighter planes, main battle tanks and submarines. India has asked Russia not only to expedite delivery of five squadrons of S-400 Triumf surface-to-air missile system under the $5.43 billion (Rs 40,000 crore) deal inked in October 2018 but it is also finalizing plans to procure 21 more MiG-29 jets, which will cost around Rs 230 crore each, as well as 12 additional Sukhois to replace the ones that have crashed. Russia is also a very important partner for manufacture of defence items in India as part of 'Make in India' program.[48] The military technical cooperation between India and Russia is one of the most important pillars of the special and privileged strategic partnership between the two countries.

Of late, there is hardening of Sino-Russian relations with Chinese laying their claims on Vladivostok. Though, it started with Chinese Internet users, followed by diplomats and officials, wherein they claimed it was Qing's Manchurian homeland but was annexed by the Russian empire in 1860 after the British and the French defeated China during the Second Opium war. Further, Russia has always been apprehensive of Chinese investments in the Russian Far-East. This sparsely populated Russian territory boasts of abundant natural resources, and traditionally looks at it as vulnerable to Chinese influence or even colonialization. China has been eager to invest here in a bid to gain influence but Russia wants to counter this dependence on China. Therefore, India gave US$1 billion line of credit to Russia for development of the Far East region.[49] China-Russia camaraderie was playing out over the last few months and that is because Russia has been sanctioned heavily by the West and its top companies pushed out of the dollar-based financial system. Ideologically, Russia will never accept Chinese communist as being superior to them, which has already been a reason for tensions between Maoist China and Soviet Russia. Russia has to be reassured that closer India-US relations do not necessarily dilute our deep bonding with them; in fact, the recent visit of India's Defence Minister Mr. Raj Nath Singh to Moscow was a step in the right direction.

Conclusion

The complete world is seized of China's aggressive stance combined with its deceptive strategy. When most of the nations are struggling to contain the Coronavirus and people are worried about their livelihood because of the economic recession, nobody wants a war. Then how to stop China's march? The commonly found solution is *"Imposing Costs on China is the only way to stop it"*. India has taken various steps, to create an impact on the Chinese economy, for example, imposing a ban on 59 Chinese mobile phone apps. Even the US Secretary of State, Mike Pompeo, welcomed this ban and said, "India's Clean App approach will boost India's sovereignty."[50] The Indian Government amended its Foreign Direct Investment (FDI) policy to prevent the hostile takeover of distressed firms, in other words restricting investment by China. Creating public awareness to boycott Chinese products is another measure. Even if India breaks trade relations with China by denying them export of a maximum of $76 billion (achieved in 2017-18) goods, will it hurt Chinese economy to the extent that China will restore status quo ante on the LAC. It is not likely, because for a $14 trillion economy, it is like taking a bucket out of the ocean. PRC will get affected, when the credibility of the Communist Party in governing the country and particularly the leadership of Xi Jinping gets challenged. That can happen when majority of the countries of the world move in unison against China on all fronts—economic, diplomatic, social and political. Probably, the time has arrived, for which China's paramount leader Deng Xiaoping had indicated while concluding his speech at the United Nations General Assembly on April 10, 1974:

> ***"If one day China should change her color and turn into a superpower, if she too should play the tyrant in the world, and everywhere subject others to her bullying, aggression and exploitation, the people of the world should identify her as social-imperialism, expose it, oppose it and work together with the Chinese people to overthrow it."***[51]
>
> ***—Deng Xiaoping***

PART II

Impact of Coronavirus and Challenges and Opportunities for India

4

The Novel Coronavirus

Historical Retrospect

Biological threats or pandemics are not new to the mankind. Not going very far in to the history, the first example of contagion caused intentionally is considered to this date was in 1346 AD. The Crimean city of Caffa (today Feodosiya), a Genoese stronghold situated on the shores of the Black Sea, was besieged by the Mongols. The Mongol Army hurled plague-infected cadavers into the besieged fortress, thereby transmitting the disease to the inhabitants. The fleeing survivors of the siege spread plague from Caffa to the Mediterranean Basin and the contagion spread throughout Europe. Europe lost one quarter to one third of its population, an estimated 30 million people to the Black Death or Bubonic plague in a period of three years, and the mortality in North Africa and the Near East was comparable.[1]

In the Twentieth Century, the Spanish flu pandemic of 1918 was the deadliest, which infected an estimated 500 million people worldwide—about one-third of the planet's population—and killed an estimated 20 million to 50 million victims, including some 675,000 Americans. Influenza or flu is a virus that attacks the respiratory system. The Spanish Flu did not originate in Spain, though its news coverage did because during World War I, Spain was a neutral country with a free media that covered the outbreak from the start, first reporting on it in Madrid in late May of 1918. By the summer of 1919, the flu pandemic came to an end, as those that were infected either died or developed immunity.[2] Since 1918, there have been several other influenza pandemics, although none as deadly. Flu pandemic from 1957 to 1958 killed around 2 million people worldwide, including some 70,000 people in the United States, and a pandemic from 1968 to 1969 killed approximately 1 million people, including some 34,000 Americans.[3]

It may be of interest to know that Centers for Disease Control and Prevention (CDC) conduct surveillance in the United States for people who see their health care provider for flu-like illness. CDC estimated that flu has resulted in between 9.3 million and 49 million illnesses each year in the United States with 140,000 and 960,000 hospitalizations each year since 2010. CDC estimated that flu-associated deaths in the United States ranged from a low of 12,000 to 79,000 every year from 2010-2011 through 2017-2018 influenza seasons[4] (In the United States, "flu season" generally runs from late fall into spring).

In the past half a century at least, the mankind has not faced a calamity of such an enormous magnitude. Only six viruses from the coronavirus family used to infect humans, which would make the new one the seventh to cause human disease. Four coronaviruses that cause only mild cold-like symptoms are: HKU1, NL63, OC43 and 229E.[5] All novel outbreaks are a public health concern because humans have no immunity against a new disease. Before the current novel coronavirus, the other two novel coronaviruses that had emerged as global health threats were the Severe Acute Respiratory Syndrome (SARS) and the Middle-East Respiratory Syndrome (MERS). SARS outbreak that started from China in 2002, spread to 37 countries and infected 8,098 people with 774 deaths, mostly in South-east Asia. MERS spread to 27 countries and infected 2,494 people and caused 858 deaths in 2012.[6] Interestingly, these novel viruses did not affect India despite causing outbreaks in neighbouring countries. SARS and MERS had a death rate of about 10 percent in 2003 and 30 percent in 2012, respectively.[7]

Epidemiology and Transmission of Novel Coronavirus

Genetic analyses have shown that the Novel Coronavirus (2019-nCoV) or Severe acute respiratory syndrome coronavirus 2 (SARS-CoV-2), which causes COVID-19, shares 79.5 percent of genetic sequence with SARS coronavirus, with the two also having the same cell entry receptor that attaches to the membrane of the host cell to cause infection.[8] SARS-CoV-2 causes infection by using its crown-like spike protein, which gives the virus its name (corona is Latin for crown) to bind to a protein named angiotensin-converting enzyme 2 (ACE2) on the surface of the human cells, from where it invades the air sacs in the lungs, leading to respiratory distress. ACE2 is found not only in lungs, but also in the heart, kidneys and tissues lining blood vessels, and there are particularly high levels in the testes. Probably that is the reason men are found more vulnerable to COVID-19 according to a study.[9] The known routes of transmission are through droplets in the air by coughing and sneezing, close personal contact including touch, touching an object or surface contaminated with the virus and then touching your mouth, nose or eyes before washing your hands, and in rare cases, faecal contamination.[10] With new evidence proving transmission begins during the asymptomatic phase, tracking the source of the infection became increasingly more difficult as the infection spread beyond initial 27 countries (including China, as on 21 February)[11] to cause localized outbreaks in communities. Till the time an effective cure is found out for COVID-19, only solution to curb this menace is to impose quarantines, order citizens to wear masks, maintain hand hygiene, ensure a social distance of minimum six feet between two individuals and shut down public places, including schools, religious places and cinema halls. People are advised to avoid shaking hands and to stay indoors. These were the same measures adopted to curb the spread of Spanish Flu.

Although very limited information on the epidemiology of this virus is available and researchers are still in the process of understanding the nature of its transmission. However, with a view to understand the future trajectory of the pandemic and to frame appropriate policy responses, essentially three epidemiological factors are to be considered:

One, **incubation period**: once a virus infects someone—a host—it takes some time for the virus to make enough copies of itself that the host begins to shed the virus, through coughs or sneezes, for instance. This is the virus' incubation period i.e., generally the time between when we are first infected and when we start shedding the virus, which may be a little before we start experiencing symptoms. The incubation period varies from virus to virus and sometimes from host to host. For SARS-CoV-2, researchers have found that the typical incubation period is about five days. About 97 percent of the people who get infected and develop symptoms will do so within 11 to 12 days, and about 99 percent will within 14 days. So 14-days quarantine is being considered the outside "safety" margin, to be certain that one hasn't developed an infection that could be spread to others. Further, it is a long-standing public health practice, and it's called 'traveler's quarantine';[12]

Two, **the serial interval**: this is the time between the onset of the illness in the primary case (infector) and illness onset in the secondary case (infectee). When the serial interval is shorter than the incubation period, pre-symptomatic transmission is likely to have taken place and may even occur more frequently than symptomatic transmission. A substantial proportion of secondary transmission occurring before illness onset indicates that many transmissions cannot be prevented solely through isolation of symptomatic cases, as by the time contacts are traced they may have already become infectious themselves and generated secondary cases. Thus, containment via case isolation alone is likely to be very challenging.[13] Research from Japan has shown that the median serial interval for COVID-19 is four days, which is less than the median incubation period of approximately five days. Therefore, containment would need to be guided by an aggressive testing and rapid contract tracing strategy; [14]

Three, the basic **reproduction number or reproduction rate** (R_0 pronounced "R-naught") is the rate at which a virus is transmitted or in other words, indicates how fast an infection is spreading. It indicates the average number of people who will contract the virus from a person who has already been infected, in a population that does not have immunity for the said disease. The virus is assumed to be introduced to a population that does not have herd immunity or vaccination against it. Mathematically, R_0 is the number of new infections divided by the number of existing infections, or the average number of new infections over an infectious period (R_0 = new infections/existing infections). The infectious period depends on the virus, which can be a few weeks, months, or even years. Higher the R_0, more contagious is the infection.[15]

When the R_0 is 1, it means the number of infected persons in a population is constant. For every person who is cured or dies of the disease there will be one fresh case in the population. By this logic, if the R_0 is greater than one, then the probability that there will be an outbreak is extremely high. The ideal scenario is when the R_0 is below 1, which means the infection is transmitted to fewer people. When such a rate is maintained over a considerable period of time, the disease is eradicated.[16] The measures adopted in the past to reduce the rate of disease transmission and applicable now also is by pharmaceutical interventions (like vaccines) or non-pharmaceutical interventions (screenings, lockdowns), or both.

The R_0 of COVID-19 was initially estimated by the WHO to range between 1.4 and 2.5, as declared in the statement regarding the outbreak of SARS-CoV-2, dated 23th January 2020.[17] However, several studies have been carried out worldwide to precisely estimate the COVID-19 R_0. A recent review written by Ying Liu *et al.* compared 12 studies covering China and overseas (1 January to 7 February 2020) and found the R_0 for COVID-19 to be much higher than WHO estimate—finding a range of values between 1.4 to 6.49, with a mean of 3.28 and a median of 2.79 (meaning that 1 infected person will on average infect 2.79 others).[18]

According to data compiled by the Times Fact India Outbreak Report, India's R_0 stood at 1.99 as of 20th April, around six days into the second phase of the lockdown. The nation's R_0 has continued its downward trend. India's effective reproduction number R for COVID-19 has come down to 1.11 as of Mid-July. The key to success in India's battle against COVID-19 will depend upon bringing its national R_0 or R to less than 1, but given the current trend it appears that India is still some way away from achieving this target.[19]

While using the factor of R_0, great caution has to be exercised in interpreting and estimating it because all individuals in a population are not alike in getting infection and recovery rate will also vary. Thus in a population sample, majority of the cases may be mildly infectious (in other words, they have an R_0 of less than one), while a small proportion of them may be highly infectious or called "super-spreaders" (with R_0 much greater than one). The variability of an R_0 plays an important role in the dynamics of an outbreak. Thus, the R_0 measure is an average—meaning "super spreaders" could infect many more, and others could infect no other people.[20]

Super-spreading Events (SSEs) are not limited to emerging infectious diseases only. In the early 20th century, Mary Mallon (Typhoid Mary), an asymptomatic typhoid carrier who worked as a cook, infected more than 50 persons. A study of tuberculosis demonstrated that many patients were not highly infectious but that 3 of 77 patients accounted for 73 percent of the infectious burden. In 1997, a study observed that 20 percent of the population contributed to more than 80 percent of transmission and suggested targeting interventions to the core 20 percent.[21] Although SSEs appear to be difficult to predict and therefore difficult to prevent. SSE prevention and mitigation depends on quickly recognizing and understanding these events and speed is essential to execute the plan. In India, Tablighi Jamaat congregation is a known example of SSE, which led to a tremendous spike in coronavirus infections.

Cause of the Outbreak

As every one knows that China had officially reported the first case of COVID-19 from Hubei's Wuhan city on 31 December 2019. But the truth is not as straightforward as China wants the world to believe.

How China has misled the world on Novel coronavirus and the complicity of World Health Organization will become clear from the following account, which appeared in media.

According to the *South Morning China Post*, a 55-year-old in Hubei province in China first contracted the coronavirus disease (COVID-19) on November 17, 2019.[22]

An article in American magazine ***National Review*** highlighted how China withheld information that proved detrimental against the COVID-19 fight. The detailed timeline of China's coronavirus cover up is elaborated as under:

> On 1st December, the symptom onset date of the first patient was identified. Five days after illness onset, his 53-year-old wife with no known history of exposure to Wuhan Sea-food market, also presented with pneumonia was hospitalized in the isolation ward.
>
> On 25 December, Chinese medical staff in two hospitals in Wuhan were found to be suspected of contracting viral pneumonia and were quarantined. Later, hospitals in Wuhan witnessed an "exponential" increase in the number of cases in late December that could not be linked back to the Huanan Seafood Wholesale Market. Whistleblower Doctor Li Wenliang warned a group of other doctors about a possible outbreak of an illness that resembled SARS. He urged them to take protective measures against infection.
>
> On 31 December, the Wuhan Municipal Health Commission declared that their investigation has *not found "any obvious human-to-human transmission and no medical staff infection."*
>
> On 3 January, Dr. Li, who was accused of "spreading rumors", signed a statement acknowledging his 'misdemeanor' and promising not to commit further 'unlawful acts'. China's National Health Commission ordered institutions not to publish any information related to the unknown disease. On the same day, *Hubei Provincial Health Commission ordered to stop testing samples from Wuhan related to the new disease and destroyed all existing samples.*
>
> On 6 January, according to a report published by The New York Times, 59 people in the central city of Wuhan were sickened by a

"pneumonia like illness". On the same day, the Chinese Center for Disease Control and Prevention issued a *level 1-travel watch*—advising *travellers to Wuhan to avoid contact with 'living or dead animals, animal markets, and sick people'*.

On 8 January, Chinese medical authorities claim to have identified the virus reiterating that it still found "no clear evidence of human-to-human transfer".

On 11 January, the Wuhan City Health Commission released a report stating no clear evidence of human-to-human transmission.

On 12 January, Dr. Li Wenliang was hospitalized, later his condition deteriorated so badly that he was admitted to the intensive care unit and was given oxygen support.

On 13 January, the first case of novel coronavirus was reported outside China involving a 61-year-old Chinese woman in Thailand, who had visited Wuhan.

On 14 January, WHO in its report stated, "Preliminary investigations conducted by the Chinese authorities have found no clear evidence of human-to-human transmission of the novel coronavirus (2019-n CoV) identified in Wuhan, China."

On 15 January, Japan reported its first case of coronavirus and its Health Ministry said the patient had not visited any seafood market in China. The Wuhan Municipal Health Commission in a statement said that the possibility of "limited human-to-human transmission" couldn't be ruled out. Despite the fact that Wuhan doctors knew that the virus is "contagious", city authorities allowed 40,000 families to gather and share home-cooked food in a Lunar New Year banquet, as per the article in National Review.

On 19 January, the Chinese National Health Commission declared the virus *"still preventable and controllable."*

On 20 January, the head of China's National Health Commission team confirmed that two cases of infection in China's Guangdong province had been caused by 'human-to-human transmission and medical staff had been infected."

On 21 January, the CDC announced the first case of the coronavirus in the US. The patient had returned from China six days ago.

> Nearly two months after the first case of the virus was reported, Chinese authorities announced their 'first steps for a quarantine of Wuhan.' By this time, a significant number of Chinese citizens have traveled abroad as "asymptomatic, oblivious carriers." Dr. Wenliang tested positive for coronavirus on February 1 and he died six days later.[23]

Complicity of the **WHO** *or its lackadaisical attitude* is another factor responsible for the spread of this virus. Though, China officially notified the World Health Organization (WHO) about several cases of an unusual pneumonia in Wuhan on 31 December 2019 but WHO officials did not take it seriously—comparing this Novel Coronavirus with earlier strains of SARS and MERS, not recommending any specific health measures for travellers to and from Wuhan and even discouraged the entry screening of passengers from Wuhan on 11 January.[24] On 14 January, the WHO officials agreed with the Chinese authorities and stated in its report that Preliminary investigations conducted by the latter found no clear evidence of human-to-human transmission of the novel coronavirus (2019-nCoV) identified in Wuhan. They could find time only on 20 & 21 January to conduct its first field visit of Wuhan.[25] The seriousness of the situation was not fathomed by the WHO officials even three weeks after it was notified by China. It took another five weeks when on 11 March 2020, the Director General, WHO declared COVID-19 as a pandemic.[26] The UN Secretary General also cannot absolve himself of the responsibility of coordinating a global response to this world crisis. Stating in a media briefing "Covid-19 is the greatest test that we have faced together since the formation of the UN" by the UN Secretary General Antonio Guterres[27] is not enough. If the United Nations is going to be absent in a global crisis where it is required most, then question will be raised on its relevance, efficacy or even continuance.

The origin story of novel coronavirus planted in the public mind is that in late 2019, someone at the now world-famous Huanan seafood market in Wuhan was infected with a virus from an animal. Scientists say it is highly likely that the virus came from bats but first passed through an intermediary animal in the same way that another coronavirus—the 2002 SARS outbreak—moved from horseshoe bats to cat-like civets before infecting humans. One animal implicated as an intermediary host between bats and humans is the endangered pangolin, whose scales are illegally trafficked in China for traditional medicine. These exotic animals are sold in the wet markets of China, that too illegally because pangolins were not listed on the inventory of items being sold in Wuhan. Another study claimed to have ruled out pangolins as an intermediary altogether. Study by a group of Chinese scientists published in the medical journal Lancet in January 2020 revealed that the first COVID-19 patient had no connection to Wuhan's wet animal market, and neither did 13 of the first 41 confirmed cases.[28]

There is another facility in Wuhan, which is on the radar of the international scientific community—its biology laboratory. The Wuhan Institute of Virology opened its very first biosafety level 4 (BSL-4) lab in Mainland China in 2015. The Wuhan BSL-4 lab took more than 10 years to complete at a cost of 300 million Yuan (US$44 million) from its conception in 2003, when the SARS virus broke out in China. This lab is dedicated to the research of severe infectious diseases. It is deemed to have the highest level of biological safety. This lab is on the cusp of being cleared to work with the world's most dangerous pathogens. The move is part of a plan to build between five and seven biosafety level-4 (BSL-4) labs across the Chinese mainland by 2025.[29]

In addition to China, the other countries that currently have BSL-4 labs in the world are the US, the UK, Canada, France, Germany, Australia, Sweden and South Africa.[30] Wuhan BSL-4 lab has a focus on the control of emerging diseases, storing purified viruses and acts as a WHO 'reference laboratory' linked to similar labs around the world.[31] Its remit includes improving defence and resilience towards biological wars/terrorist attacks and maintaining national biosecurity.[32] This lab is located only 30 km away from the South China Seafood Wholesale Market (In fact "Express" of UK has brought out that the Wuhan Centre for Disease control laboratory, WCDC is less than one mile from the disease epicenter at Wuhan fish market). This "wet market" in Wuhan was closed on 1st January 2020 after it was found to be most likely starting point for the outbreak of COVID-19 pandemic. In 2017, scientists such as U.S. molecular biologist Richard H. Ebright expressed concern of previous escapes of the SARS virus from Chinese high-level containment labs in Beijing and the pace and scale of China's plans for expansion in to BSL-4 labs. In January 2020, the Institute of Virology was rumored as a source for the novel coronavirus outbreak as a result of allegations of bioweapon research. According to a report by the Central News Agency quoting Beijing Today, Huang Yanling, a postgraduate student of the Wuhan Institute of Virology of the Chinese Academy of Sciences, was the first "patient zero" infected with the Wuhan pneumonia and began to spread the virus; however, researchers at the virus lab denied these claims and guaranteed that no one was infected by the virus. The claim was discarded as a conspiracy theory by *the Washington Post* in an article titled, "Experts debunk fringe theory linking China's coronavirus to weapon's research". The Newspaper cited U.S. experts who explained why the Institute was not suitable for bioweapons research, as most countries had abandoned bioweapons as fruitless, and that there was no evidence to establish that the virus was genetically engineered.[33] Still, a considerable number of scientists believe that SARS-CoV-2 actually escaped by default because of lax safety protocols from this laboratory where it was being either studied or genetically engineered as a bio-weapon.

Either the WHO was misled by the Chinese or its dubious leader Dr. Tedros Adhanom Ghebreyesus was arm-twisted not to inform the world about the true facts so that the Chinese could shirk responsibility at best and cover up at worst about the origin, nature and scale of the pandemic.[34] In any case, China should give full access to international scientists and investigators to Wuhan wet markets, Institute of Virology and the city of Wuhan in general to try and establish the origin of the virus rather than creating impediments. An impartial and independent investigation could absolve China of this virus conspiracy but probably the truth may never come out as they have officially destroyed all existing samples on 3rd January and locating a "zero patient" is like 'finding a needle in the haystack'.

A war of words has broken out between China and the United States over the outbreak of novel coronavirus pandemic. China pushed a new theory about the origins of the coronavirus: It is an American disease that might have been introduced by members of the United States Army who visited Wuhan in October. The notion received an official endorsement from China's Ministry of Foreign Affairs.[35]

On 18th May 2020, the United States President Donald Trump wrote an official letter to Director General WHO and posted it on Twitter, bringing out reasons for suspending the US contribution (on 14 April 2020) to WHO pending an investigation by his Administration of the organization's failed response to the COVID-19 outbreak. He has illustrated complete timelines showing connivance between WHO and Chinese officials. Mr. Trump categorically specified that the International Health Regulations require countries to report the risk of a health emergency within 24 hours. But China did not inform the World Health Organization of Wuhan's several cases of pneumonia, of unknown origin, until 31 December 2019, even though it likely had knowledge of these cases days or weeks earlier. He argued that Dr. Tedros strongly praised China's strict domestic travel restrictions, but was inexplicably against his closing of the United States border, or the ban, with respect to people coming from China. According to Mr. Trump, the world has suffered because of the deadly political gamesmanship of Dr. Tedros and governments relying on his comments, delayed imposing life saving restrictions on travel to and from China. Further, before locking down Wuhan, Chinese authorities had allowed more than five million people to leave the city and that many of these people were bound for international destinations all over the world. Till as late as, on 3 March 2020, the World Health Organization cited official Chinese data to downplay the very serious risk of asymptomatic spread, telling the world that "COVID-19 does not transmit as efficiently as influenza" and that unlike influenza this disease was not primarily driven by people who are infected but not yet sick." Mr. Trump highlighted that by the time Director General, WHO finally declared the virus a pandemic on 11 March 2020, it had killed more than 4,000 people and infected more than 100,000 people in at least 114 countries around the world.[36]

Without even waiting for 30 days, which he gave to the WHO in the aforesaid letter to show major substantive improvements, President Trump terminated all ties with the WHO on 29 May 2020, stating "Because they have failed to make the requested and greatly needed reforms, we will be today terminating our relationship with the World Health Organization." He further said that he would redirect its funding from the Geneva-based WHO towards other global public health organizations.[37]

Another role in exacerbating the pandemic has been played by the religious fundamentalist organizations. Most Prominent is ***the Tablighi Jamaat,*** reportedly a nursery for recruiting and indoctrinating Islamist terrorists. Since 2001, traces of links have been found between Tablighi Jamaat and Islamists involved in acts of terror. The French intelligence calls Tablighi Jamaat the 'antechamber of fundamentalism' and it has found to be behind various terrorists attacks in France, UK, Spain and the United States.[38] Tablighi Jamaat held large gatherings in Malaysia, Pakistan and Indonesia and thereby exported the pathogen to multiple countries, from Southeast Asia to West Asia. India inexplicably allowed the Tablighi Jamaat activists, including foreigners, to congregate in the Markaz, as the Jamaat headquarters is known, located in Nizamuddin West area of Capital from March 13, a day after Delhi state declared an epidemic and shut all schools, colleges and movie theatres. The New Delhi congregation stretched for 18 days until April 1, when 2,346 individuals were evacuated.[39] According to Health Ministry, the Tablighi Jamaat congregation has significantly contributed to the doubling of coronavirus (COVID-19) cases in India. Earlier, the number of confirmed cases doubled in around 7.4 days on an average, the event has resulted in doubling them in 4.1 days.[40] The government claimed more than 8,000 people, including foreigners, visited the headquarters in early March. As on 6th April, more than 25,000 Jamaat members and their contacts had been quarantined across nearly 15 Indian states.[41] The other such organizations, which played similar role in spreading COVID-19 are: South Korea's secretive Shincheonji Church of Jesus (More than half of South Korea's COVID-19 cases have been linked to this doomsday sect) and Qom became the center of Iran's contagion.[42]

Only a detailed investigation and research will reveal why the impact of COVID-19 was far more pronounced in the United States and Europe than in China, from where it had originated. Was it a pure coincidence that being an authoritarian regime, China withheld and delayed the release of information or was it by design for some ulterior motives or some non-state actors jumped in to the bandwagon to accentuate the contagion.

5

The Multitudinous Effects of the COVID-19 Pandemic

Thomas L. Friedman, in his 1999 classic "The Lexus and the Olive Tree" that has been translated in 30 languages, and later in an international best selling book "The World is Flat: The Globalized World in the Twenty-First Century", identified three great eras of Globalization: Globalization 1.0—primarily the globalization of countries that lasted for four centuries from 1400s to 1800; Globalization 2.0—the globalization of companies that lasted roughly for two centuries from 1800 to 2000, interrupted by the Great Depression and World Wars I and II; and Globalization 3.0 that started since 2000 pertained to the globalization of individuals, who are to collaborate and compete globally through digitization.[1]

But the COVID-19 pandemic appears to have reversed the whole process of globalization. Globalization was used as a way to resolve problems of the world ranging from natural disasters to international crises. But when the lives of individuals are getting threatened by the coronavirus with the death toll increasing at an exponential rate, international organizations have faltered when most needed—WHO behaved irresponsibly and in a suspicious manner and should be made accountable for dereliction of its duty, UN Security Council took so long to meet (and that too inconclusively) to discuss a truly global catastrophe; each country is responding to this menace individually in a de-globalized manner. Though it started as a global health crisis, the pandemic has exposed many weaknesses in the global system. The pandemic has created a decision dilemma between the public health and economic well-being of the country. The emerging social pattern and social etiquette may create a greater social divide, which can only be filled by digitization and innovative use of technology. The control and exploitation of technology itself will be the guiding force for the future. The current international organizations having lost their relevance, new ones may come up but that will depend upon the emerging leadership post-COVID-19.

Thus impacts of COVID-19 pandemic need to be studied in detail on the socio-economic environment and the public health, being the main cause of concern.

Economic Fallout

Most analysts are of the opinion that the impact of COVID-19 pandemic on the global economy may be far greater and more widespread than that of the Great Depression of the 1930s. The International Monetary Fund (IMF) said in its latest forecast that the global economy would experience its "worst recession since the Great Depression, surpassing that seen during the global financial crisis a decade ago."[2] Even before the onset of this pandemic, the global economy was confronting turbulence on account of disruptions in trade flows and attenuated growth. A global recession now seems inevitable. Extended lockdowns, uncertainty and panic are expected to cause demand worldwide to decline in a precipitous manner. Inevitably, this leads to a vicious downward cycle, where companies close down, resulting in more layoffs and a further drop in consumption. This will consequently lead to a precipitous decline in GDP. To compensate for this loss, massive inflows of funds would be required but most governments including India might find it difficult to manage adequate resources for this purpose. Equally important, such funds, to be effective, would be required immediately, before the situation gets spiraled out of control.

COVID-19 has thus aggravated the economic situation by inflicting the triple shock of demand, supply and liquidity.

There are countries whose major source of income depends on tourism industry; they will have to bear a larger impact on their economies, such as Australia. Disruptions in the import and export of critical raw materials and probably rise in price will impact domestic industries adversely.[3] Service driven economies will witness huge economic fallout of lockdown due to a complete stoppage of all economic activity. On the other hand countries, which have manufacturing driven growth will also see shuttered factories and equally significant contraction. Is there any template to measure the extent of economic fallout? Economists and banking organizations are churning out figures almost daily.

Assuming a scenario in which the pandemic would fade in the second half of 2020, the International Monetary Fund (IMF) in its biannual World Economic Outlook had projected the global economy to contract sharply by 3 percent in 2020 but in its latest report of July, IMF further revised it to—4.9 percent. Earlier, the IMF had given a rosy estimate of 1.9 percent economic growth for India in 2020-21 but now it expects the country's economy to shrink by 4.5 percent in the same period. It also revised its estimate for the following year, 2021-22 from 7.4 percent to a much more modest 6 percent.[4] The IMF forecast is broadly in line with what most economists have been predicting for India, a contraction of anything between 3 percent and 5 percent. Looking at the current trends, agriculture or rural sector may help to rejuvenate the economy. However, Investment Bank Barclays on 14 April pared its growth forecast for India to 0 percent for calendar year 2020 from its earlier projection of 2.5 percent. Further, combined with the disruption in several service sectors, Barclay's Research estimated that the economic loss would be close to $234.4 billion (8.1 per cent of GDP), assuming that India would remain under a partial lockdown at least until the end of May. This was much higher than the $120 billion it had estimated earlier for roughly the same time period.[5]

According to the Federation of Indian Chambers of Commerce and Industry (FICCI), close to 40 million jobs are at risk during the period April-September 2020 and these are from the organized sector.[6] To revive India's economy, the financial package recommended by economic advisers to Industry bodies ranged from Rs. 10 lakh crore to Rs 20 lakh crore (i.e., 5 to 10 percent of the GDP for 2019-20 respectively).[7] They sought economic package akin to the one announced by the US, which was $2.2 trillion, around 10 percent of that country's GDP, the largest economic rescue package in the United States' history. The US government would send checks to more than 150 million American households, set up enormous loan programs and much more.[8] On 12 May 2020, Prime Minister Narendra Modi launched Aatma-nirbhar Bharat Abhiyan or Self-reliant India Mission by announcing a Rs 20 lakh crore stimulus package, which is about 10 percent of India's GDP in 2019-2020. Rs 20 lakh crore included Rs 1.7 lakh crore that the government had given as relief package (of free food grains to poor and cash to poor women and elderly) on March 26 as also the steps taken by the Reserve Bank of India (RBI) such as liquidity enhancing measures and interest rate cuts. While the March stimulus was 0.8 per cent of GDP, RBI's cut in interest rates and liquidity boosting measures totaled to 3.2 per cent of the GDP (about Rs 6.5 lakh crore).[9] The government is working out a further economic stimulus. However, fight of figures will always be there between the government on one side and the business leaders /academics on the other side. The government will talk in terms of combined package (monetary, fiscal and liquidity measures) while business leaders will seek absolute fiscal commitment as a percentage of country's GDP.

Public Healthcare

This virus is capable of overwhelming any country's health systems preparedness. The crisis in the United States is illustrative. The United States has resources, research capacity, infrastructure, talent and world-class health care system, yet COVID-19 has crippled the country, just as it shook the fundamentals of China and also destabilized Europe. In fact, lockdown became a bone of contention between economists and healthcare professionals. The economists were of the opinion that bringing economy to a grinding halt through a lockdown could have a far greater impact than Coronavirus whereas medical fraternity argued that the misery caused by spread of COVID-19 would be unimaginable if there were no restrictions imposed. Reportedly, the dilemma between public health versus country's economy compelled the US President Donald Trump to resist the advice by doctors, apprehending that the impact of the countrywide lockdown on world's largest economy would be unprecedented—leading to a compromised position as against the Chinese economy.[10] Aiming for his re-election this year, President Trump knew a declining US economy could hurt his election campaign significantly. But ultimately, with the COVID-19 cases mounting, restrictions have finally been imposed in the United States.

The pandemic has exposed the chinks in the armor of every country. No nation has the ability to manufacture every variety of medical equipment and manufacture all varieties of drugs with in its borders. India is the world's largest manufacturer of hydroxy-chloroquine. Interestingly, China does not make hydroxychloroquine and India is the lead global supplier.[11] Even a mighty nation like the United States and 54 other nations were supplied hydroxychloroquine by India as grants as well as on commercial basis. On the other hand, even in to the fourth month of the pandemic, India was importing tonnes of protective gear and testing kits from all over the world.[12] The same is true even for the developed nations of the Western World.

The enormity of the pandemic has brought back the welfare state in to cognizance. In the most developed capitalist democracies, it has never faded entirely but the State adhered to its core function of providing basic public health services and acted as a regulator, and leaving the rest for the market to determine. But the governments will now have to intervene in every aspect of economic life—for the poor, food and direct cash transfer will become a norm; for citizens across the board, free or subsidized health care will have to be provisioned and so on.

The world will need to invent new international public health systems that can reduce the risk of another pandemic, and help save lives in the current one. The sooner we as human beings start thinking about how to do this, the better it is. To do it successfully, we will have to invent a new philosophy. Just as in the aftermaths of previous incidents of mass death, social disarray and economic collapse, as in the wake of World War II, human civilization will need to invent a new understanding of what it means to be human.[13] Both in the developed and the developing world, health care paradigms and national economic priorities, especially social safety nets for the most vulnerable sections of society will have to be reimagined and budgeted accordingly.

Dr. Henry A. Kissinger, former Secretary of State of the United States has categorically pointed out that "Leaders are dealing with the crisis on a largely national basis, but the virus's society-dissolving effects do not recognize borders. While the assault on human health will—hopefully—be temporary, the political and economic upheaval it has unleashed could last for generations." Hence he advised that the necessities of the moment must ultimately be coupled with a global collaborative vision and program so as to achieve global resilience to infectious disease. New techniques and technologies are required to be developed for infection control and commensurate vaccines across large populations. Cities, states and regions must consistently prepare to protect their people from pandemics through stockpiling, cooperative planning and exploration at the frontiers of science.[14]

Social Environment

There is a direct correlation between the way a society functions and the economic activity. The nature of this pandemic is such that there is an inherent tension between preserving lives and economic activities—the former involves large scale lockdowns, quarantines, social distancing, restrictions on all types of public travel, closure of schools, institutes, cinemas, entertainments, religious and social gatherings, all opposed to the latter which are based on mobility, migration, supply chains, trade, demand and consumption. The governments across the world have intervened, in varying degrees, to minimize the stress.

An additional fallout from the current pandemic may probably be the extent to which inequality in incomes would impact segments of the population, facing a common threat. Developing countries, like

India, lacking a comprehensive nationwide health system would find this an even more difficult situation to handle. An example is the unskilled migrant workers settled in and around the metropolitan cities. Due to sudden announcement of prolonged lockdown, finding themselves unsure of future employment and without any medical cover, it resulted in mass exodus of families toward their native places—not only creating a law and order problem for the states but also acting as suspected carriers of the virus to their villages, which have almost negligible medical support. U.N. Secretary General Antonio Guterres argued in a videoconference before the U.N. Security Council on 10 April 2020, "the pandemic also poses a significant threat to the maintenance of international peace and security—potentially leading to an increase in social unrest and violence that would greatly undermine our ability to fight the disease."[15]

Most significantly, the advancement in technology has come to the rescue of mankind. The technology advances were already driving economic integration in unprecedented ways before the Coronavirus struck. That is what has made work from home possible otherwise the society would have come to standstill. Universities, colleges and technological institutes across the world have been able to function normally through conduct of virtual classes.

In this world, no one is self-sufficient. Nature has designed us in such a way that connections will never disappear. The society will soon adapt to the changes enforced by the pandemic. Individuals will become more interconnected but the connection will be digital. Work from home will become a norm for software companies.

One possible aspect of this pandemic is likely to be the thrust it could provide to the extensive employment of Artificial Intelligence (AI) combined with Big data analytics and advanced surveillance means to control the spread of such infectious diseases in large populations. China's authoritarian methods, by using these technologies, seem to have helped it in containing the spread of the virus—at least for the time being. Some other countries have also started employing somewhat similar techniques. Other leaders across many nations, though being democratic, may find it too tempting to emulate China, in controlling their population digitally. This is also being referred as 'digital authoritarianism'. The rise of digital autocracies may possibly lead to digital repression, and with AI-powered surveillance, create a capacity for predictive control, as this is also being referred to as 'social management'.[16] AI will be the cause (though unintentionally) of our next big existential challenge as Vint Cerf, Google chief Internet evangelist who is widely known as "Father of the Internet," had warned about AI and machine learning, "There will be abuses and bugs, some harmful, so we need to be thoughtful about how these technologies are implemented and used."[17]

The Coronavirus has brought the human species in to a new world, where humans are locked inside the houses; and animals and birds are reclaiming their space. In other words, nature is telling the humanity that humans are not the masters but they are co-habitants of this Universe like other species and there is somebody else who is controlling the Universe. The only positive aspect of this pandemic is that measures adopted to control the spread of virus have resulted in sharp reduction of air pollution and carbon dioxide. A recent report of Carbon Tracker, a London-based not-for-profit think tank, revealed that China staved off a quarter or more of its CO_2 emissions in two weeks by stopping work at manufacturing units and construction sites to quarantine its workers. The European Space Agency and NASA images showed a drop in pollutants like nitrogen oxide that lead to respiratory diseases.[18] However, once the pandemic is under control, we might see a massive rise in economic activity, just as in the aftermath of World War II, and we should take care that it is not at the cost of the environment. This state of crisis has given us the opportunity to heal the planet by decarbonizing our economy. Significant policy shifts aimed at decarbonizing our economies could help improve lives.

6

Emerging New World Order (Post-COVID-19)

Nobody could have imagined that a deeply inter-connected globalized world—a boon for the mankind—would itself become a medium for the spread of a deadly virus, resulting in to a global crisis. Like all global crises in the past, the COVID-19 crisis will also have a significant impact on the global power configuration. The global elite is waiting with bated breath to know what kind of new world order will emerge once the crisis is over. Is it going to be a Unipolar, Bipolar or Multipolar world? Is it going to be Sino-centric, US-centric or some other power centres will have a decisive role?

After World War II and prior to the disintegration of Soviet Union in December 1991, i.e., in the so-called Cold War period, it was conveniently referred to as a bipolar world, which was based on the military power or rather the nuclear weapons capability of the North Atlantic Treaty Organization (NATO) countries led by the United States and Warsaw Pact countries led by the Soviet Union. Though economy mattered but Economic power was not talked about. For example, in 1985, the Soviet Union's GDP was only $741.9 billion compared to Japan's $ 1,220 billion. But while Japan was an economic lion, it was a military mouse. The impoverished Soviet Union, on the other hand, had a military machine on par with the USA's.[1] Hence, the Soviet Union was considered superpower, competing with the United States. As the Cold War was ending, emphasis began to shift from military to economic power. In 1990, Edward N. Luttwak first coined the term "geo-economics" and described how in the post-Cold War period, the main arena for rivalry between states would be economic rather than military. In fact, the main cause for the collapse of the Soviet Union was economic weakness. Three years later, Samuel Huntington also emphasized the importance of economic activity in inter-state relations, in a more forthright manner.[2] The emphasis on economic power considerably increased after China's rise. Though, academics will always evaluate the 'Comprehensive National Power' (CNP) of countries but the overt trend now is to establish the economic supremacy of one country over another, with military power taking the back seat.

As long as the nations compete with each other to achieve their geopolitical ends, the traditional concepts of national security and balance of power will continue but post-COVID-19, emphasis will be on economic recovery and it will be the new economic world order for which nations will seek new politico-economic alignments or partnerships. Various experts opine that the world will pass "peak virus" within months but the economy, governments, and social institutions will take years to recover in the best-case scenario.[3] The various scenarios of economic world order, which are likely to emerge can be guesstimated: One, Emergence of a China-centric World Order; Two, Weakening of China's Economic Footprint; Three, Dynamic Balance of Economic Alliances between West and East.

Emergence of a China-centric World Economic Order

Some analysts argue that the post-COVID-19 era may be the beginning of a China-centric world order and China-centric globalization. They are of the opinion that as the financial crisis of 2007-2008 led to the strengthening of right and left-wing populist parties all over the world, similarly the current crisis may further strengthen authoritarian states if they perform well.[4] Reports emerging from China indicate that China has somehow managed the spread of COVID-19 well and its industrial production is recovering even as that of every other country is taking a hit. The oil price slump will make this recovery even faster.[5] Such a scenario may give a huge global competitive advantage to China, which it may use to help the recovery efforts of the other international actors. China's President Xi Jinping had intensive telephonic conversations with the UN Secretary General and leaders of other countries. China has shown support to more than 130 countries, including all those on the agenda of the Security Council. China provided medical supplies, shared experiences, sent expert teams and assisted with commercial procurement.[6] China's richest man Jack Ma spearheaded the private sector's fight against the pandemic. The Chinese propaganda machinery will magnify this and refer its efforts as equivalent of a new "Marshall Plan". China will, in return, expect the continuation of an open trade regime for its manufactured goods and technological products.

Chinese actions are a smart economic investment for geopolitical gains. Beijing will like to assert its claim to global leadership by pushing Huawei 5G trials as a bargain and rejuvenate the Belt and Road Initiative as the future of global connectivity.[7] For instance, Italy was the first country of the Group of Seven industrialized nations to join the Chinese Belt and Road infrastructure project.[8] To what extent China will succeed in its endeavours, it will become clear in the coming months.

Weakening of China's Economic Footprint

Reminiscent of the 2008 global financial crisis, where China provided the largest stimulus in the country's history (RMB 4 trillion (US$575 billion)—equivalent to about 13 percent of China's 2008 GDP)[9], there is a general belief that China will again come out with a significant stimulus package to revive its economy back to life. However, China's economic condition is now much different:

- China's economy shrank by 6.8 percent in the first quarter of 2020, confirming the damage done to it by the pandemic. Its GDP stood at 20.65 trillion Yuan (about $ 2.91 trillion) in the first quarter of 2020 and according to the government data it was the first time that the Chinese economy had contracted since the Cultural Revolution, which ended in 1976. Chinese State media reports said the 6.8 percent contraction translated to an economic loss of about 1.44 trillion Yuan ($203.4 billion).[10]

- According to Andrew Small, the author of bestseller book "The China-Pakistan Axis" and an authority on China, "China does not have the same fiscal and monetary firepower to deploy as it did after the financial crisis (of 2008)."[11]
- Before the novel coronavirus hit, China was already walking a fine line between spending enough to prop up economic growth and cutting down high levels of debt that pose a structural threat to its economy's sustainability.
- Thus China would be dependent on recoveries in its major markets, especially the United States. Its investments in the grand Belt and Road Initiative (BRI) are not going to deliver anything meaningful in the near future because the host countries are not in a position to service the debt.[12]
- According to S Narayan, former economic advisor to the Prime Minister of India, unless China manages to ramp up quickly and its domestic consumption picks up, its economic growth could shrink to as low as 2-3 per cent, far lower than the 6 per cent estimated before the pandemic outbreak.[13] The World Bank in its latest Economic Update of July 2020, has brought down China's GDP growth to 1.6 per cent this year from 6.1 per cent in 2019,[14] whereas according to IMF's latest report of June 2020, China's economy is expected to grow only at 1.0 percent in 2020 (compared to earlier 1.2 percent of April 2020 Report).[15]
- China is the world's biggest holder of reserves, with $3.1 trillion as of the end of January. Investors may consider the foreign exchange reserve to be a buffer against severe economic dislocation but that would be a mistake. Reserves aren't profits. In addition to net export payments, they include foreign investment. The asset (reserve investments) is offset by a liability (the amount owed to foreign investors). Based on International Monetary Fund criteria used to calculate the

minimum required level of reserves, China needs around $3 trillion—roughly what it has now.[16]

- D Sampath Kumar, former Editor of *Business Line* highlighted that foreign investors have parked $ 900 billion in Chinese equities, which is 'hot money'—the reserves would be needed to pay the investors if they choose to pull out. Alongside, China's reserves are (mostly, at least) invested in US Treasury bonds.[17] Given the current blame game between the United States and China for the origin of Coronavirus, *there is a risk of US freezing China's reserves, as damages for what US sees as China being responsible for releasing the virus.*
- The $14 trillion Chinese economy is powered by manufacturing; and the American and Western markets are essential for Chinese manufacturing and export. This situation may change if the production and supply lines gradually shift back to the U.S. or to other Chinese alternatives. Rising production costs in China already had been driving the momentum of manufacturing and production location toward cheaper labor destinations in Southeast Asia.[18] John Garver of the Georgia University of Technology, Atlanta, US, and Mandarin-speaking expert on China opined "As long as Donald Trump is in the White House, the US would strive to bring home production of critical items, or at least out-source them outside China—maybe India."[19]
- To power its factories and other physical infrastructure, the Chinese are under tremendous debt. Undue focus on creation of physical infrastructure, decision to pour billions of dollars into One Belt One Road (OBOR) and hunt for mineral rich nations in Africa have all come at a huge cost, that is debt.[20] The Debt to GDP ratio for China is one of the highest in the world—China's corporate debt to GDP ratio is 156.7 percent.[21] Debt requires servicing; it requires the economy to run on full steam, it requires the giant factories and huge supply chains to run overtime. The debt bubble for China is a reality and economic disintegration is a possibility given the ambitious over spending that has happened in the last decade.

As China recovered from the novel coronavirus, government authorities have likely turned their attention from crisis management to restoring the economy. The stimulus that was likely to come in 2020 differed from 2008 in size, target and strategic priorities. According to *Reuters*, the Chinese government has considered spending up to RMB 2.8 trillion (US$394 billion) in local government special bonds to spur infrastructure investment—a much smaller percentage of GDP than the 2008 stimulus.[22] Whereas China's 2008 stimulus helped build high quality but relatively basic infrastructure like high-speed rail line, train stations, metro systems, and airports, the stimulus in 2020 will likely be more targeted towards "new infrastructure" that will help China transition from polluting, export-led manufacturing economy to a high-tech and service-driven economy. Broadly speaking, "new infrastructure" includes, for example, big data centres, 5G infrastructure, and charging stations for new energy vehicles (NEVs), among other areas. Whereas China previously needed infrastructure to help move large numbers of people and massive quantities of goods, now China needs infrastructure that will help the economy to operate more efficiently and sustainably. The return on investment on new infrastructure is more risky and less certain than is the case with hard infrastructure. For example, when building a bridge to connect two cities, there is a fairly certain economic and social benefit that can be calculated in advance, regardless if a project meets challenges. In contrast, new infrastructure involves areas that are still in their emerging stages of development. NEV technology, for example, is far from established, and Internet of Things (IoT)-enabled technology will not take off in earnest until 5G infrastructures are running and its networks are widespread. While investments in such fields very well may prove prudent, it is less clear what role new infrastructure will play even one or two decades from now. The new infrastructure may be better executed by private firms like the tech giants Alibaba, Tencent, and Baidu, as well as start-up enterprises rather than by state owned enterprises (SOEs).[23]

In view of the faulty and used medical equipment supplied by China to the needy countries for fighting the coronavirus and suppressing information on the outbreak of coronavirus for first two months in connivance with WHO officials, it has badly dented China's reputation. China badly needs reputation management but that calls for substantial wherewithal.[24] Experts are not too sanguine about China's ability to throw money around and buy loyalties and that too when all other countries of the world have suffered heavy casualties.

Dynamic Balance of Economic Alliances between West and East

The United States with a GDP of $21.4 trillion (in 2019) is the world's leading economy;[25] hence its relevance will not be lost completely. Post-COVID-19, there will be a lot of domestic transformation and much will depend upon the re-election of Mr. Donald Trump. According to Dr. Henry Kissinger, "The U.S. administration has done a solid job in avoiding immediate catastrophe. The ultimate test will be whether the virus's spread can be arrested and then reversed in a manner and at a scale that maintains public confidence in Americans' ability to govern themselves."[26] It is very much likely that the United States will change its policy concerning China and use its resources differently to balance China.

Italy, Spain, France, Germany and the whole of Europe was celebrating the *'Hug the Chinese'* campaign but they are now regretting their actions, having been hit hard by the Coronavirus. [27] As of 16 August 2020, there have been 210,289 deaths in Europe overall due to the coronavirus (COVID-19) since the first recorded European death in France on 15 February.[28] Further, China exploited this humanitarian crisis not only by making quick profit through supply of sub-standard and used medical kits and protective gear but reportedly tried to acquire distressed assets in strategic sectors globally as economies struggle during the COVID-19 pandemic. The European Union, Germany, France, Spain, and Italy have taken measures to counter this move by tightening their foreign investment rules (Of the 27 EU members, 14 already have FDI screening mechanism in place). A false perception was created by China's propaganda machinery that China came to the rescue of Italy with a plane load of medical emergency, at a time many Italians thought "Europe" was abandoning one of EU's founding members? But this was no more than a blip, and the perception was wrong. Germany and France together donated, as opposed to sold, more medical equipment to Italy than China.[29] This could lead Europe to carry out a rethink of their economic policy. Political leaders, close observers, analysts and experts in Europe are considering a range of possibilities, which can be summarized as:

- COVID-19 crisis is being compared to the wartime effects, with the economy collapsing and unemployment skyrocketing.
- This crisis has shown that Europe's open, market-orientated economy is very fragile.
- The fragility of global supply chains has been exposed. Businesses will now diversify their ways of supply and source certain pieces at least in several Asian countries and not just in China ... Some might even create redundant supply chains at home to be fired up in times of crises.
- Need is being felt to take control again of crucial sectors such as health care, energy, transport and even the textile industry—so as not to depend on other countries for everything.
- The state will also play a bigger role—the balance of power will shift away from the market towards the state.
- According to Niclas Frederic Poitiers, trade economist and research fellow at Brussels-based economic think tank Bruegel, "The crisis will give momentum to protectionism, which is already on the rise, especially since US President Donald Trump was elected," Poitiers further added, "But this will come at a price for the consumer—producing more at home instead of in countries where production is cheaper means prices will go up."[30]

Meanwhile, foreign companies are increasingly looking at India as a viable investment destination as more investors seek to exit China in the wake of the COVID-19 outbreak and its political management. Around 1,000 foreign firms are presently engaged in conversations with Indian authorities, and at least 300 are actively pursuing production plans in India—in sectors such as smartphones, electronics, medical devices, textiles, and synthetic fabric.[31]

Japanese Prime Minister Shinzo Abe wants high value-added product manufacturing bases located in China to come home to Japan. In its emergency economic package adopted on 7th April, the Japanese government called for the re-establishment of supply chains that have been hit by the virus's proliferation. It earmarked more than 240 billion yen (about $2.2 billion) in its supplementary budget plan for fiscal 2020 to assist domestic companies to move production back home or to diversify their production bases into Southeast Asia.[32] Similarly, the United States is also considering shouldering the relocation costs of American companies returning home from China.

If the U.S. and Japan, the world's biggest and third-biggest economies respectively, move away from China, then China's long-standing growth model and consequently its GDP is going to be in a great trouble. Thus environment in post-COVID-19 may provide greater opportunities to India and ASEAN to seek profitable economic alliances with the West establishing a dynamic balance between the West and East.

But the one factor that could be equally decisive in shaping the new world economy will be crude prices—at historic lows. This has ramifications not just for oil producing countries—Russia, USA and OPEC—but also for oil guzzling nations like India and China. If these prices continue, it could reshape not just crude economics but also alter economic positions. Only time will tell Russia's gamble to drive down oil prices will hurt Moscow or will it actually be a death knell for American Energy companies. Recently, Russia has become far more economically and politically stable and an important power broker in West Asia.[33]

The World Economic order that we are used to is destined to change in the coming months and years. The new world economic order will witness a lesser role for China—both due to the possibility of a debt bubble and due to unwillingness of other countries to trade. In the initial phase of BRI, China through its predatory economics had acquired assets in Asia and Africa but that did not affect the Western world. Now when the epicentre of COVID-19 has shifted to the West with their casualties' rate rising to unmanageable proportions and

businesses are virtually closed, China, leaving aside all norms of humanity, is on a profit-making spree—selling used and substandard medical kits and protective gears at exorbitant rates but claiming themselves as saviours through false propaganda; and investing money to acquire their distressed assets in key sectors. Unlike the Communist country run by the authoritarian regime, where dignity of human life has no value, it is unlikely that democratic countries with liberal values will prefer trade relations with China when better options are available elsewhere.

In his daily White House briefing, the US President Donald Trump has warned that China should face consequences if it was "knowingly responsible" for the coronavirus pandemic. However, he did not elaborate on what form that might take.[34] *China has been using tenets of Asymmetric Warfare to seek vulnerabilities of the United States. Destroying the social and economic fabric of an adversary through the spread of pandemic falls in the category of Non-traditional security threats and if the United States finds any evidence for that, it may not fall under the category of open warfare between the two states but an equal and appropriate response from the United States can not be unexpected. If the United States and its allies from North Atlantic Treaty Organization (NATO) perceive this as a combined threat against the lives of their people, they may move together to deny trading space to China—a non-aggressive counter measure and a modified application of Article 5 of NATO; invoked only once in its history—in response to the terrorist attacks of September 11, 2001.*[35] *Moreover, Article XX of GATT / WTO permits countries "to take any actions it considers necessary to protect it's national security interests".*

7

Challenges and Opportunities for India

Incidentally, COVID-19 crisis has come at a time when India's economy was in the midst of one of the worst slowdowns with GDP growth at sub-5 percent per annum.

In the absence of adequate public health care facilities and the medical resources to handle the pandemic of this magnitude; against which developed countries of the West have buckled up, India has chosen the right measures of complete lockdown and social distancing so as firstly to prevent the disease from spreading and secondly to gain time to deploy appropriate resources to test, trace, isolate and treat people. For a people considered the world over to be noisy, undisciplined, argumentative and individualistic, Indians have shown how a populous and diverse nation comes together in a crisis.[1] The credit for this goes to the perspicacious leadership of Prime Minister Narendra Modi, who not only ascertained the real nature of the crisis, but he motivated and helped 1.35 billion people to prepare for a graded response[2]—initially one day voluntary Janta curfew on 22 March, followed by 68 days national lockdown in four phases from 25 March to 31 May 2020. State leaderships also demonstrated synergy with Centre, thereby establishing the success of federal democracy in India. Modi had categorically brought out in his message to the nation on

April 14, "Had India not adopted a holistic and integrated approach—taking quick and decisive action; the situation in India today would have been completely different."[3]

Initially, the overall growth in number of cases in India had been linear, compared to other countries where it had been exponential. On 25 April, India's tally of coronavirus disease (COVID-19) cases crossed the 26,000 mark and that was one month in to the lockdown period. According to Dr. Balram Bhargava, Director General, Indian Council of Medical Research (ICMR) and Secretary, Department of Health Research, "The case positivity rate had been about 4.5 percent throughout, so we can safely say that we have managed to flatten the curve." Flattening the curve refers to the strategy of bringing down new infections to match health care capacity, an approach particularly crucial for a highly contagious disease like COVID-19. Positivity rate refers to the proportion of people who test positive among all individuals tested on a particular day. However, the total number of tests carried out across the country was still a mere 420 per million of population. The country touched a million infections on 16 July and posted its second million in exactly 21 days thereafter on 7 August. India's journey to two million cases took 158 days, with at least 90 percent of these cases coming after the lifting of the hard nation wide lockdown—a strategy used to gain precious time for the country to set up isolation centres, add hospital beds and testing infrastructure. With India now heading toward the target of one million tests a day, the numbers of detected infections are bound to increase and then the curve will start flattening as it has been proven in case of New Delhi. In view of the crippling economic costs piling up, it became essential to commence unlocking in June, when the outbreak was on a sharp upward trajectory. However, by then the government has been able to augment health infrastructure and testing facilities. Union Health Minister Harsh Vardhan, while addressing a virtual meeting of the WHO for Southeast Asia on 6th August said, "From one lab (for COVID-19 testing) in January, India has 1,370 laboratories at present. Indians anywhere can access a lab within three hours travel time and 33 of the 36 states and UTs exceed WHO's recommendation of testing 140 people per million per day. India's proactive and graded multilevel institutional response to COVID-19 made it possible to have very low cases per million and deaths per million in spite of having a high population density and low fractional GDP spending… as compared to other developed countries." The number of people who have recovered from COVID-19 in India touched 1,375,797 on 6 August, bringing the proportion of recoveries to 68.01 percent, against the global average of 64.2 percent of all cases recovered.[4]

India's recovery rate is expected to eventually soar to over 90 percent, once the outbreak nears its end. If we are able to contain this pandemic, we will emerge victorious with our national image burnished and we can prove to the rest of the world as an example of how one sixth of humanity can achieve results democratically.

As regards economy, it is estimated by experts that India would require at least up to six months even after the entire course of the COVID-19 epidemic is over to restore normalcy and business continuity.[5] There are different estimates by different study reports regarding the loss to India's economy due to the lockdown. According to report from DataLabs from Inc42, the COVID-19 pandemic is expected to hit Indian economy with about $320 billion in terms of daily GDP loss after 40 days of lockdown. The daily GDP of India is estimated to be approximately $8 billion.[6] It is being considered in various forums that India has opportunity to build a more resilient and diverse economy after COVID-19 pandemic. India's Union Minister of Road Transport and Highways and MSME, Nitin Gadkari in a session on post-COVID entrepreneurship opportunities and challenges organized by Bharatiya Shikshan Mandal on 13 April, said, "This should be seen as a blessing in disguise," for Indian industry. He elaborated, "USA is also looking for allies outside of China. The world is thinking in this direction. Naturally, those countries that do not want to deal with China, will look at other countries with potential for quality products at reasonable price and India has that potential."[7]

It is not that India will be getting the opportunity for building up its economy for the first time due to COVID-19. Earlier also, opportunities came on our way but we missed them. We neglected manufacturing during the 1980s, when global supply chains and manufacturing shifted to East Asia and again we did not make use of the global financial crisis in 2009. According to a study by Nomura, a Japanese financial group, out of 56 companies that relocated their production out of China between April 2018 and August 2019—only three went to India, two to Indonesia, 26 relocated to Vietnam, 11 to Taiwan and eight went to Thailand.[8]

India's Challenges

Thus challenges being faced by India are manifold: Firstly, we have to free ourselves from the scourge of novel coronavirus and ensure resumption of economic activity simultaneously; and secondly, we need to introspect our system about the lacunae as to why despite best of our intentions to promote manufacturing we have not succeeded so far.

The severe economic challenges faced by India due to COVID-19 pandemic are:

- Volatility and precipitous fall in financial markets and commodity prices, and financing gap due to shrinking fiscal revenues and COVID-19 expenditure.
- Liquidity crunch, disruptions in international trade and travel, depletion of foreign exchange reserves, devaluation of currency and subsequent fall in export revenues are causes for concern.[9]
- India could face a remittances crisis largely due to fall in the wages and employment of migrant workers, who tend to be more vulnerable to loss of employment and wages during an economic crisis in a host country. According to the World Bank report, remittances to India are likely to drop by 23 percent from $83 billion last year to $64 billion this year due to the coronavirus pandemic.[10] The remittances may further go down, if migrant workers from these countries start returning back to India.

Resilience and rebound will depend on the duration of the lockdown and social distancing compliance by citizens. Uncertainties around health security driven economic decision-making need to be removed by establishing a right balancing between health and the economy. According to a government assessment in end-April, 130 districts in 20 states and five Union Territories were identified as red zones. Additionally, there were 284 orange zones in the country, and the rest of India's 733-odd districts were classified as green zones. Firming up his idea that India would need to focus on a two-pronged approach—preserving public health and reviving economic activity—Prime Minister Narendra Modi laid emphasis on green zones to be used as the hub of future activity.[11] Though the last two phases of lockdown were also accompanied with a set of relaxations, the period between June 1 and June 30 was declared by the government as Unlock 1.0 so that a range of economic activities could be allowed with citizens following the rules of social distancing.

However, India has to ensure that in the interregnum, a banking/credit crisis does not occur, liquidity at household and corporate level is maintained, and there is minimal disruption in capital formation and investments. Labor displacement is to be minimized and encouraged to stay in place or return after the lockdown ensuring their reutilization. Alternatively, the jobs should be created for the migrant labor in their home states.

Presently in India, manufacturing sector is 16 percent of GDP (compared to 42 percent in China and around 30 percent in South Korea). However, manufacturing contributes almost 50 percent of India's exports and every job created in manufacturing has a multiplier effect creating three jobs in the services sector. It implies that with the rise of manufacturing, there will be a four-fold job creation. Under the "Make in India" initiative, the Government of India aimed to increase the share of the manufacturing sector to the GDP to 25 per cent by 2022 and to create 100 million new jobs.[12] However, the scheme hasn't been able to boost up the share of the manufacturing industry. Rather, the percentage of the manufacturing industry in India's GDP came down to 15 percent in 2017, according to World Bank data.[13] Coinciding with the above period, China-based Korean companies were looking for alternate turf somewhere in Southeast Asia because of the mounting operational costs, Chinese firms imitating Korean technologies and the growing political tension between South Korea and China. According to Yoo Chang-Ho, Minister Counselor for Political Affairs, Republic of Korea, these companies had sought opportunities in India as it has a vast domestic market, a good workforce, and also from India they can export to other countries. At present, there are hardly 700 South Korean companies in India whereas Vietnam hosts 7000 of them. Tiny countries like Cambodia and Laos comparatively did better in hosting Korean companies than India. In the last 4-5 years, India miserably failed to attract the China-based Korean companies. They did attempt to come to India but went back after having bitter experience. The Minister Counselor said "most of these companies skipped India because of too many bureaucratic hurdles and red-tape." Most of the companies have gone to Vietnam as it offered them a very good business environment. Vietnam also provided them with incentives and in Vietnam; there is a single point of contact, a person who takes care of everything from the government side. South Korea was fully aware that India is comparatively a better destination and a long-term market. Big companies could afford to wait for a long time to get bureaucratic hurdles to clear off in India but small companies cannot wait for 5-10 years as they need to make money quickly because of the limited amount of capital.[14]

On the heels of South Korean companies relocation, followed the US-China Trade War, where tariffs made exports from China more and more expensive for US importers. Many firms started doing their calculations and have been looking for new locations to re-site their manufacturing operations.

However, re-locating manufacturing facilities to a different country is not an easy task. To start with, it requires the high initial set-up costs, as also simultaneously involves other essential factors like infrastructure, communications, connectivity, good and cost-effective warehousing, transportation and other logistical support. Then comes the challenge of finding the right skilled manpower and thereafter putting the new workers through training specific to their production process. After satisfying these requirements, comes the factor of 'Ease of Doing Business' in a new country, which includes—governmental support, a favourable tax regime and legal framework, and the ease and speed of starting a business in that country.[15]

India has the ideal demographics and its labour cost is half that of China's to become a global manufacturing powerhouse to rival China but the comparison finishes there only. First of all, having a large population, in itself, cannot attract foreign investment or foreign companies to establish their manufacturing base over here. The biggest stumbling block is the lack of skilled manpower. Taking in to account the advantage of demographic dividend in India's favour, Prime Minister Narendra Modi launched ***Skill India*** campaign on 15 July 2015 which aimed to train over 40 crore (400 million) people in India in different skills by 2022. According to the 2018 annual report of National Skill Development Corporation (NSDC), a public-private partnership, it trained 3.98 million students that year, through 11,035 training centres across 40 skill development programs. Only about 12 percent of those who were trained under NSDC programs found jobs, according to government statistics.[16] However, just 25 million youths have been imparted skill training so far under various government schemes.[17] Lack of a trained work force will not only impede the growth of manufacturing sector but will also increase the ratio of unemployment, thereby turning the demographic dividend in to disadvantage. We must concentrate less on number of people trained but more on quality and certification should meet the international standards.[18] Apple's iPhone is a striking illustration of this deficiency. Apple's manufacturing venture in India began in 2016, and since then it has been producing four models in the country, all of them old models. However, the new models are still being manufactured in Shenzhen, China.[19] Beside the extensive global supply network, which China has established in terms of components manufacturing and end-assembly, greater skills are required for higher generation equipment manufacturing.

India moved 14 places to be 63rd among 190 nations in the World Bank's ease of doing business ranking released in end-October 2019 on the back of multiple economic reforms by the Narendra Modi government. However, it failed to achieve government's target of being at 50th place.[20] Whereas the countries of Southeast Asia, remains much ahead in this ranking: Singapore, 2nd; Malaysia, 15th and Thailand, 27th.[21] However, there are instances where some companies came to India with some hopes and certain state governments gave them the location, power supplies, tax holidays and they were able to make agreements very quickly and set up fast. But some companies were not met with the same enthusiasm hence they went back.[22] The government is planning to focus on six areas to take India to the top 50 by 2021 in World Bank's Ease of Doing Business. The six parameters include enforcing contracts, resolving insolvency, starting a business, registering property, paying taxes and trading across borders. The next ranking list is expected to be released in October 2020.

Therefore, if India wants companies to establish their manufacturing bases over here and shift their supply lines from China, then the government must act fast to create better environment by removing administrative hurdles, providing more incentives and give a massive push to create robust infrastructure. This will need investments for ensuring regular power supplies and efficient rail, road and port operations. Rather than becoming the end-point for assembly of old generation electronics, India should also undertake manufacture of parts and components of high-tech equipment so as to become a support base for global supply chains. Reforming land and labour laws, legal reforms, greater ease in custom clearance and tax breaks for foreign investors are some other essential aspects. The tax incentives should be focused toward desired areas of manufacturing like high-tech and technology-intensive electronics equipment. The recent cut in the corporate tax rates from 25 percent to 15 percent for new manufacturing companies was a positive step as this has made the country one of the lowest tax jurisdictions in South and Southeast Asia.[23] However, the impact of cut in corporate tax rates is yet to be seen in terms of expansion in manufacturing sector.

In the present context, when the Central and state governments are moving in concert to defeat the Coronavirus in the true spirit of federalism, the Prime Minister shall be able to convince the states' leaders to enact long-pending reforms pertaining to 'ease of doing business' forthwith so that foreign manufacturers can set up their manufacturing bases in India. Rather, the much sought after economic stimulus by states should be released proportionately based on each state's competitive index to attract foreign investment.

Opportunities for India

In response to overcome the economic crisis created by COVID-19 pandemic, the catchy solutions or rather phrases appearing in the media are—'India must seize the moment', 'India should turn crisis in to opportunity' and 'the government must release the economic stimulus package worth Rs 16 lakh crore immediately' otherwise we will miss the bus as all other major economies have released it (the United States—$2.3 trillion, Japan—$1 trillion, Germany—€750 billion ($814 billion), Italy—€750 billion, China—$394 billion, UK—£65.5 billion)[24]. Conceding to the suggestions of industry bodies and their economic advisors, when a final economic package of Rs 20.97 Lakh crore was announced, experts said that the actual fiscal cost of the package ranged from Rs 1.47 Lakh crore to Rs 4 Lakh crore and the package is heavily skewed towards monetary measures.[25] Union Finance Minister Nirmala Sitharaman told that the comprehensive economic package was announced after comparing announcements of other countries and every country has thought of a basket of measures including fiscal and monetary steps. She said that the government has come up with measures, which will lead to more liquidity in the economy. She said, "Everything has been studied. Every country has brought in a basket of measures—fiscal, monetary, guarantee, central liquidity and so on."[26]

Though, India is the fifth largest economy in the world with annual GDP of $2.94 trillion (IMF data for year 2019)[27] but its per capita GDP is $2199[28] hence we cannot afford to splurge money or in other words equate ourselves with other major economies in terms of stimulus. The government is intending to provide relief to every sector in a calibrated manner so that the limited resource can be utilized most effectively.

The most valuable lesson learnt from this pandemic is the importance of self-reliance and self-sufficiency. Prime Minister Narendra Modi in his address through videoconference to India's 250,000 gram panchayat heads on National Panchayati Raj Day on 24 April has elaborated that, "Every village has to be self-sufficient enough to provide for its basic needs. Similarly every district has to be self-sufficient at its level, every state has to be self-reliant at its level and the whole country has to be self-reliant at its level."[29] Thus we need to have a balanced approach to bring back our economy on the growth track hence the economic opportunities should encompass:

- First and foremost, boost and enlarge the scope of rural economy;
- Second, Recognize the relevance of Health industry and exploit our strengths in Vaccine development and Pharmaceuticals;
- Third, Accelerate 'Make in India';
- Fourth, Relocation of Global Supply Chains and Reconfigure Local Supply Chains;
- Fifth, Technology Absorption and Innovation;
- Sixth, Shift from Fossil Fuels to Clean and Renewable Energy.
- Seventh, Provide Leadership to create New Multilateral Institutions.

Rural Economy

In India, 68 percent of country's population resides in rural areas and agriculture provides livelihoods to 53 percent of India's population, contributing 15 percent of national GDP. Out of 53 percent of population who are dependent on agriculture, around 65 percent of them are marginal farmers who cultivate in less than one hectare farmland while 18.5 percent of them are small farmers, cultivating on one to two hectare of land.[30] Can agriculture sustain the 53 percent population of the country with merely 15 percent of country's GDP?

In China also, the average production unit was the farm household employing 1.4 persons on less than half a hectare. But with the launching of agricultural reforms in 1981, farmers could get better prices for their produce and greater access to markets. The effect was immediate. Agricultural production began to rise, and many farmers were soon not only feeding their families well but also earning money by selling produce in the 'free markets'. With marked improvements in their lives, farmers were able to buy things for the first time, stimulating a slight consumer boom in the countryside, raising rural living standards.[31] Further, there has been an official encouragement for new crops, multi-cropping, higher yields and diffusion of Best Practice Technology.[32]

Modi government is sensitive on this account, therefore, in 2016, it had rightly set an ambitious target to double farmers' income by 2022 because with more money in the hands of two-thirds of country's population that is the best way to boost consumption, create more demand and thereby enhance the GDP growth. But the continuing low food prices resulted in to a squeeze in farmers' income. Agricultural reform is an important post-pandemic agenda for Prime Minister Narendra Modi as he has directed his top ministers and bureaucrats to cut down on archaic regulations, raise farm-gate prices, unify domestic markets as well as integrate the farm economy into global value chains. Essentially, Prime Minister Modi wants to establish **"one nation, one market"**. Further, the Prime Minister's focus is on last–mile dissemination of technologies developed by agricultural research bodies.[33]

However, agriculture alone is not adequate to sustain this huge population. There is a need to set up alternate sources of employment in village areas to boost the rural income. Here again China serves as the best example. Deng Xiaoping allowed small factories called Township and Village Enterprises (TVEs) to be started up by farmers using their savings. TVEs began to mushroom in the 1980s; some started by group of farmers and some as private investments by local governments. Most of these were tiny companies employing fewer than half a dozen people and performing functions like food processing or making spare parts for farm equipment, but some have flourished and developed into major industrial corporations—particularly in the South in Guangdong. There are now an astonishing 120 million TVEs, and they have played a key part in China's economic boom.[34] Some are now selling produce all round the world.

Since independence, all the Indian governments have emphasized the importance of Panchayati Raj and importance of rural economy but none has bothered about the holistic development of rural economy. There are about 6,50,000 villages in India[35] and if small-scale industries had been promoted in these villages, they would have been structured to produce: environmental friendly bio-fertilizers or organic manure, thereby reducing the import burden of chemical fertilizers; Khadi natural products like fragrant soaps, massaging oils and cotton yarn/apparels which have a great demand in urban areas and in foreign countries; processed farm products; farming tools and implements. Regulatory bodies could have been established to ensure quality control and standardization for export. For instance, at the scale of 20 per village, employing 25 to 50 persons in each, there would have been functional 130 lakh small-scale industries or the so-called small to medium- business enterprises in the country. In an emergency situation like in COVID-19 pandemic, where availability of face masks became a global criticality, even if one enterprise per village dedicated for apparel making was tasked to produce cotton masks or face covers, the nation would have produced 650 million masks per day (considering that small enterprise of 25 people shall be able to produce 40 simple masks per person per day) and covered the complete global requirement in 10 days. Amazon is selling a washable cotton mask in Europe for €8 to €10 (₹664 to ₹830) per piece and it would have costed us maximum ₹8 to ₹10. Unlike price gouging by China, we would have provided it to the whole world with a reasonable profit or even as philanthropy and earned their good will.

In Army parlance what we call is *"Back to Basics"*, i.e. if we want holistic development of economy, village must be treated as a *Basic Entity*. The Centre in concert with states should lay down number and types of small or medium scale industries required in each village. Adequate loans should be catered for the entrepreneurs from the recently announced comprehensive economic package, against setting up the pre-designated industries in a village so that there is a planned development of the rural economy. Industrial clusters in rural areas have been talked about in the stimulus package but these must be based on growing demand and centrally planned and organized, rather than leaving these to individual entrepreneurs. The contribution of rural India in national growth can only come though massive investment in rural infrastructure development.

Health Industry and Pharmaceuticals

Public health infrastructure needs to be strengthened because any unexpected outbreak of pandemic in future where common people do not have access to necessary medical facilities will have grave consequences for the country. India's well-known strength in the fields of biotechnology, pharmaceuticals, medical supplies and equipment and related infrastructure need to be leveraged to enhance our health sector capacity.

Development of Vaccine. The spread of COVID-19 has proved that evolving new techniques and technologies for infection control and commensurate vaccines across large populations in a shortest possible timeframe is the necessity of the day. As regards the current pandemic, China had shared the genetic sequence of Sars-CoV-2 with the WHO on 12 January 2020. Since then global efforts to develop a vaccine have been progressing at an unprecedented pace with at least 321 vaccine projects in various stages of development, launched by different countries.[36] For developing coronavirus vaccines, a variety of techniques are being used to train the human immune system to identify the Sars-CoV-2 virus and block or destroy it before it infects the body. An effective vaccine is one that generates neutralizing antibodies to give protection. The vaccines being developed can be categorized in to four different types: One, ***Virus vaccine***—at least seven teams are employing this technique using the SARS-CoV-2 virus in a weakened or inactivated form similar to the ones against measles and polio. In the weakened virus, its genetic code is altered so that viral proteins are produced less efficiently, whereas in vaccines based on inactivated virus, the virus is rendered un-infectious using chemicals, such as formaldehyde or heat; Two, ***Nucleic Acid vaccine***—at least 20 teams are using coronavirus genetic material (DNA or RNA) to prompt an immune response from human cells. RNA- and DNA-based vaccines are safe and easy to develop as their production involves making genetic material only and not the virus but they are unproven and no licensed vaccines use this technology; Third, ***Viral-Vector vaccine***—a weakened virus, such as measles or adenovirus, is genetically engineered to produce coronavirus proteins in the body without causing disease. About 20 groups said that they were working on viral-vector vaccines. With in this also, there are two types of weakened viruses, those that can replicate within cells (such as weakened measles)—newly approved Ebola vaccine is an example, and those that cannot replicate because key genes have been disabled (such as adenovirus)—Johnson & Johnson singled out by President Trump and Oxford University are using this approach; Four, ***Protein-Based vaccine***—fragments of proteins or protein shells, that mimic the coronavirus's outer coat, are injected directly in to the body. 28 teams are working on vaccines with viral protein subunits, focusing on the virus's spike protein and five teams are working on 'virus-like particle' vaccines.[37]

According to a study published by PLOS ONE, the standard vaccine development, on average, takes 10.71 years from the preclinical phase and has a market entry probability of 6 percent.[38] In the history of vaccine development, Merck's Mumpsvax vaccine holds the record as it took little less than four years from start (1963) to finish (1967).[39] Vaccine development can be broken into two phases—a pre-clinical study and once this phase is done, the clinical study phase starts. The latter is the time-consuming part, a very risky and expensive business involving billions of dollars and unless there will be a market when the vaccine is eventually ready, no company will like to back the research. Generally, the clinical study of a vaccine has three phases—Phase 1 could last between one and two years (it involves administering the vaccine to a few people to see if it is safe and provokes an immune response in them) but the vaccine candidates for COVID-19 have crashed this timeline to months; Phase 2 normally lasts anything between two and three years and is called randomized double-blind placebo-controlled study. In this study phase, test subjects are randomly divided in two groups—one group is given placebos and the other group is administered the candidate vaccine. Neither the researchers nor the subjects know who is getting what, that is the reason it is called double-blind. Phase 2 usually involves testing the vaccines on hundreds of subjects who have the condition (say COVID-19) but do not suffer from any other complications. The results are studied for safety, efficacy and to determine the correct dosage of the vaccine; Phase 3 is similar to Phase 2 but it could last for anything between two and four years. In this phase, the vaccine is administered to thousands (if not tens of thousands in cases) of subjects who are representative of the larger population. Besides studying the safety and efficacy, clinical outcome is the most important part of this phase (as Phase 2 studies do not measure clinical outcomes) so that the researchers should have enough data to show that the 'benefits outweigh the risks'. Most vaccine candidates for COVID-19 have combined Phase 2 and Phase 3 trials, trying to reduce the time involved to about a year. ICMR have also contemplated to reduce the time it takes to conduct Phases 1, 2 and 3 trials for a vaccine candidate of Hyderabad-based Bharat Biotech to 45 days.[40]

Nations are aiming to develop, test and manufacture the COVID-19 vaccine on a scale of hundreds of millions of doses within 12 to 18 months. India is the powerhouse of vaccine manufacturing. India produces 60 per cent of the world's vaccines and accounts for 60-80 per cent of the United Nations' annual vaccine procurement. The Pune-based Serum Institute of India (SII) is the world's largest vaccine maker by number of doses produced and sold globally. The 50-year-old company makes 1.5 billion doses every year, mainly from its two facilities in Pune. SII has taken the initiative to mass-produce the experimental vaccine ChAdOx1 nCoV-19 (will be marketed as AZD1222) being developed by the University of Oxford. Oxford University has licensed the experimental vaccine to AstraZeneca, which in turn has selected SII. Human trials of the vaccine having been started in Britain in the fourth week of April, Serum Chief Executive Adar Poonawalla said he hoped trials of the Oxford vaccine, due to finish in about September, would be successful and he aims to produce up to 400 million doses next year if all goes well.[41] This vaccine hoped to tackle COVID-19 by injecting a weakened adenovirus into which genetic material from SARS-CoV-2 had been inserted—something that should generate an immune response. The adenovirus being used is one that causes cold in chimpanzees, which determines the name of the vaccine (Ch for chimpanzee and Ad for adenovirus). We as humans share 99 percent of our DNA with chimpanzees and bonobos (another ape).[42]

The industry believes that India is ahead of the COVID-19 curve and should take the lead in producing the vaccine. More than 30 coronavirus vaccines are in various stages of development in India and some are heading to the trial stage.[43] SII has also partnered with the U.S. biotech firm Codagenix and Austria's Themis on two other COVID-19 vaccine candidates and planned to announce a fourth alliance. India should be the only country to sell the vaccine at the lowest possible price due to its mass production ability. SII envisages a price of 1,000 rupees per vaccine.[44] In fact, a number of Indian firms, other key players in the global vaccine industry—Hyderabad-based Bharat Biotech, Ahmedabad-based Zydus Cadilla group and mid-rung companies like Gurugram-based Premas Biotech, Ahmedabad-based Hester Biosciences and start-ups Neuberg Supratech and Mynvax are collaborating with their foreign partners to develop COVID-19 vaccine.[45]

The Prime Minister Narendra Modi's office reportedly is "very closely" involved in the vaccine production. The Prime Minister Modi has appreciated the potential of Indian companies as innovators for research into early-stage vaccine development.[46] On 9th May, the Indian Council of Medical Research (ICMR) announced a tie-up with Bharat Biotech International Limited (BBIL) to develop a fully indigenous vaccine for COVID-19 using the virus strain isolated at the National Institute of Virology (NIV), Pune. ICMR has shared one of the 11 virus strains that it managed to culture with Bharat Biotech. The industry partnership is to develop the vaccine candidate and ICMR has transferred the technology to them.[47] Further, Bharat Biotech has also partnered with the US-based Thomas Jefferson University (TJU) to develop its experimental vaccine Coravax—that uses a proven deactivated rabies vaccine as a carrier for the genetic code of the Sars-

CoV-2 spike protein, which the virus uses to enter human cells and cause infection. Bharat Biotech is the world's largest supplier of rabies vaccine and the rabies carrier vaccine being used is approved for use in the whole population, including children and pregnant women.[48]

India is in the process of striking a pre-production deal with the vaccine developers, which are in the race for a successful candidate—a strategy several advanced economies are following to jump what might be a long waiting line. According to the Union Health Minister Harsh Vardhan, "the expert group is holding consultations with vaccine manufacturers to plan ahead for the production, pricing and distribution of the vaccine, whenever it is ready".[49] The United Kingdom's Oxford-AstraZeneca (AZD 1222 vaccine) and the United States' Moderna NIAID (mRNA-1273 vaccine) are the global front-runners for coronavirus vaccine. The five Indian companies that are being consulted are: SII, Bharat Biotech, Zydus Cadilla—all three have vaccine candidates in human trials—and other two are Biological E, Hyderabad and Gennova Biopharmaceuticals, Pune—both having candidates in pre-clinical trials. Nine other vaccine development programs—including ones in Germany and Israel—are also being looked at. The Russian vaccine, Sputnik V is in its second phase of trials but little is known about its performance in the first phase. Zydus Cadilla (ZyCov-D vaccine) also started Phase 2 clinical trials to establish efficacy of its indigenously developed vaccine candidate. The other indigenously developed vaccine is COVAXIN by Bharat Biotech-ICMR.[50] The Centre has already decided to take charge of the procurement of the vaccine as and when it is ready. There is no final number of vaccines at the moment for pre-order but roughly 680 million vaccines are being talked about including primary and booster shots. The delivery mechanism will be digital to ensure last mile delivery on a real-time basis. India is also likely to receive some doses as part of multilateral mechanism such as the WHO-led Covax facility—meant to ensure equitable distribution between rich and emerging economies.[51]

Though there is still enough time for vaccines to come in the market and the efficacy of vaccines under development is not even known but there is a global rush to finalize the deals with prospective COVID-19 vaccine developers. Reportedly, the countries have struck deals or announced commitments for almost 4.5 billion doses of vaccines from nine vaccine developers. Interestingly, the UK has committed to buy 340 million doses, whereas its population is a little less than 70 million. The US, the European Union and Japan have also committed to buy enough to vaccinate every one of their residents at least once.

Indian medical fraternity is not only experimenting with the available medicines like hydroxychloroquine or other anti-viral drugs to treat COVID-19 but is continuously working to find new medicines to cure the patients. Besides working on a vaccine project with Seagull Biosolutions, Biocon, a leading Indian biopharmaceutical company, is developing two new generation repurposed drugs for treatment and an antibody diagnostic kit.[52]

All the Biotechnology giants are of the firm opinion that India must take a leadership role and establish itself as a central and significant player in this pandemic. The industry is praising the government effort for easing regulatory norms and handholding companies that need support in every stage of the development of vaccine.

Pharmaceuticals. India is the world's single-largest exporter of generic drugs but the Pharma industry largely depends on imports from China. Bulk drugs or active pharmaceutical ingredients (APIs) are the raw materials used for making formulations or medicines. These are used to manufacture at least 12 essential drugs such as paracetamol, acetylsalicylic acid, amoxicillin, ascorbic acid, etc. Intermediates, on the other hand, are chemical compounds that are used in producing APIs. India imports almost 80 percent of APIs and intermediates from China. Of the 373 drugs listed under India's national essential medicines list, some 200 are imported as APIs, mostly from China.[53] Department of Pharmaceuticals in the Ministry of Chemicals and Fertilizers has consistently maintained that the imports from China are due to economic considerations.

What are these economic considerations? In the early 1990s India was self-sufficient to produce both formulations as well as API. However, in the last two decades, the situation has completely changed. Today majority of our API comes from China. Most API production units in India run at 30 per cent of their capacity as against capacity utilization of 70 per cent in China. Even industry sources agree that the production cost of API in China is about 20-30 percent less than that in India. In fact, it is well documented now that India has already lost its manufacturing base for API to China. The three factors responsible for over-dependence on Chinese imports are—wage cost, infrastructure facilities and tax benefits. In the case of wage or labor cost, India still has an advantage over China as labor has now become more expensive in China. As regards, infrastructure or tax benefits, reportedly the Indian government hasn't done much in the last 20 years. For a manufacturer, it's always about turnover and profit; hence they are bound to import API from China. Drug companies blame the government, saying that low-cost imports have forced many manufacturers to close down. Some have now given up producing ingredients for other drug manufacturers and gone on to produce more complex formulations themselves, which they then export to developed markets in the US and Europe.[54] This Chinese strategy of destroying the domestic industry is applicable in all other fields. If we talk of the Chinese items, which proliferate our markets during festive seasons, about a decade back, the traders often used to source products—toys, plastic items, idols of Indian gods, among others—from domestic manufacturers. Reportedly, they have all shut down and now import from China. Cheaper and better Chinese imports have wiped out the domestic industry, particularly toys. Similarly, despite having numbers of local manufacturers, over 80 percent of India's solar component supplies have been hijacked by the Chinese.[55]

India also more than doubled the import of antibiotic drugs from China in recent years and the trade is now worth billions of dollars. There are now no domestic producers left for penicillin and its derivative. There was always a fear of a public health crisis if China were to ever stop its supply. This has now come true after COVID-19 created a shortage of essential medicines, as India has been dependent on China for many APIs. The current crisis also gives an opportunity to India to challenge China's stronghold on supplying basic drug ingredients.[56]

Incidentally in the recent past (2016-2018), lakhs of Chinese API facilities remained shut to step up their environmental compliance. Therefore, India depended on countries like the US, Italy, Singapore and Hong Kong for import. Though supplies from China got stabilized but prices of some APIs have increased. The supply crunch has done good for the Indian bulk drug industry, as API makers increased their capacity. In a way, it created the opportunity for India to develop APIs and intermediates and fill some of the supply gaps. As a result, China along with 174 destinations started purchasing APIs from India during 2018-19. Reportedly, India's exports of bulk drugs grew for a year or so but due to cost of production for API being higher, it hampers the export competitiveness of India's products. The Pharmaceutical Exports Promotion Council of India (Pharmexcil), a body under the Union Ministry of Commerce and Industry data also reveals that exports of Indian APIs throughout the last year grew by over 20 percent.[57]

GlobalData has said that the impact of the coronavirus COVID-19 outbreak has exposed the dependence of India on China for its API requirements. Apart from the dependence on legal imports, a large number of illegal imports of APIs from China were also a cause of worry for the regulator. In fact, considering the historical unstable political relationship with China, risk of economic overdependence should have been avoided and the contingency planning for breakdown in trade or supply should have been done. For India's pharma industry, this is a 'wake-up call' to reduce dependence on China.[58] To reduce the reliance on China, it is important that the raw material used for manufacturing APIs is also made in India. The API industry should be promoted under the 'Make in India' initiative and the government should give its manufacturers free land, long term tax holidays, low-cost utilities such as water, steam and power and negligible financing costs. It should also liberalize policies for clinical trials and approval of already approved drugs in other countries.[59]

So it is time for India to become self-reliant in APIs to prevent another shortage like the one the coronavirus has inflicted on it.

Bureaucracy and lack of environmental clearances in India had also made it uneconomical to produce raw materials anymore. If China takes about six months to set up the factory and produce raw materials, India, on the other hand, takes about six years to build a factory for the production of raw materials. Indian API industry has a complex license renewal system. They need to approach various authorities for the renewal of application.[60] According to Pharmexil, ***"If the government wholeheartedly provides the monetary help in one cluster, it can become a success in two years and in five years, that model can be replicated throughout the country."***[61]

After announcing a 140-billion-rupee ($1.8 billion) fund last month for setting up three drug manufacturing hubs, the government has identified 53 key starting materials and APIs whose output will be boosted on priority. These include fever-medicine paracetamol and antibiotics such as penicillin and ciprofloxacin. Viability of reviving the loss-making state-owned drug makers Hindustan Antibiotics Ltd. and Indian Drugs and Pharmaceuticals Ltd. is also being considered to speed up this process and ensure affordable medicines.[62]

Medical Equipment and Infrastructure. India needs to build up a manufacturing base for ventilators and personal protective equipment (PPEs) not only to contain the present spread of COVID-19 but for the future also.[63] Though the current requirement is well under control since a small percentage of patients are needing such support but the capacity needs to be build up by combining and synergizing the capabilities of private and public sectors. There was a huge shortfall in state capacities, as there were only 48,000-odd ventilators in the various hospitals across India, with around 40,000 in the pipeline. Experts say India will need 80 to 100 times the number of ventilators if the virus spreads.[64] State-run companies like Bharat Electronics Ltd were manufacturing PPEs and ventilators and there was an opportunity for local private companies to tap the growing demand for such equipment.[65]

The industry has promised to involve the automobile sector to use its production line to manufacture ventilators and several companies such as Maruti, Mahindra, Tatas, Bharat Forge and others have committed to build a supply chain for such equipment, both for use domestically as well as for exports.[66] Automobile companies are re-engineering their manufacturing capabilities to bring out ventilators. Mahindra & Mahindra, in partnership with two public sector units, is working on a basic ventilator model that would cost between Rs 5,000 and Rs 7,500, as against Rs 5-10 lakh it does now.[67]

The state-owned Defence Research and Development Organization (DRDO) is addressing the shortage of PPE by using a special adhesive which finds its application in submarines. Scientists are testing this adhesive to make full-body suits at low cost at a scalable level. This adhesive can be used as a special coating that can strengthen high-performance fabrics. DRDO uses this adhesive for making suits of paratroopers. DRDO has shared this technology with two companies, which are now looking to manufacture around 15,000 to 20,000 suits every week.[68] Naval Dockyard at Vishakhapatnam succeeded in innovating a device with which one Oxygen cylinder can be used for multiple patients. Indian Navy designed an innovative 'Portable Multi-feed Oxygen Manifold (MOM)' using a 6-way radial header fitted to a single cylinder. This innovation would enable one Oxygen Bottle to supply six patients concurrently thus enabling critical care management to a larger number of COVID patients with the existing limited resources. The assembly has been tested and manufacturing has also begun.[69]

Items like face masks, gloves and goggles can be produced by medium and small-scale enterprises at village level—ensuring quality control through regulatory mechanism, giving employment to rural youth and linking up with logistics supply chain. According to a garment exporter based in NOIDA, a normal mask comes to about Rs 6-8 per piece but it was sourced from China at the rate of 60 paisa per piece.[70] While launching the Self-reliant India mission and announcing Rs. 20 lakh crore package, Prime Minister Modi said, "When the corona crisis began, there was not a single PPE kit made in India. N-95 masks were produced nominally in India. Today the situation is that India is producing 2 lakh PPE and 2 lakh N-95 masks everyday".[71]

It may not be an exaggeration to state that *in the near future the face masks and hand gloves will become part of everyone's personal attire and persons will like to have designer face masks and gloves matching with their dress.* Thus the fashion industry must be involved in this venture now only, even to cater for export requirements.

India has the potential to manufacture the ventilators, PPEs and even test kits at a very reasonable cost, which need to be leveraged by using economy of scales for global supply. The innovations in this field should be patented to gain the status of original equipment manufacturers (OEMs).

Telemedicine. Telemedicine in India is currently at a nascent stage. Systems like those adopted by US administration to counter COVID-19, when powered with the network of the future—5G, will give a tremendous boost to telemedicine in India. It will also open up opportunities for entrepreneurs to set up back-end operations in remote, inaccessible and remote parts of India, which in turn would also create job opportunities.[72]

Accelerate 'Make in India'

In his maiden Independence Day speech from the Red Fort, New Delhi on 15 August 2014, India's Prime Minister, Narendra Modi introduced the concept of 'Make in India', "I want to tell the people of the whole world: Come, make in India. Come and manufacture in India. Go and sell in any country in the world, but manufacture here. We have the skill, talent, discipline and the desire to do something. We want to give the world an opportunity that come make in India."[73] The agenda of 'Make in India' was announced on 25 September 2014, covering about 25 sectors of Indian economy, which range from automobile to Information Technology (IT) & Business Process Management (BPM) and is being led by the Department of Industrial Policy and Promotion (DIPP), Ministry of Commerce and Industry, Government of India.[74] The aim is to ensure that investors not only contribute to the FDI but also set up industries in India itself.

FDI is a good indication of external investor confidence in the success of economic reforms and prospects as it is a sign of how much foreign corporations are willing to commit to long-term investments in a country. FDI is necessary for a developing economy to create jobs, absorb excess labour supply and plug financial gaps. But India today pulls in a miserly 0.6 per cent of GDP in manufacturing FDI.[75] According to World Investment Report 2019, the abundance of cheap labour in addition to a strong business ecosystem, low taxes and not-so-strict regulatory compliances, along with competitive currency practices are the main drivers of attracting FDI.[76]

Why "Make in India" campaign has not taken off the way, the Indian government has desired? Rather, the contribution of manufacturing sector to GDP has shrunk—the possible reasons have been discussed in detail under 'India's Challenges' above.

Consequent to COVID-19 pandemic, the entire world is re-assessing its overdependence on China's manufacturing and supply chains. India provides a suitable alternative destination for companies looking for relocation but so also countries like Vietnam, Bangladesh, Myanmar, Indonesia, Thailand and even Ethiopia, from whom India faces stiff competition.[77] However, the overwhelming advantage, which India offers is the market size. For instance, if the manufacturing of a commodity is done in a country like Vietnam or Bangladesh, the final product would be most likely exported due to the low consumer market in these countries. Many companies are looking towards India with interest because of its own sizeable market and additionally as an export hub in the region. Various proposals are already being reviewed at various levels—central government, state industry departments and Indian missions abroad. India needs to act fast, lest the other countries grab the opportunity by taking advantage of the situation.

India's generous behavior towards the international community in terms of providing medical supplies and equipment during the current pandemic despite its own burden has reinforced its soft power credentials. For example, India supplied essential medicines, test kits and protective gears worth about Rs 82 crore to 89 countries.[78] Even in these difficult times, India has remained dependable and responsive in living up to its international commitments. As India is showered with international adulation, China at the same time faced severe criticism for not only covering up the initial outbreak of the virus but also indulged in propaganda and misinformation in its aftermath. This will definitely hold India in good stead as a favourable destination for foreign companies looking for relocation from China.

The experts of the Technology Information, Forecasting and Assessment Council (TIFAC), an autonomous technology think tank under the department of Science and Technology is preparing a white paper to strategize on the revival of post-COVID-19 Indian economy. The white paper would mainly focus on "strengthening Make in India initiatives, commercialization of Indigenous technology, developing a technology-driven transparent Public Distribution System (PDS), efficient rural health care delivery, reduction of import, adoption of emerging technology domains like AI, Machine Learning, Data Analytics and many more."[79]

The government plans to aggressively push its 'Make in India' program by offering domestic and foreign manufacturers policy and fiscal incentives to manufacture locally. India needs to assure both its domestic and foreign investors that it will also protect them from any import surge, particularly from China. The new incentives are aimed at burnishing India's attraction as an investment destination for manufacturing companies. A thorough review of import duties is now underway with the objective of encouraging manufacturing or value addition in India and according to officials, "Import of raw materials will be made increasingly cheaper, but higher duties will be levied on finished goods."[80]

Federation of Indian Export Organizations (FIEO) president Sharad Kumar Saraf has brought out that the post-COVID era is likely to see the shift of manufacturing of all types of products away from China but issues related to land, labour and uncertainty in taxation are limiting the success of 'Make in India'.[81] Radical reforms are needed in all three areas. The Uttar Pradesh government suspended key labour laws for three years on 6 May through an ordinance and Madhya

Pradesh government also announced on 7 May that it was taking a similar course to put all labour laws on hold for the next 1,000 days. Some economists have welcomed the move for clearing structural bottlenecks, possibly leading to greater investment and positioning India in a better position to take advantage of disruptions in global supply chains. Gujarat and Uttarakhand are also likely to follow suit. The Gujarat government has taken another initiative "A total of 3000 hectares in the industrial estates of Gujarat will be made available from the state's land bank and also different nodal officers will assist incoming industries from other countries. New industries will be exempted from labour laws other than the Minimum Wages Act, Industrial Safety and Health Act, Labour Compensation Act for 1,200 days from the start of production in the state."[82] Under the Constitution, labour falls under the concurrent list, which means the Union government and states have joint jurisdiction. Changes by state need to be ratified at the federal level. According to people having knowledge of the matter, none of the ordinances has received approval from the President.[83] Labour reform is the key aspect for attracting foreign investment, therefore states and central governments must move fast and act together. According to the World Bank, with less restrictive laws, India could approximately add on an annual basis "2.8 million more good quality formal sector jobs."[84]

Relocation of Global Supply Chains and Reconfigure Local Supply Chains

If one has to single out the most spectacular achievement of globalization that has benefitted the majority population of the world, it is the Global Supply Chain. It has led to an exponential rise of economic activity and consequently lifted the GDP of multiple countries linked to the chain. But the vulnerabilities of the system have been thoroughly exposed by the COVID-19 pandemic. Even before the imposition of the lockdowns and the spread of this pandemic across the world, the severe disruptions in China were having a ripple effect on global trade flows. While most companies across the globe had been working to make their supply chains leaner, the novel coronavirus dealt the final deathblow to the existing linkages.

The current supply chains across industries have evolved over time but how they got intertwined with China, for this, one has to study their genesis. Three decades ago, with the sole aim of keeping the production costs low and maximize financial gains, the Western governments allowed their multinational companies to set up their manufacturing and industrial bases in China. China took advantage of this outsourcing by developing its own manufacturing prowess in a manner that not only it became a world's factory but it simultaneously developed a complex web of internal supply chains and interoperability that has made relocation extremely difficult. China has become a preeminent supplier of goods and components across nearly all industrial sectors—technology, automotive, electronics, pharmaceutical, equipment or consumer goods.[85] Thus, *the so-called global supply chain is essentially China-dominated one*, which the whole world suddenly realized after the outbreak of this pandemic. According to Dun & Bradstreet, a business intelligence company, 51,000 companies have one or more direct suppliers in Wuhan, while 5 million companies have one or more tier-two suppliers in the region.[86] From another survey by the Institute for Supply Management, it became evident that it is not only Southeast Asia but a majority of global companies are simply unprepared to address continued supply disruptions from China. For instance, US tech giant Apple, which despite having shifted some production to India and Vietnam, remains critically dependent on China.[87] Due to the disruption caused by the pandemic, there is a sudden urgency to diversify and relocate manufacturing and supply chains out of China.

The available evidence points to the likelihood that long-lasting structural shifts in the global supply chains are in the offing. Many companies, supported by their governments are rushing to relocate some of their production lines from China to avoid getting caught again in a pandemic like situation where entire global supply chain collapsed due to over-reliance on a single source. For instance, Japan's Honda and Toyota and South Korea's Samsung have already started to adopt "China plus One" strategy, signaling their intent to diversify their supply chains regionally with a view to offset future risks in operating solely from China. The US companies are also looking to realign supply chains closer to home in countries such as Mexico, while also diversifying them to reduce future exposure risks by relocating to India and ASEAN states.[88]

The global supply chain has three connotations for India: One, Integrate in to the relocated global supply chains; Two, Reduce supply chain vulnerability of Indigenous Industries and; Three, Reconfigure existing consumer product supply chains to function effectively in post-COVID-19 environment.

- **Integrate in to the Relocated Global Supply Chains.** Nisha Desai Biswal, who served as the Assistant Secretary of State for South and Central Asia during the previous Barack Obama Administration, and is now the president of US India Business Council (USIBC) said that India was expected to benefit as the businesses would like to de-risk in having too much of a supply chain concentrated in one area and try to diversify and disperse. She told in an interview on 13th April, "USIBC is committed to working with India on positioning for kind of a post pandemic opportunity… also allow India to become more and more integrated into a global supply chain." She further added, "But India will also have to make sure that it takes the steps that it needs to create more efficient opportunities for supply chains to be located in India, whether it's on economic incentives, whether it's on labor".[89]

  Once the conducive business environment is created under the 'Make in India' project, scores of multinational companies are likely to establish their manufacturing facilities in India and consequently the global supply chains would be linked to these manufacturing hubs. This will not only increase the share of manufacturing as part of India's GDP but also create large-scale employment. To achieve a close-knit integration in to the global supply chains, India will have to undertake manufacturing of parts, components or essential ingredients for the final products.
- **Reduce Supply Chain Vulnerability of Indigenous Industries.** Industries in India have become more and more dependent

upon China for import of raw materials such as Pharmaceuticals for 80 percent of APIs and intermediates; Automobiles for 10 to 30 percent of raw materials and base components; and Solar Energy for 80 percent requirement of solar panels.[90] The chemical industry, a sector worth $163 billion, covering more than 80,000 commercial products, which is projected to reach $304 billion by 2025, is now struggling due to disruption in supplies of raw material and capital goods etc.[91] As regards, electronics (including mobile handsets), though India progressed from assembling to manufacturing of low-end electronic components, import dependency remains high with 67 percent of electronic components coming from China. From mobile phone manufacturing to printers, to personal computers (PCs) to set-up boxes and inverters are being affected since printed circuit boards (PCBs) were being sourced from China. These were just being assembled in India. For a large number of electronics manufacturers, it is far easier, and financially viable to import the Semi Knocked Down (SKD) or Completely Knocked Down (CKD) equipment from China. According to Rajoo Goel, Secretary General, Electronic Industries Association of India (Elcina), "As a result of the Coronavirus outbreak, the sector is in dire strait as the entire supply chain is now severely affected. Even those supplies that have already arrived in India require an advanced level of sanitization before these are allowed to be dispatched to various markets. The tragedy is, no worker is willing to touch any device sourced from China as of now." Even in case of consumer durables, India imports 45 percent completely built units from China.[92]

COVID-19 pandemic is an urgent wake up call for Indian industry to realize the need to have indigenous sourcing units. In respect of pharmaceuticals, the government has acted promptly in deciding to manufacture critical Key Starting Materials (KSMs)/Intermediates and APIs with in the country.[93] Alternatively, in the near term, companies should seek to diversify supply chains with a view to reduce supply-side risk from one country. Multiple sources of key commodities or strategic components should be identified and protocols devised to activate alternative sources of supply at short notice.

- **Reconfigure Existing Consumer Product Supply Chains**. A consumer product supply chain in a country like India, where infrastructure is not fully developed with low demand in earlier days, has multiple layers between the manufacturer and the end consumers, with many days of inventory in the chain. This supply chain got further complicated with number of small distributors having intermediated between the manufacturers and customers.[94] This pandemic lockdown has resulted in either emptying the supply chains of their inventory or reducing the same substantially, thus presenting an opportunity to the organizations to reconfigure their supply chains completely.
  - The lockdown has forced the customers to adopt home delivery and they were seen willing to pay the delivery charges. Even after the lockdown, social distancing will become a norm and people will tend to avoid crowded places for regular shopping. The Amazon Pantry, Big Basket or Grofers were not able to meet the demands as they got overloaded with small orders but much more in number. The supply chains will have to be designed to handle smaller packs.
  - Organizations will have to avoid single points of potential failure, be it a supplier, manufacturing site, or distribution centres by building redundancies in to the system to cater for failure of imports.
  - Digitization enables smooth functioning of this chain even during COVID-19-like disruptions. Therefore extensive digitization is required to ensure that all information and cash flows in the supply chain is digitized.
  - Equally, the increasing need for traceability of products and assets in the supply chain will encourage organizations to evaluate and adopt technologies like Blockchain.[95]

Indeed, after the first announcement of a nationwide lockdown on March 24 in the wake of COVID-19 outbreak, the kirana stores—that control 98 per cent of India's $360-400 billion grocery retail market—were the ones to be hit the hardest.[96] The Department for Promotion of Industry and Internal Trade (DPIIT), along with traders body Confederation of All India Traders (CAIT), is planning to develop a national e-commerce platform that can be used by over 70 million kirana stores to accept orders online and ensure last mile contactless delivery. The DPIIT is looking for solutions including e-commerce solutions, messaging platforms, logistics solutions, digital payment gateways, and app development, among other things, to help *kirana* stores in taking and delivering online orders.[97] The platform will connect domestic manufacturers, distributors, wholesalers, retailers and consumers.

Technology Absorption and Innovation

The advancement in technology provides the momentum to the economic growth and allows a country to remain ahead of others in the international arena. Therefore the developed countries keep the intellectual property rights (IPR) of their products as a closely guarded state secret. Accordingly, none of these countries will part with its latest technology in any technology transfer to another country. It will provide its second-best or rather third-best technology, that too at a huge cost. Having acquired the basic design, the recipient country should absorb the technology and further innovate on it to be ready to produce the next generations of products with which it can compete with others in the world market. For instance, with a view to pursue quick profits, China initially imported equipment without caring for software such as patents, know-how, blueprints etc. Once the equipment was imported, almost no financial resources were given to absorption, assimilation and innovation. As a consequence, few Chinese enterprises owned independent intellectual property rights in core technologies, as it is apparent from the data available on patents. Because of their interest in utility model and design patents, Chinese firms lagged far behind their foreign counterparts in invention patents. Thus China developed rapidly but it was processing—and assembly focused, low-end product-oriented and foreign-invested enterprise-led.[98] With its quest for upgrading the technology, China resorted to theft of intellectual property through cyber-espionage, lack of enforcement of IPR and heavy-handed or forced technology transfer (FTT) policies. China reportedly causes approximately $ 600 billion a year intellectual property thefts costs to America.[99] The U.S.-China Trade war, which was started by President Trump to reduce the massive trade deficit with China, concentrated more on technology-transfer matters. Washington had not only demanded Beijing to end its practice of forcing foreign joint venture partners to transfer technologies to their Chinese collaborators, but was also scrutinizing the works of Chinese researchers based in the US.[100]

Thus while importing manufacturing plants or undertaking joint ventures with foreign countries or multinationals, India's endeavour should be to assimilate the technology and innovate on it to produce indigenous advanced versions. For example Shinkansen bullet train from Ahmedabad to Mumbai is being built with Japanese assistance and 81 percent of the total project cost Rs 88,087 crore (US$13 billion) is being met through a 50-year loan at an interest rate of 0.1 percent with a moratorium on repayments up to 15 years.[101] It will be a great achievement if India can fully absorb the technology, train its manpower in a manner that it could undertake future bullet train projects on its own within the country as also win the bids in other countries. Another aspect is that we should invest adequately in disruptive technologies likely to be evolved during the ongoing Fourth Industrial Revolution and try to seek the "first-mover" advantage over other nations. A nation needs not to go through the hierarchical phases of development because of the technological breakthroughs. The President of the World Economic Forum (WEF), Borge Brende, firmly believes that Fourth Industrial Revolution can help India leapfrog traditional phases of development and accelerate its transition to a developed nation. He said, *"India is well positioned to enhance its global leadership in a post Fourth Industrial Revolution era"*.[102]

Shift from Fossil Fuels to Clean and Renewable Energy

Oil and gas are still considered as key elements of the economy, playing an important role in achieving prosperity for both producers and consumers. While oil-producing countries make money from each barrel of oil sold, oil-consuming countries also generate an income on oil through the tax system at the state level and through dividends in saving funds, pension funds and the like, which are owned by individual citizens. In some countries, the revenue from these taxes is used to finance green infrastructure projects. The collapse in oil prices due to COVID-19 pandemic lockdown has benefitted the large energy-consuming countries by significantly reducing their energy expenditure. For example, every $4 decrease in commodity prices leads to about $5 billion in import bill savings for India, which is the world's third-largest energy consumer.[103] The Country can use these savings for reinvestment in a more diversified energy system.

Though the overall support for fossil fuels has been decreasing in India, there is still a significant gap between usage of fossil fuels and renewable energy. A report "Mapping India's Energy Subsidy 2020: Fossil fuels, renewables, electric vehicles" prepared by two think tanks working on environmental issues—the International Institute for Sustainable Development (IISD) and the Council on Energy, Environment and Water (CEEW)—revealed that subsidies for fossil fuels are still over seven times more than subsidies for alternative energy in India. The report stated, "In Financial Year 2019, subsidies for oil, gas and coal amounted to Rs. 83,134 crore ($ 12.4 billion), compared to Rs. 11,604 crore for renewables and electric mobility."[104] Interestingly, one of the authors of the report, Karthik Ganesan pointed out that India's major energy subsidies amount to Rs. 1.74 lakh crore—higher than the initial economic package of Rs.1.70 lakh crore that the Indian government announced for tackling COVID-19 pandemic.[105] The government needs to reassess this large subsidy outlay and rationalize this across end-consumers.

While reviving the economy, the government should focus on clean and renewable energy as the fossil fuel sources cause the most damage to public health and the climate. By resetting its energy spending in favour of clean energy, the government will enable citizens to continue enjoying the unprecedented clean air and blue skies bestowed by the lockdown.

As per findings of the World Bank, low-emission and resource-efficient greening of India's economy is possible at a very low cost in terms of GDP growth. By attracting global and domestic investors, deploying renewable energy will have a positive effect on the GDP of our country. Investment in renewable energy at this juncture will not only lift up the rural economy but will also provide employment to migrant population rushing back to villages. Twenty leaders from top think tanks, renewable energy companies, industry groups, and health care services wrote to Prime Minister Narendra Modi on April 30, recommending to solarize over 39,000 unelectrified health sub-centres—the first point of contact between the primary health care system and the local community—serving 230 million people in rural India. According to Ulka Kelkar, director, climate program, World Resources Institute India, in remote rural hospitals where electricity supply is erratic, solar power could be used to run ventilators and other medical equipment at a lower cost.[106]

India's new green job creation can be a game-changer for the economy of the nation, particularly for the rural folks with the majority of the jobs being available for unskilled and semi-skilled workers. People who are considered ineligible for several permanent and well-paid jobs can get maintenance and operations, installation and sales jobs in this sector. According to the World Resources Institute, permanent jobs in this sector don't just benefit the workers with regular pay but also provide training opportunities, healthcare benefits, safety standards and therefore enables people to plan for their family's future. This would also help in reducing income inequalities and in creating a sustainable equitable environment.[107] According to the International Renewable Energy Agency (IRENA), decarbonization of the global energy system can grow the global economy and create up to 28 million jobs by 2050.[108] IRENA report also recorded that the renewable energy industry in India accounted for almost 7,19,000 jobs in the year 2018. The further expansion of the renewable energy sector would lead to the emergence of new employment opportunities in the country.[109] Experts believe that investing in renewables is not only a necessity but also a smart economic choice.

Provide Leadership to create New Multilateral Institutions

Though the instant reaction by all nations to control the spread of coronavirus pandemic was to switch from globalization to localization and the 'Isolation' or 'Protectionism' appeared to be the only solution to keep the virus away from one's country. But with no respite in the mounting coronavirus infection cases, the whole world has come to realize that the virus is not going away so easily therefore one has to live with it. The only way to control COVID-19 pandemic and also prevent a future crisis like this is to build stronger and more effective public systems across countries. That means more global cooperation with transparent mechanisms will be needed.

We should remember that we all breathe the same oxygen and share the same blood to survive on this earth. It means an infection anywhere that can enter into our bloodstream or in our breathing pipe, is a threat to mankind everywhere. Therefore, the international public health system should be responsive or rather prompt in action, accountable and transparent. The manner in which the WHO has responded to the outbreak of this pandemic has not only brought its top functionaries in to the sphere of suspicion but the organizational effectiveness itself has become questionable. The international institutions, which came up in the aftermath of World War II, like the World Health Organization a specialized agency of the United Nations (UN) responsible for international public health and even United Nations Security Council, one of the principal organs of the UN, have become overtly partisan and lost their credibility today. S Jaishankar, India's External Affairs minister said recently, "The United Nations is far less credible today than it has been through its history".[110] In fact, Japan's deputy PM Taro Aso was more forthright in calling WHO as the Chinese Health Organization, excoriating it for refusing to declare COVID-19 a global emergency in January.[111] China has already manoeuvred Party officials into top spots in at least four of the U.N.'s 15 specialized agencies—the International Civil Aviation Organization, the International Telecommunication Union, the Food and Agricultural Organization, and the U.N. Industrial Development Organization.[112] According to experts, China's efforts to influence the WHO, the health arm of the U.N. are a good example of its strategy of expanding influence in international bodies.

According to the Council on Foreign Relations (CFR), China contributed approximately $86 million to the WHO over the agency's two-year funding cycle, an increase of 52 percent since 2014. That is a modest sum when compared to the United States' $839 million over the same period, but it reinforces the idea that China is increasing its influence with in the UN. China has exerted indirect political influence at the same time. Beijing was a strong backer of the nomination of the current Director General Tedros Adhanom Ghebreyesus, a former senior Ethiopian government official, and Beijing invited him to speak in China before his 2017 election to the position.[113] It remains unclear just how much sway such moves have actually yielded Beijing inside the WHO but the agency's response to China's role in the COVID-19 outbreak has drawn criticism from many quarters.

Holding aloft its principle of ***"Vasudhaiva Kutumbakam"*** i.e., 'Whole Earth is One Family', India has stood out for its values during the ongoing pandemic, despite its own problems. India has supplied medicines to over 120 countries during this pandemic. India is a world leader in pharmaceuticals and vaccine development and is a model of vibrant and liberal democracy for the entire world.[114] In mid-March, the Modi administration launched a regional cooperation program in South Asia. First, India pledged $10 million towards a 'SAARC COVID-19 Emergency Fund'. Later, India explored an Information Exchange Platform (IEP) to facilitate exchange of expertise among South Asian health professionals.[115] G-20 Summit happened because of Prime Minister Modi's initiative and in his address at a video conference of the G-20 leaders on 26 March, Modi pitched for developing a new crisis management protocol and procedures to deal with global health crisis besides significantly boosting capability of organizations like the WHO.[116] In the global platforms, Prime Minister Modi has also been championing the cause of climate change and environmental issues.

Mr. Ram Madhav, BJP's National General Secretary, writes, "With the US facing its worst nightmare, and the credibility of the Chinese leadership at an all-time low, the presumption that Modi should step into the role that Roosevelt played 75 years ago sounds logical".[117] The United States had emerged as the most powerful nation in the world militarily, economically and technologically after the World War II. Therefore when US President Franklin D. Roosevelt promoted the idea of the United Nations, it was readily accepted because the United States had muscle and money power both. Undoubtedly, Prime Minister Narendra Modi has the charisma, ingenuity and innovativeness of a great leader but India does not have the type of money and muscle power required to launch a nascent organization. However, looking at the current world disorder created by the COVID-19 pandemic, health has emerged as the strategic issue, which has to be addressed with utmost priority. Health care is a low investment but high-dividend field. India has the expertise in biotechnology and medical science and has all the credentials to provide leadership role. Having lost faith in the functioning of an autonomous world organization like WHO and concealment of facts by a communist country, the majority world will like to have transparency and open sharing of details when it comes to the health of their people. There is a need for countries with open, transparent and fair healthcare and medical research facilities to come together not only to address the present crisis but for long-term benefits of global public health. India can act as a bridge or platform to bring the affected countries together and Prime Minister Modi is a world leader, who easily connects with other leaders. Initially Prime Minister Modi should launch **Health 7 (H 7)**—a group comprising of India, the United States, Japan, Germany, UK, France and Russia—who can pool resources, be transparent in sharing their scientific knowhow and invest without being "indebted" but based on more overt principles of fairness—to fight and defeat the pandemic together. In the current world setting, there are corporations with GDPs bigger than many countries in the world, which can also join this grouping. The group can provide assistance to other countries of the world.

Later the **H 7** can be expanded, which India should prefer to call *"Vishwa Swasthya Setu"* or **"World Health Bridge" (WHB)** with the nodal point of this omnidirectional health bridge in India. India should act as a node to transmit and receive all knowledge and expertise on healthcare in a transparent manner and draft rules and regulations to ensure that healthcare facilities are made available to all citizens of the member nations at affordable rates. All countries agreeing with the laid down charter of this organization can become members. Pune, Bengaluru or Hyderabad, being the Biotechnology and Pharmaceutical hub of the country; any one of these should be the place where Headquarters of WHB should be located.

8

Self-Reliant India

Having been hit hard by the novel coronavirus, all nations of the world (leaving aside China) have drawn inwards to rebalance their economy and restore confidence of their people. Launching of *"Self-reliant India"* mission or *"Aatma-nirbhar Bharat" Abhiyan* by Prime Minister Narendra Modi on 12 March 2020 is appropriately timed for preparing the nation, to put it back on the path of economic recovery. Considering *"Self-reliant India"* as the only path for India in the state of the world today, Prime Minister Modi drew a parallel with what is given in our scriptures—*Eshah Panthah, i.e., self-sufficient India.*[1] Though, some may consider the approach to be equivalent of 'Swadeshi' economics of the past, where videshi or foreign stuff was avoided but the Prime Minister made it amply clear by stating that "India does not advocate self-centric arrangements when it comes to self-reliance. India's self-reliance is ingrained in the happiness, cooperation and peace of the world." He further added, "India's progress has always been integral to the progress of the world."[2]

Prime Minister Modi elaborated that this magnificent building of self-reliant India would stand on five **Pillars**: First, ***Economy*** that brings Quantum Jump rather than incremental change; Second, ***Infrastructure*** that becomes the identity of modern India; Third, ***Our System*** that is

driven by technology to fulfill the dreams of the 21st Century; Four, ***Our Demography***; and Five, ***Demand*** the cycle of demand and supply chain in our economy.[3]

Focus on Rural Sector

It is a war of very different kind—while every nation is engaged in a battle to save precious human lives but at same time it has to employ the human resources to build up the economy on a war footing. And to achieve victory in war, the time-tested principles of war need to be followed. First and foremost is the 'Selection and Maintenance of Aim' that is 'to give a quantum jump to the Economy with a view to build 'Self-reliant India'. How do we achieve it? Follow other principles—'concentration of force' (or rather resources) at the point of decision or in other words at the 'centre of gravity' at the right time. With two-third of the country's population residing in rural areas comprising of 6,50,000 villages and almost 10 million of migrant labor (of an estimated total of 23 million)[4] having shifted from urban to ***rural areas,***[5] this ***is the 'centre of gravity' in post-COVID period where economic resources and effort should be concentrated to leverage the demographic dividend***. Though Unlock 3.0 has commenced since 1st August, industries in urban areas, which were dependent upon migrant workers are still at loss due to their absence and are functioning at around 50 percent of their full capacity. They were trying hard to reach out to migrant workers to facilitate their early return by wooing them with better wages and other incentives.[6] However, the physical sufferings combined with trauma created by COVID-19 pandemic on migrant workers are so great that those having moved to their villages may not come back so early.[7] But the lure of money is so strong that once the shock of pandemic is over within next six months or so and if migrant workers are not absorbed in rural areas, they will return back to their familiar urban surroundings. Therefore the governments, both central and states, must act expeditiously and in concert to ensure that returned migrant workers are gainfully engaged, imparted requisite skills for the demand-oriented small- and medium-scale industries, which should come up in a planned manner in the rural sector. These industries can fall in any of the categories: food processing, fruit juice, farm implements, textile to include face covers and PPEs, leather goods, khadi cosmetics, village craft and so on. It is going to be the nature's way of rebalancing the population where villages will no longer be emptied of young people and urban industries will be compelled to value their workers according to their skill. Rural economy will get a well-deserved boost and contribute a greater share of the GDP. The government is believably conscious of this aspect. Rather, the Uttar Pradesh government has done skill mapping of 24 lakh workers out of 32 lakh workers returned from other states. Yogi government has decided to employ those who are skilled and those who are unskilled will be imparted skill training[8] for the long-term benefit to the state as also for the individual workers.

Demand is the most important ingredient that runs the economy of a country. Where does demand come from? In a modern economy, it comes from ***three sources: investment, domestic consumption and exports***—not in any order of priority.

Physical Infrastructure

Investment in physical infrastructure directly promotes growth because construction of roads, bridges, oil and gas pipelines, power generation etc. employs not only lot of labour, creating millions of jobs but rejuvenates the industries producing steel, cement, paints and other raw material, thus creating a self-sustaining cycle of supply and demand as long as the projects continue. The famous "Marshall Plan", under which the United States provided more than $15 billion (a generous 5 percent of the US GDP at that time) as aid to Western Europe for its economic redevelopment after World War II was primarily used to reconstruct cities, industries and infrastructure heavily damaged during the war.[9] Prior to that, massive investment in public works was used as major means to end the 'Great Depression' of the 1930s.[10] One of the key features of China's economic rise is the massive investment in building infrastructure—rail, road, bridges, canals, pipelines, airports, seaports, power generation and so on. In fact China's 'One Belt, One Road' (OBOR) or 'Belt and Road Initiative' (BRI) is the utilization of its surplus infrastructural building capacity on foreign shores. Many experts regard China's BRI as an emulation of 'Marshall Plan'.

The Indian government must spend a major portion of its economic stimulus package on infrastructure, which should pay multiple dividends i.e., not only for economic recovery through infrastructure development cycle as discussed above but also to attract foreign companies for shifting their manufacturing bases in India as part of our 'Make in India' mission. For example, Sagarmala Project, which is aimed at accelerating economic development in the country by harnessing the potential of India's coastline and inland waterways and was approved by the Union Cabinet on 25 March 2015,[11] should be completed in time (See Map of Sagarmala at Annexure). The project is promising. If one goes by the example of Shenzhen in China since 1978, it helped created an estimated 7 million jobs and the city's GDP grew 50 times to $180 billion after the development of ports.[12] Further, in the Shenzhen cluster of China's Special Economic Zones (SEZs), companies were provided road, water and electricity infrastructure free of cost, and quick access to ports. The government also built accommodations close to work sites for labor brought in from remote areas. Single-window clearances for projects were in 30 days or less. The duty on exports was a flat 15 percent.[13] It is expected that Sagarmala could boost India's merchandise exports to $110 billion by 2025 but its real potential will be exploited when foreign companies move in to set up their manufacturing bases and India gets amalgamated in to global supply chain. Further, completion of five industrial corridors approved by the government viz., Delhi Mumbai Industrial Corridor (DMIC), Amritsar Kolkata Industrial Corridor (AKIC), Chennai Bengaluru Industrial Corridor (CBIC), East Coast Economic Corridor (ECEC) with Vizag Chennai Industrial Corridor (VCIC) as Phase-1and Bengaluru Mumbai Industrial Corridor (BMIC)[14] should be expedited. Industrial corridors have been planned with the aim to attract potential investors both domestic as well as foreign to set up their manufacturing units at National Investment and Manufacturing Zones (NMIZs).

Household Consumption

As regards, India's ***household consumption, traditionally it had been on a much higher side***. According to the International Monetary Fund, the household consumption share of the economies of Brazil, Russia, India and China were 62.8 percent, 54.1 percent, 57.3 percent and 35.1 percent of their GDPs respectively in 2011.[15] Notwithstanding its major contribution to economic growth the household consumption in India is not equally distributed over the complete strata of society. There are, as usual, rich versus poor and urban versus rural divide and depending upon money in their hands, the demand and consumption of consumer goods will vary. The slowdown in economy, prior to the pandemic was being attributed to lower demand due to lower incomes. On the rural front, it is believed that a sharp fall in food inflation shifted the terms of trade against agriculture. With farmers getting less money for their produce, it resulted in a big squeeze on farm incomes and accordingly drop in the household consumption. The World Bank report cited a drop in private consumption growth—from 7.3 percent a year ago to 3.1 percent in the last quarter (quarter ending September 2019) and negligible manufacturing growth as the main reasons for India's slowdown.[16]

Post-COVID, the pattern of private consumption is likely to be different. The rich strata of the society, which were forming 20 percent of the society but were earlier contributing almost 50 percent of the domestic consumption according to 2011-12 NSSO data,[17] will likely reduce their spending. This will happen because precautionary savings by rich people will tend to rise under conditions of income uncertainty caused by the pandemic lockdown and will continue at least for the next few years.[18] Since, India's private consumption is skewed towards the rich, any cutback in consumption demand will make economic revival even more difficult. Unlike a communist regime, in a democratic set up, an elected government cannot force individuals to decide between more consumption or savings. The government can only create conducive conditions for more spending. There is merit in focusing on the bottom 80 percent of the population.[19] Investment in a well-designed social protection architecture is critical for driving the broader economic recovery. The government has rightly chosen the schemes such as the ***National Rural Employment Guarantee Scheme (NREGS) for employment security and public distribution system (PDS)*** for food security costing 0.5 percent and 1 percent of GDP respectively. Evidence has found that by reducing leakages, payment delays and uncertainty, NREGS implementation has been improved leading to a substantial reduction in rural poverty. Similarly, recent research has found that PDS can insulate the poor from price fluctuations of food-grains, and increase the proportion of the population that can reach minimum nutrition standards. Knowing fully well the linkage between nutrition and productivity for labor-intensive tasks, PDS likely contributes not only to food security but also in boosting the productivity of the poor. Economic experts opine that the government's decision to increase the budgets for NREGS and PDS make a lot of sense as the benefits will likely exceed the costs.[20] But economic recovery and India's development need much more. The government is planning for a third social protection pillar, based on modest but near-universal income transfers that will promote both public welfare and an economic recovery. Reportedly, implementation of a ***Universal Basic Income*** (UBI) is under examination and active consideration of the government.[21]

Exports

Net export (exports minus imports) is one of the main pillars of GDP growth of a nation. Due to rapid developments in transportation and speed of communications, the quantity of exports has become a game changer in the growth of economy of a country. China is the best example. China has adopted a triangular structure for trade with its most important trading partners. China imports about twice, as much as it exports, from five East Asian neighbours including Korea and Taiwan, rather in case of Taiwan, China imports four times as much as it exports. By contrast, China exports more than three times as much as it imports to the big three export markets of the United States, European Union and Hong Kong.[22] Thus overall trade balance is more important, rather than comparing the trade deficit or trade surplus with individual countries.

India's export growth until the 2008 financial crisis was progressing well but it declined post-2008. With rise of protectionism and trade wars in the past few years followed by the shock of this pandemic, exports are unlikely to revive anytime soon and even the global trade is in jeopardy. Though for India not having joined any major mega regional trade treaty like Regional Comprehensive Economic Partnership (RCEP), it may be considered as an impeding factor for its export growth. But this period must be considered as heaven-sent opportunity for India to reorient and expand its manufacturing sector to produce items, which have greater export potential and where India should have the 'first-mover' advantage. It is worth studying the example of China.

From virtually an industrial backwater in 1978, China is now the world's biggest producer of cement, steel, aluminum, coke, ships, chemical fertilizers and textiles and has world's largest automobile market. The number of industrial firms rose from 377,300 in 1980 to nearly 8 million in 1996.[23] A major change began in the late 1990s as the government shifted emphasis from light industrial development to heavy industry. Take the example of steel—Chinese steel output was just 37.1 million metric tons in 1980; while it quadrupled to 128.5 million metric tons in 20 years i.e., 2000 but in next six years in 2006, it reached 418.8-million metric tons, one third of global production.[24]In 2018, China produced an astonishing 928.3 million metric tons of crude steel (almost 50 percent of global production) as against106.5million metric tons by India, 104.3 million metric tons by Japan and 86.7 million metric tons by the United States.[25] It means that China is capable of moving world markets for commodities like iron ore. How did this happen?

Mao wanted China to become steel super power, with ancient city of Handan as a capital of steel but that did not happen during his lifetime. Handan had two advantages: rich veins of coal and iron ore and easy access to a major North-South railway line. Hangang, as the local steel mill in Handan was called, was a government favourite. Hangang was created by an act of Mao and it survived for decades on state subsidies, providing benefits for its 30,000 workers but made low-quality ferrous metals that earned poor returns. In the 1990s, Hangang came under pressure to turn a profit. Its managers decided to start making sheet metal, for home appliances and cars, as well as their usual output of construction material, which required a major upgrade. Backed by state bank loans and a listing on the Shanghai stock market, Hangang embarked on an overhaul. But its ambitions far exceeded its budget. The company needed a cheap and radical solution to transform the mill. The answer came from Europe and in particular Germany as their steel mills were earmarked for closure and probably heading for the scrap. Chinese bought dozens of Germany's relatively sophisticated blast furnaces for a small fraction of what new ones would have cost. Starting with Dortmund in 1998, Chinese workers arrived in hundreds and labeled every part of the seven-story furnace, then disassembled it, packed it in thousands of wooden crates and shipped to China. Chinese then proceeded to buy second-hand blast furnaces from France and Luxembourg. Following in to the footsteps of Hangang, other Chinese companies also flocked to Europe to buy these assets. Working 24 hours a day, 77 large steel mills like Hangang and hundreds of small rivals have made China a world leader in steel production. It is a different story that same steel mills have been spewing particulates in to the air, thereby adding to the world pollution at a much faster rate.[26]

The situation now is much different as compared to when China entered in to the world market. The global market has become increasingly competitive and we cannot challenge China in fields where she is already the world leader. India's exports are too diverse and lack a sustainable competitive advantage. Therefore, India has to develop global dominance in certain sectors in which we have the expertise and can sustain ourselves through 'first-mover' advantage. We must focus on developing pockets of excellence to support exports. There are three fields for which human need will never diminish but form will only change, irrespective of any country in the world. These are: **Health upkeep**, for which people will become even more conscious post-COVID; **Food**—should be both healthy and tasty; and **Dress**—should be comfortable, contemporary and fashionable. Once these needs are met, then human beings will look for their education/

knowledge enhancement, luxury and entertainment. Ultimately, there has to be ultra-high speed, ***real-time digital connectivity combined with means of communications*** to enable our products to reach the consumers in every corner of the globe as per their needs.

In the sphere of **health upkeep**, necessity of remaining ahead in manufacture of medicines and vaccine development is very important. As regards innovation, India is already a significant player in global health research and development. This expertise gives India's vaccines industry a significant advantage in developing cost-effective and quality-assured vaccines. That's why reputed foreign research institutes have tied up with around 30 Indian companies for mass manufacturing of potential novel coronavirus vaccines. In addition, India already manufactures many anti-viral drugs that could be re-purposed and scaled-up for use in mild cases of COVID-19. Further, it is not only the ability to develop vaccines and medicines but India has a proven track record to manufacture these to a high standard, in high volumes and at a low cost.[27] India has the ability and it must pursue rapid development of diagnostics and medical devices ranging from rapid test kits to ventilators and high-end medical equipment. The ayurvedic herbs and potions, which have been our ancient heritage and are claimed to be building the body immunity, need to be given value addition through scientific evaluation and international certification for their worldwide acceptance. Yoga and *Pranayama* should be made popular for building up the body strength against diseases.

In Western countries, **Indian traditional cuisines** were being promoted because of their pungent taste and wholesome cooking as one of the preventive measures against novel coronavirus. Every state in India has its own peculiar cuisines, which should be made popular. In the post-COVID period, majority of the people will avoid going out for eating and stay at home. Thus Indian food should be packaged in raw form, with simplified recipes enclosed or alternatively semi-cooked with only natural preservatives, which people should enjoy preparing at home and remain healthy.

Garment manufacturing and linked to it fashion industry and their selling techniques will undergo a big overhaul in the post-COVID period. Due to the peculiar spreading character of coronavirus, shopping malls displaying the huge inventory of clothing, with customers at liberty to try the dresses before buying may now become a taboo. Even for shopping online, exchange or return offer of clothes may be out of question because people will not like to buy clothes already tried out by others. Since majority population is going to stay at or work from home, cloth designing will undergo a change—torn or patchy jeans and whacky dresses made of synthetics may give way to comfortable and natural fabrics. Now, coming to the strength of India's rural sector. Textile sector is the second largest employer in rural India, with an estimated 16 million crafts-people living over there. They constitute a highly skilled workforce, with huge knowledge of specialized and complex textile processes, learnt from master craftsmen over centuries.[28] They produce aesthetically appealing, ecologically friendly and superior natural fabric handloom products but they need the support of modern marketing and retailing techniques for projecting their products as the best in the world. The world today produces textiles using sophisticated machinery. On the other hand, India has weavers, embroiderers and creators of embellishments, which no one in the world can match. This is the time when the government must step in and support the entrepreneurs to invest their talent in this sphere. They can organize these craftsmen in to clusters according to their skills; market the products in a professional manner, offering competitive prices making intelligent use of Internet. Fashion designers can be involved to offer dress material to the customers in a form that either it is semi-stitched or in a Do-it-Yourself (DIY) form.

Digitization is essential for the global outreach of Indian export products, both for their promotion and marketing. Digitization has two components: software and hardware. Indian software engineers have been known for their professional expertise and have proven their mettle. However, for hardware we are dependent upon foreign countries for critical components. All the gadgets viz., Personal computers, tablets and mobiles/smart phones require semiconductor chips to function. India is a large net importer of semiconductor chips.

While India has done well in terms of chip design and electronics manufacturing, there have been challenges in setting up of Semiconductor Wafer Fabrication (FAB) units in India for a long time. It is not that India does not possess the scientific capabilities to manufacture semiconductor chips. In fact, the level of technical know-how is so high that the government even considered a Rs 2,500 crore feasible study based on Gallium Nitride semiconductor fab at the Indian Institute of Science (IISc) in order to build a local semiconductor industry. Gallium Nitride based semiconductors skip altogether the already mature silicon-based fab technology dominated by countries like the US and China.[29]

However, Silicon-based semiconductor fab is the most popular and proven technology. Fab manufacturing units require not only massive investment but its technology is possessed by Western multinationals. Semiconductor industry or chip making is a fast-moving arena because innovations in this technology are continuous and highly cumulative. It is essential for firms to innovate quickly, accumulate intellectual property rights and use profits to reinvest in R&D to fund the next round of advances. Those falling behind, see their products lose value and then disappear entirely from the market. It is best to learn from the example of China. China's semiconductor firms have so far not been able to innovate at the speed necessary to compete with the best in the world. To illustrate this, an example is the 909 Project, where Shanghai government invested 10 billion RMB to establish 'Huahong', which is now one of China's most advanced chip manufacturers. 'Huahong' was tasked to manufacture semiconductors using 8-inch wafers and it enlisted the support of Japan's NEC to manage production.[30] It is known that by the time project took off, most advanced companies were already using 11.8-inch (300mm) wafers in semiconductor manufacturing. In fact, there is a clear plan to move towards 450 mm (18 inch) wafer size.[31]Thus China has not able to keep pace with global innovation, as in semiconductors, cutting-edge technology becomes obsolete every two years. Shanghai-based Semiconductor Manufacturing International Corporation (SMIC), founded in 2000, is considered one of the world's top five semiconductor foundries in the world. However, it is three generations—or at least six years—behind its rivals.[32]

If India has to become fully digitalized, then we have to reduce the dependency on chip imports and create semiconductor-manufacturing units within the country. For this we have to make proper investment not only for initial setting-up of units but for subsequent research & development to remain ahead in the race. Focus must also be made on small- and medium-enterprises to take up chip manufacturing, as is the case in China, Taiwan, and Thailand. This will certainly, make India self-reliant as well as self-sufficient in semiconductor chip production.[33]

Vocal for Local to make it Global

The Pandemic lockdown has revealed the importance of Local manufacturing, Local market and Local supply chain. In the time of crisis, local products fulfilled our demand. The Prime Minister in his speech of 12 May explained, "The Global Brands you feel today were sometimes also very local like this. But when people started using them, started promoting them, branding them, proud of them, they became Global from Local Products". He emphasized that *"Therefore, from today every Indian has to become vocal for their local, not only to buy local products, but also to promote them proudly."*[34]

In fact, most of the global brands were initially launched as local companies by entrepreneurs with the vision to go global. For example, LG Electronics was founded as GoldStar (Hangul) in 1958 with the objective of domestically producing consumer electronics and home appliances. By 2005, LG (adopting the new name as Lucky-Goldstar in 1995) was a Top 100 global brand; playing a large role in the global consumer electronics industry and it was the second-largest LCD TV manufacturer worldwide as of 2013.[35] Similarly, **Red Bull** is an energy drink sold by Red Bull GmbH, an Austrian company, which was created in 1987. Now, Red Bull has the highest market share of any energy drink in the world, with 7.5 billion cans sold in a year (as of 2019).[36] One example is of White goods or consumer durables and another is of daily consumables.

Promising Indian startups should be motivated and encouraged from the above examples. Prime Minister Modi during his speech of 12th May praised, "Today, the demand and sales of both Khadi and handloom have reached record levels in a very short time. Not only that, you also made it a big brand."[37] But for Khadi to become a global brand, tremendous efforts will be required in encouraging young entrepreneurs to accept it as a challenge in establishing number of small and medium industries to produce Khadi products of highest quality as also by the government for promotion and marketing of the same abroad. Natural organic products have great demand in the West and are being sold at 10 times the cost compared to that in India. Another aspect is the real time information about the emerging demands in foreign countries. For example, changing climatic conditions are throwing up new challenges for human beings at unexpected places on the globe. People across Western Europe suffered through intense heat wave, with Britain, Germany, France and the Low countries reaching life-threatening, record breaking temperatures during the last summer.[38] People over there are not used to such weather, structures are not built for it and homes in general don't have air conditioning. That was the time, when India could have supplied non-air-conditioned, environmental friendly, economical but effective appliances to meet their short-term requirement.

Only a person with fine business sense, present in that country, can sense such an opportunity and sensitize his country about the urgency of requirement. Ideally, the Indian embassies and consulates should be promoting the trade by providing inputs to the industry about the new demands but India's diplomatic corps is miniscule compared to its counterparts in the United States, China and even Brazil. According to the Ministry of External Affairs, India's diplomatic corps consists of around 1,750 officers (750 IFS Grade-A officers, 250 IFS Grade-B personnel, defence attaches and other officers).[39] If we want to be proactive in enhancing our exports, we should create post of Commerce Attaches on the lines of Defence Attaches, who should monitor that country's business environment and provide regular feedbacks about the emerging demands. They can act as interface between the business communities/industrialists of two countries.

If the objective of India is to become a $5 Trillion economy by 2024, then irrespective of the setback caused to the economy by this pandemic, the ultimate aim should never be lost sight off. Whether it is economy or life, it never follows a linear path. The Universe follows the law of momentum i.e., mass x velocity. If mass is represented by money or resources and velocity by efforts then economy can gain momentum by increasing either of these and growth will be exponential. When money is available in a limited quantity, then it is wise to maintain adequate reserves, which should be launched in the projects gaining momentum to further accelerate the growth. The principle is simple—"You always reinforce 'success' and not failure".

9

Conclusion

History is replete with examples; whenever there were extreme human sufferings or crises of unparalleled magnitude in the past, old structures gave way to new ones and nations adopted altogether different courses for the betterment of its people. 'League of Nations' of World War I gave way to 'United Nations'; The World Bank and International Monetary Fund (IMF), known collectively as the Bretton Woods Institutions were founded to support the structure of the world's economic and financial order. It was a 'decade of catastrophe' under Chairman Mao's "Great Proletarian Cultural Revolution" (1966-76) during which millions of Chinese people died and they had untold sufferings, which stimulated Deng Xiaoping to launch 'Four Modernizations' in 1979, leading China to become a great economic power in four decades, ready to dislodge the United States from its Numero Uno position.

In 1991, it was the crushing balance-of-payment crisis, which forced P V Narsimha Rao's government to liberalize the Indian economy. Despite his best of the intentions and efforts, Prime Minister Narendra Modi could not succeed in his first tenure in executing the much-needed second phase of economic reforms. Prime Minister Modi's second tenure started with the downfall of economy and then followed the catastrophe of novel coronavirus. COVID-19 pandemic has provided once-in-a-century opportunity to the Modi government to undertake deeper reforms for long-term economic goals so that critical sectors are unshackled and foreign investment is brought in to make India as a manufacturing hub. On 12 May, Prime Minister Modi announced Rs 20.97 lakh crore economic package equivalent to 10 percent of India's GDP under the 'Aatma-nirbhar Bharat Abhiyan' (Self-reliant India Campaign) that includes Rs 1.7 lakh crore relief package announced earlier on 26 March and about Rs 5.7 lakh crore of monetary measures announced by Reserve Bank of India since 27 March.[1] The government is pushing for key reforms in land, labour, capital, technology and infrastructure.

Pandemics have been striking with greater frequency primarily because of deforestation, environmental degradation, rapid urbanization, overpopulation, migration and growing animal and human conflict.[2] Experts have been warning about these causes since long but the nations or the people didn't heed to this warning because of their wanton greed to plunder the nature for uncontrolled development. Now the COVID-19 pandemic has struck the mankind with severity and too little is known about the disease or the future course it will take. Researchers, world over, have resorted to computer simulations modeling to predict different ways the pandemic could play out.

On 16 July, when the country touched a million cases, nearly 56 percent of all cases could be traced to the three regions that were the original hot spots of the disease in India—Maharashtra, Tamil Nadu and Delhi. However, the trend has shifted and the new hot spots are now believed to be emerging in Andhra Pradesh, Karnataka, West Bengal and Uttar Pradesh. The focus of the battle against the pandemic needs to shift to the hinterland and the peninsula—both high population density regions. Virologists and microbiologists opine that aggressive testing is crucial to control the outbreak. Though on mass testing, much higher number of infected people will be identified and initially the tally of positive cases will go up. But this is the only way forward being followed all over the world i.e., to test as many people as possible so as to track and isolate those people who are infected and thereby curtail the spread of the disease in the community.[3] Aggressive testing is considered as key to the turnaround in Delhi, where the positivity rate of tests—the proportion of people found positive for the disease from among those tested—dropped from 37 percent a month ago to about 6 percent.[4] The country's maximum caseload, which is about 80 percent of the cases, is restricted to 50 districts out of about 740 total districts. On 11 August, Prime Minister Narendra Modi, while addressing the chief ministers of the 10 hardest-hit states, cited the example of COVID-19 response in Delhi and said that the states must focus on containment and surveillance, tracking and testing of close contacts of any infected person within 72 hours, and ramping up testing further to bring down the test positivity rate. The Prime Minister said, "We have seen that increasing testing helps us identify and contain the spread...And once we increase testing even further, we will see that the goal of bringing the fatality rate below 1 percent will be achievable."[5] The ICMR had set a target of one million tests per day by the end of August and India already crossed that milestone on 21 August with a total of 1,023,836 tests having been conducted across the country. The testing lab network in the country is also being strengthened as it consists of currently1511 labs (of which 983 labs are in the government sector and 528 are private labs) and more are being added day by day. Overall, India has conducted 34,491,073 COVID-19 tests as of 21 August, since the first swab sample was diagnosed on January 22. Even with such a high level of testing, the positivity has remained low at 8.81 percent.[6] The WHO identifies 8-12 percent as the ideal range for test positive rate in a country with an active outbreak.

If we look at the positive aspects, so far India's average COVID-19 death rate (as on 31 August) is 47 per million against the global average of 109.7 deaths per million. The mortality rates in respect of the United States, Brazil and Russia are 567, 571 and 118 deaths per million of population respectively.[7]

The figures are based on data analytics to create statistical records, which are of help to prepare for managing the increasing patients load. These cannot provide any knowledge about the biological behaviour of the virus. Therefore, the most relevant question asked is when will the COVID-19 disease peak in India because after that curve is likely to flatten. In the first two weeks of August, the new cases in the US and Brazil were seen hitting a plateau; one can say the third wave of infections has started showing flattening of the curve. The global COVID-19 curve has flattened twice before—first, when the Chinese outbreak peaked and the contagion was yet to reach the West; the second, when cases dropped in Europe—however, it has risen again with more ferocity both times as the virus has spread to new regions.[8]

Some experts had said that the disease was expected to peak in July in India. While a study funded by Indian Council of Medical Research arrived at the conclusion that the disease would peak in November. An infection wanes under two conditions: One, it has run its course, which means enough of the population has been exposed to the pathogen, and has, therefore, become immune. This is called 'herd immunity' that is said to be achieved if 60-65 percent of the population is infected. It is a phenomenon where a virus or any other pathogen can't infect too many people because it soon runs in to someone who has already been infected, and is therefore immune, breaking the chain of infections.[9] According to one mathematical model developed by researchers at the University of Nottingham and Stockholm University, the herd immunity for COVID-19 could be around 40 percent.[10] But none of the country is close to that; Two, its chain has been broken either through a cure or a vaccine, or by physically removing chances of an infection. In the absence of a cure or vaccine, best option is to break the chain—by testing, tracing, isolating and treating the affected, and by persuading the rest of the population to adopt preventive measures—masks, hand-washing and social distancing.

According to a study published in the journal 'Nature Medicine' on 18 June, the asymptomatic people may produce antibodies that can fight the viral disease for just a few months. Though based on a small group, the study suggests that unlike a few other diseases, where after being infected once, a person gets lifelong immunity (chicken pox is an example), contracting the coronavirus disease once doesn't mean a person will not contract it again. This study creates a doubt that some asymptomatic infected people may or may not become immune.[11] Thus, the solution lies in the discovery and availability of a vaccine for the coronavirus disease. There are number of vaccines in various stages of testing and trial, but these could be ready by next year only. That too, it will not be widely available immediately. The world will require seven billion doses (and if it is similar to flu shots then one may have to take one every year) and not everyone will get it. According to a recent Bloomberg article, the first vaccines may not be able to prevent the coronavirus disease.[12]

Viruses always mutate and come back—the influenza pandemic of 1918 had three major waves. Starting in March 1918, its peak came during a second wave late that same year. That second wave was a stronger mutation than the first version of the virus. We are already seeing what may become, officially, a second wave of the novel coronavirus. There are new cases in China, Russia, and even South Korea, which had earlier been praised for its containment of the first wave.[13] In the wait for a vaccine or cure, the nation cannot stay in a prolonged lock down. India cannot wait for COVID-19 pandemic to be over. If life and livelihood has to go together then a balance has to be maintained. Therefore, Prime Minister Modi, while speaking at the beginning of a two-day meeting with chief ministers on 16 June, said, "We must focus on both life and livelihood, boost health infrastructure, testing and tracing as well as increase economic activity".[14] This is the right time for India to leverage its expertise and capacity in healthcare sector for establishing mutually beneficial relationships with coronavirus affected countries. Rural economy should be treated as the basic building block of national economy and if organized properly it will also be able to absorb the migrant youth returning back due to lockdown in big cities.

On the economic front, Prime Minister Modi said that efforts of the past few weeks have resulted in the revival of the economy. He said, "We are seeing green shoots in the economy. Power consumption, for instance, has increased, the sale of two-wheelers is now at 70 percent of pre-lockdown numbers." He further added that the increase in the sale of fertilizers in May and increase in kharif sowing and digital payments were the other "green shoots" that could be witnessed. The rural economy has gathered pace—area of kharif crop this time was 12 to 13 percent more than the previous year.[15] The Indian economy is ready to bounce back fast.

During his address at a Confederation of Indian Industries (CII) event on 2 June, Prime Minister Narendra Modi listed out five 'I's to make India a self-reliant economy. The ***intent, inclusion, investment, infrastructure and innovation*** are of utmost importance to make a self-reliant India.[16] No one can doubt the honest intent of Prime Minister Modi and his relentless endeavours for inclusivity. However, home-generated investment will always be insufficient to adequately fuel the economy. Therefore, land, labour and tax reforms should be pushed in along with requisite infrastructural development to attract the foreign companies to set up their manufacturing bases in India. Innovation is a constant endeavour because if you want to remain ahead in the market, you have to keep innovating and upgrading—the quality of product as also the techniques of marketing. To the five 'I's, a sixth one can be added—***Implementation*** or rather speedy and timely implementation of government's intent and policies. In spite of best of the policies and projects during the first term of Modi government, the laid down objectives could not be achieved because of tardy implementation, e.g., Skill India, Clean Ganga (Namami Gange) etc. and the accountability for that should rest with the bureaucrats. If India gets it right this time, in both domestic and international terms, we would be embarking on the road to taking our rightful place in the world.

Lastly, it is human tendency that your neighbours will always be envious of your progress and prosperity and that too if they feel that it was their legitimate share that has been snatched. Once the foreign countries start shifting their manufacturing bases from China to India, as some of them have already started the process, China will respond aggressively both in traditional as well as non-traditional security domains. Recent deadly clash of troops in at least 45 years on 15 June evening in the Galwan Valley along the Line of Actual Control (LAC) in Eastern Ladakh, should be accepted as a warning shot. Even in the time of adversity, when the economy has yet to start recovering, adequate safeguards must be ensured against both external and internal security threats by allocating proportionate share of the GDP.

To bolster self-reliance for its defence industrial base, India on 9 August released a list of 101 weapons and platforms that will be banned from import over the next seven years. The items on the list, worth a total of $53.4 billion, are to be manufactured in India, with local companies as prime contractors. Defence Minister Rajnath Singh called it "a big step toward self-reliance in defence production in accordance with Prime Minister Narendra Modi's 'Aatma-nirbhar Bharat,' " or "Self-Reliant India."[17] It signals the strong intent of government to boost domestic defence production.

If we are welcoming friendly foreign countries to invest in India by setting up their industries or shifting their logistical supply chains as part of our 'Self-reliant India' mission, then it will be equally wise to forge reciprocal alliances with like-minded nations in the security domain. ***The shared prosperity amongst the nations will lead to shared security as a natural phenomenon.***

NOTES

Chapter 1: Introduction

1. "Modi's vision 2022: A 'new, inclusive India' for poor, middle class and women", *Hindustan Times*, 13 March 2017, available at https://www.hindustantimes.com/assembly-elections/election-results-the-foundation-of-a-new-inclusive-india-pm-modi/story-retKz0dyLeZlC5hYgaPkEI.html
2. "PM slams 'professional pessimists', says India poised to become $5-trillion economy by 2024", *Business Today*, 6 July 2019, available at https://www.businesstoday.in/current/corporate/pm-slams-professional-pessimists-says-india-poised-to-become-5-trillion-economy-by-2024/story/362195.html
3. "COVID-19 CORONAVIRUS PANDEMIC", available at https://www.worldometers.info/coronavirus/ (accessed on 10 September 2020)
4. R Sukumar, "Covid-19: What you need to know today", *Hindustan Times*, 26 August 2020, available at https://epaper.hindustantimes.com/Home/MShareArticle?Orgld=26820c0cc9f&imageview=0
5. "Major economies shrink sharply in June quarter", *Hindustan Times*, 01 August 2020, available at https://epaper.hindustantimes.com/Home/MShareArticle?Orgld= 189f854396&imageview=0 ; and "Eurozone suffers deepest contraction on record", *BBC News*, 31 July 2020, available at https://www.bbc.com/news/business-53606101
6. "World Economic Outlook Update, June 2020", available at https://www.imf.org/en/Publications/WEO/Issues/2020/06/24/WEOUpdateJune2020
7. "Indian Economy sees a record fall", *Hindustan Times*, New Delhi, Tuesday, 01 September 2020.
8. V.R. Ferose, "A forecast of the post-covid new world order", *Livemint*, 03 April 2020, available at https://www.livemint.com/opinion/quick-edit/a-forecast-of-the-post-covid-new-world-order-11585907017571.html
9. "'Mission Self-Reliant India': COVID-19 crisis opportunity, says PM Modi as he announces Rs 20 lakh crore package", *DNA*, 12 May 2020, available at https://www.dnaindia.com/india/report-mission-self-reliant-india-covid-19-crisis-

opportunity-says-pm-modi-as-he-announces-rs-20-lakh-crore-package-2824591

10. Geeta Mohan, "China's growing territorial aggression amid coronavirus crisis", *India Today*, 26 June 2020, available at https://www.indiatoday.in/mail-today/story/china-growing-territorial-aggression-amid-covid-crisis-1692787-2020-06-26
11. "Strong, self-reliant India stands for greater good of world: Modi", *Hindustan Times*, New Delhi, Sunday, 16 August 2020.

Chapter 2: Emerging Geopolitical Environment

1. Francis P. Sempa, "Forget About a 'New' Cold War. The Old One Never Ended", *The Diplomat*, 27 May 2020, citing James Burnham 'The War We Are In' available at https://thediplomat.com/2020/05/forget-about-a-new-cold-war-the-old-one-never-ended/
2. Robert Farley, "Was the Sino-Soviet Split Borne of Ideology or Geostrategic Consideration?", *The Diplomat*, 06 March 2017, available at https://thediplomat.com/2017/03/was-the-sino-soviet-split-borne-of-ideology-or-geostrategic-consideration/
3. Deborah Welch Larson, "Will China be a New Type of Great Power?", *The Chinese Journal of International Politics*, 2015, Vol. 8, No. 4, p.333., available at https://fas.org/nuke/guide/china/doctrine/0046.htm
4. Robert Farley, "Beijing 'Lost' the Sino-Soviet Split, But That Didn't Matter in the End", *The Diplomat*, 22 January 2016, available at https://thediplomat.com/2016/01/beijing-lost-the-sino-soviet-split-but-that-didnt-matter-in-the-end/
5. Deborah Welch Larson, op.cit., p.333.
6. "Rapprochement with China, 1972", US Department of State, Office of the Historian, Milestones: 1969-1976, available at history.state.gov/milestones/1969-1976/rapprochement-china
7. "Speech By Chairman of the Delegation of the People's Republic of China, Deng Xiaoping, At the Special Session of the U.N. General Assembly", 10 April 1974, available at https://www.marxists.org/reference/archive/deng-xiaoping/1974/04/10.htm
8. Barry Buzan, "The Logic and Contradictions of 'Peaceful Rise/Development' as China's Grand Strategy", *The Chinese Journal of International Politics*, Vol. 7, Issue 4, Winter 2014, Pages 381–420, 03 June 2014, available at https://academic.oup.com/cjip/article/7/4/381/2365898
9. Ezra F. Vogel, Deng Xiaoping and the Transformation of China (Cambridge: Belknap Press of Harvard University Press, 2011), pp. 359-360.
10. Deborah Welch Larson, op.cit., p.335.
11. "Hu Yaobang's Report to the 12th National Congress of the Communist Party of China", *Beijing Review*, 13 September, 1982', Vol. 25, No. 37 (1982), 'Adhering to an Independent Foreign Policy', p.29., available at https://www.marxists.org/subject/china/peking-review/1982/PR1982-37.pdf
12. Dingding Chen and Jianwei Wang, 'Lying Low No More? China's New Thinking on the Tao Guang Yang Hui Strategy', *China: An International Journal*, Vol. 9, No. 2 (2011), pp. 197–98.
13. Philip Shenon, "Manila Sees China Threat On Coral Reef", *The New York Times*, 19 February1995, available at https://www.nytimes.com/1995/02/19/world/

manila-sees-china-threat-on-coral-reef.html

14. Robert S. Ross, "The 1995–96 Taiwan Strait Confrontation: Coercion, Credibility, and the Use of Force", *International Security*, Vol. 25, No. 2 (Fall 2000), pp. 87–88., available at http://people.duke.edu/~niou/teaching/Ross.pdf
15. Deborah Welch Larson, op.cit., p.337.
16. Pichamon Yeophantong, "Governing the World: China's Evolving Conceptions of Responsibility", *Chinese Journal of International Politics*, Vol. 6, Issue. 4 (Winter 2013), p. 331., available at https://academic.oup.com/cjip/article/6/4/329/467530
17. Deborah Welch Larson, op.cit., p.338.
18. Rosemary Foot, "Chinese Strategies in a U.S.-hegemonic Global Order: Accommodating and Hedging", *International Affairs*, Vol. 82, No. 1 (January 2006), p. 85.
19. Elizabeth Freund Larus, "China's New Security Concept and Peaceful Rise: Trustful Cooperation or Deceptive Diplomacy?", *American Journal of Chinese Studies*, Vol. 12, No. 2 (OCTOBER 2005), pp. 222-223, https://www.jstor.org/stable/44288800?read-now=1&refreqid=excelsior%3Ae054f567d134893d6d89ddc2b3aff0c0&seq=1# page_scan_ tab_contents (accessed on 10 July 2020)
20. Ibid., p.224.
21. Deborah Welch Larson, op.cit., p.339.
22. Elizabeth Freund Larus, op.cit., p.225.
23. Deborah Welch Larson, op.cit., p.340.
24. Barry Buzan, "The Logic and Contradictions of 'Peaceful Rise/Development' as China's Grand Strategy", *The Chinese Journal of International Politics*, Vol. 7, Issue 4, Winter 2014, pp. 381–420, available at https://academic.oup.com/cjip/article/7/4/381/2365898
25. White Paper on China's National Defense 2004.
26. Zheng Bijian, "China's 'Peaceful Rise' to Great: Power Status", *Foreign Affairs* 84, No.5, September-October, 2005, pp. 21-24.
27. Wikipedia, World Bank WDI figures.
28. Wikipedia, "Historical GDP of the People's Republic of China", China NBS figures.
29. Richard E. Poole, "China's 'Harmonious World' in the Era of the Rising East", *Inquiries*, Vol. 6, No. 10, 2014, pp. 1-2, available at http://www.inquiriesjournal.com/articles/932/chinas-harmonious-world-in-the-era-of-the-rising-east
30. "Harmonious society not just utopian dream", Global Times, October 27, 2010 available at www.globaltimes.cn/opinion/commentary/2010-10/586744.html and "Harmonious World: China's Ancient Philosophy for New International Order", available at bw.china-embassy.org/eng/xwdt/t 367341.htm
31. Bonnie S. Glaser and Melissa E. Murphy, 'Soft Power with Chinese Characteristics', in Carola McGiffert, ed., Chinese Soft Power and its Implications for the United States: Competition and Cooperation in the Developing World (Washington, D.C.: Centre for Strategic and international Studies, 2009), pp. 15-16.
32. Ibid., pp. 13-14.
33. Weihong Zhang, 'China's Cultural Future: From Soft Power to Comprehensive National Power', *International Journal of Cultural Policy*, Vol. 16, No. 4 (2010), p. 395.
34. Richard E. Poole, op.cit., p.2.

35. Deborah Welch Larson, op.cit., pp. 341-342.
36. Martin Fackler and Ian Johnson, "Japan Retreats With Release of Chinese Boat Captain", New York Times, 24 September, 2010, available at https://www.nytimes.com/2010/09/25/world/asia/25chinajapan.html
37. Deborah Welch Larson, op.cit., p. 343.
38. Richard E. Poole, op.cit., pp.2-3.
39. Elizabeth Freund Larus, op.cit., p.225., citing Qin Yaqing, "Strategic Culture and Security Issues" presentation for the workshop China's Perspective on National Security Issues, CFAU, Beijing, China, June 7, 2004.
40. Ibid., pp. 225-227.
41. Ambassador Chas W. Freeman, Jr. (USFS, Ret.), "Indo-Pacific Dynamics in Trans-Pacific Perspective," *Middle East Policy Council*, 16 April 2012, available at https://www.mepc.org/speeches/indo-pacific-dynamics-trans-pacific-perspective
42. Phillip C. Saunders, "The Rebalance to Asia: U.S.-China Relations and Regional Security", Strategic Forum, August 2013, National Defense University, p.1., available at https://ndupress.ndu.edu/Portals/68/Documents/stratforum/SF-281.pdf
43. John Ford, "The Pivot to Asia Was Obama's Biggest Mistake", *The Diplomat*, 21 January 2017, available at https://thediplomat.com/2017/01/the-pivot-to-asia-was-obamas-biggest-mistake/
44. Ibid.
45. Brigadier (Dr.) Rajeev Bhutani (Retd), "Profile: China's President Xi Jinping", *Centre for Joint Warfare Studies*, New Delhi, Issue Brief, Vol. XII, No. 2 / May 2018.
46. Graham Allison, "What Xi Jinping Wants", The Atlantic, 31 May 2017, available at https://www.theatlantic.com/international/archive/2017/05/what-china-wants/528561/
47. Zheping Huang, "China's President Xi Jinping Now Has a Dozen Titles, and Counting", *Quartz*, 23 January 2017, available at https://qz.com/892208/chinas-president-xi-jinping-now-has-a-dozen-titles-and-counting/
48. "Xi Jinping named as "commander in chief" by Chinese state media", *The Guardian*, 4/2016, https://www.theguardian.com/world/2016/apr/21/xi-jinping-named-commander-in-chief-chinese-state-media
49. Hampton Stephens, "Will the 'One Belt, One Road' Gamble Bring the World to China?", *World Politics Review*, 29 March 2019,available at https://www.worldpoliticsre view.com/insights/24984/will-the-one-belt-one-road-gamble-bring-the-world-to-china
50. Wade Shepard, "Why China Just Added the Belt and Road Initiative to its Constitution", *Forbes*, 25 October 2017, available at https://www.forbes.com/sites/wadeshepard/2017/10/25/why-china-just-added-the-belt-and-road-initiative-to-its-constitution/#5750e00f42ab
51. Brigadier (Dr.) Rajeev Bhutani, "Sino-Indian Equation: Competition + Cooperation-Confrontation", Pentagon Press LLP, New Delhi, 2019, p.97 and p.148.
52. Cary Huang, "Just what is Xi Jinping's 'Chinese dream' and 'Chinese renaissance'?", *South China Morning Post*, 06 February 2013, available at https://www.scmp.com/news/china/article/1143954/just-what-xi-jinpings-chinese-dream-and-chinese-renaissance

53. Graham Allison, op.cit.
54. Ibid.
55. Brigadier (Dr.) Rajeev Bhutani (Retd), "Transformation of Chinese People's Liberation Army: Reforms, Restructuring & Modernization", Centre for Joint Warfare Studies, New Delhi, 2016, pp. 1-3.
56. Zhao Lei, "PLA to be world-class force by 2050", *China Daily*, 27 October 2017, available at http://www.chinadaily.com.cn/china/2017-10/27/content_33756453.htm
57. Ian James Storey, "Living with the Colossus: How Southeast Asian Countries Cope with China", *Parameters*, Vol. XXIX, No.4, Winter 1999-2000, p.117.
58. James Tunningley, "The South China Sea Dispute: China's Polygonal Defence of Core Interests", *RUSI*, 12 July 2016, available at https://rusi.org/commentary/south-china-sea-dispute-chinas-polygonal-defence-core-interests
59. "Chinese South China Sea Claims", Global security.org, available at https://www.globalsecurity.org/military/world/china/south-china-sea.htm
60. Brigadier (Dr.) Rajeev Bhutani, "Sino-Indian Equation: Competition + Cooperation-Confrontation", op.cit., pp. 11-13.
61. "Chinese Troops Outnumber Indian Army 6:1 In Galwan Valley; Deploys Latest Missiles, Heavy Artillery", *The Eurasian Times*, 3 July 2020, available at https://eurasiantimes.com/chinese-troops-outnumber-indian-army-61-in-galwan-valley-deploys-latest-missiles-heavy-artillery/
62. M.K. Narayanan, "Making sense of China's calculations", *The Hindu*, Monday, 29 June 2020.
63. Brigadier Anil Gupta, "Karakoram Highway: A security challenge for India", *Indian Defence Review*, 02 October 2015, available at http://www.indiandefencereview.com/news/karakoram-highway-a-security-challenge-for-india/
64. Haider Talat, "5 Ways India's Going to Be Affected When CPEC Changes World Trade", *The Quint*, 23 March 2017, available at https://www.thequint.com/voices/blogs/ways-india-going-to-be-affected-when-china-pakistan-cpec-changes-world-trade-gwadar
65. Ankit Panda, "The Political Geography of the India-China Crisis at Doklam", *The Diplomat*, 13 July 2017, available at https://thediplomat.com/2017/07/the-political-geography-of-the-india-china-crisis-at-doklam/
66. Prof. Sachidananda Mohanty, "The Chinese Betrayal, Early Warnings Unheeded Lessons from Sardar Patel and Sri Aurobindo", *Tibet.net*, 7 July 2020, available at https://tibet.net/the-chinese-betrayal-early-warnings-unheeded-lessons-from-sardar-patel-and-sri-aurobindo/
67. Dan Blumenthal, "China's Steps Backward Began under Hu Jintao", *Foreign Policy*, 4 June 2020, available at https://foreignpolicy.com/2020/06/04/china-xi-jingping-hu-jintao-aggression-ideology/
68. Antara Ghosal Singh, "The stand-off and China's India policy dilemma", *The Hindu*, Wednesday, 15 July 2020.
69. J.P. Yadav, "When Shah thundered on Aksai Chin: 'Iske liye jaan de denge'", *The Telegraph Online*, 18 June 2020, available at https://www.telegraphindia.com/india/india-china-clash-when-amit-shah-thundered-on-aksai-chin-iske-liye-jaan-de-denge/cid/1781717

70. Brigadier (Dr.) Rajeev Bhutani, "Hybrid Warfare to Warfare in 'Gray Zone': a Smart Transition", *Synergy*, February 2020, Centre for Joint Warfare Studies, New Delhi.
71. David Carment and Dani Belo, "War's Future: The Risks and Rewards of Grey-Zone Conflict and Hybrid Warfare", *Canadian Global Affairs Institute*, October 2018, p.5, available at https://www.cgai.ca/wars_future_the_risks_and_rewards_of_grey_zone_ conflict_and_hybrid_warfare
72. Qiao Liang and Wang Xiangsui, "Unrestricted Warfare", Beijing: PLA Literature and Arts Publishing House, February 1999, available at https://archive.org/stream/Unrestricted_Warfare_Qiao_Liang_and_Wang_Xiangsui/Unrestricted_Warfare_Qiao_Liang_and_Wang_Xiangsui_djvu.txt
73. US DoD, "Military and Security Developments Involving the People's Republic of China 2011", Annual Report to Congress (Washington, DC, 16 August 2011), http://www.defense.gov/pubs/pdfs/2011_CMPR_Final.pdf, p.26.
74. Dylan Gerstel, "It's a (Debt) Trap! Managing China-IMF Cooperation Across the Belt and Road", *CSIS.org*, available at https://www.csis.org/npfp/its-debt-trap-managing-china-imf-cooperation-across-belt-and-road
75. "India takes on China at another battlefront: A Sri Lankan airport", *Economic Times Online*, 14 October 2017, available at https://economictimes.indiatimes.com/news/international/world-news/india-takes-on-china-at-another-battlefront-a-sri-lankan-airport/articleshow/61079813.cms
76. "How China's debt trap diplomacy works and what it means", *TRT World*, 13 December 2019, available at https://www.trtworld.com/africa/how-china-s-debt-trap-diplomacy-works-and-what-it-means-32133
77. Tim Fernholz, "Eight Countries in Danger of Falling into China's Debt Trap", *Quartz.com*, 08 March 2018, available at https://qz.com/1223768/china-debt-trap-these-eight-countries-are-in-danger-of-debt-overloads-from-chinas-belt-and-road-plans/
78. Plaban Gupta, "What Does China's Belligerence in Eastern Ladakh, Power Play at South China Sea Mean for India & the World", *News18.com*, updated 10 July 2020, available at https://www.news18.com/amp/news/opinion/what-does-chinas-belligerence-in-eastern-ladakh-power-play-at-south-china-sea-mean-for-india-the-world-2709895.html
79. Maneesh Pandeya, "Debt diplomacy, a dampener for Dragon", *Sunday Guardian Live*, 23 May 2020, available at https://www.sundayguardianlive.com/world/debt-diplomacy-dampener-dragon
80. Christine Lagarde, "Belt and Road Initiative: Strategies to Deliver in the Next Phase," International Monetary Fund (IMF), April 12, 2018, available at https://www.imf.org/en/News/Articles/2018/04/11/sp041218-belt-and-road-initiative-strategies-to-deliver-in-the-next-phase
81. Maneesh Pandeya, op.cit.
82. Plaban Gupta, op.cit.
83. Minxin Pei, "Will China let Belt and Road die quietly?", *Nikkei Asian Review*, 15 February 2019, available at https://asia.nikkei.com/Opinion/Will-China-let-Belt-and-Road-die-quietly
84. Giancarlo Elia Valori, "India and China in the Clash for Ladakh", *Modern Diplomacy*, 11 July 2020, available at https://moderndiplomacy.eu/2020/07/11/india-and-china-in-the-clash-for-ladakh/

85. Ibid.
86. "Majority of China's BRI projects abroad adversely affected by COVID-19 pandemic: Official", *The Economic Times*, 28 June 2020, available at https://economictimes. indiatimes.com/news/international/business/majority-of-chinas-bri-projects-abroad-adversely-affected-by-covid-19-pandemic-official/articleshow/76673279.cms?from=mdr
87. Anurag Vishwanath, "Xi Jinping plays the nationalism card – it's nothing new", *Financial Express*, 08 June 2020, available at https://www.financialexpress.com/opinion/xi-jinping-plays-the-nationalism-card-its-nothing-new/1984326/
88. Palden Sonam, "Making sense of China's border belligerence", *The Tribune*, 4 June 2020, available at https://www.tribuneindia.com/news/comment/making-sense-of-chinas-border-belligerence-94209
89. Indrani Bagchi, "Beijing's Aggressive South China Sea Push Amid Pandemic Worries India, US", *The Times of India*, 26 April 2020, available at https://timesofindia. indiatimes.com/india/beijings-aggressive-south-china-sea-push-amid-pandemic-worries-india-us/articleshow/75393720.cms
90. "ASEAN takes position vs China's vast historical sea claims", *India Today*, 27 June 2020, available at https://www.indiatoday.in/world/story/asean-takes-position-vs-china-vast-historical-sea-claims-1694663-2020-06-27
91. Colin Clark, "US To China: You Do NOT Control South China Sea", *Breaking Defense*, 13 July 2020, available at https://breakingdefense.com/2020/07/us-to-china-you-do-not-control-south-china-sea/
92. Ibid.
93. Jesse Johnson, "Three U.S. aircraft carriers operating on doorstep of South China Sea", *The Japan Times*, 21 June 2020, available at https://www.japantimes.co.jp/news/2020/06/21/asia-pacific/three-us-aircraft-carriers-south-china-sea/#.Xx_Nn_gzbVo
94. Xuan Loc Doan, "Is Xi's 'Chinese dream' still realistic?", *Asia Times*, 25 February2019,available at https://asiatimes.com/2019/02/is-xis-chinese-dream-still-realistic/
95. John Ruwitch, "As China Imposes New Hong Kong Law, U.S. and Allies Take Steps To Retaliate", *NPR*, 02 July 2020, available at https://www.npr.org/2020/07/02/886587827/as-china-imposes-new-hong-kong-law-u-s-and-allies-take-steps-to-retaliate
96. Zachary L. Morris, "China's Conscription Cycle: Challenges, Vulnerabilities and Opportunities", *Small Wars Journal*, 29 January 2018, available at https://smallwarsjournal.com/jrnl/art/chinas-conscription-cycle-challenges-vulnerabilities-and-opportunities
97. Shrikant Bedekar, "Indian Army Set To Become World's Largest Armed Force Overtaking China", *The Eurasian Times*, 19 March 2020, available at https://eurasiantimes.com/indian-army-set-to-become-worlds-largest-armed-force-overtaking-china/
98. Frank O'Donnell and Alexander K. Bollfrass, "The Strategic Postures of China and India: A Visual Guide", *Belfer Center for Science and International Affairs*, March 2020, available at https://www.belfercenter.org/publication/strategic-postures-china-and-india-visual-guide

99. Henry Boyd, "2019 Pentagon report: China's Rocket Force trajectory", *IISS, Military Balance Blog*, 15 May 2019, available at https://www.iiss.org/blogs/military-balance/2019/05/pla-rocket-force-trajectory
100. Vijay Mohan, "Fiberglass Mats for Quick Runway Repairs," *Tribune*, 3 February 2019, available at https://www.tribuneindia.com/news/archive/nation/fiberglass-mats-for-quick-runway-repairs-722957
101. Sajid Farid Shapoo, "The China-India Standoff and the Myth of a New Cold War", *The Diplomat*, 13 June 2020, available at https://thediplomat.com/2020/06/the-china-india-standoff-and-the-myth-of-a-new-cold-war/
102. Maria Del Pero, "The US-China rivalry is not a new cold war, and it's dangerous to call it that", *The Guardian*, 14 July 2020, available at https://www.theguardian.com/commentisfree/2020/jul/14/the-us-china-rivalry-is-not-a-new-cold-war-and-its-dangerous-to-call-it-that
103. "Coronavirus exposes Xi Jinping's feet of clay", *The Times of India*, 30 March 2020, available at https://timesofindia.indiatimes.com/world/china/coronavirus-exposes-xi-jinpings-feet-of-clay/articleshow/74885933.cms
104. Bonnie S. Glaser and Kelly Flaherty, "US-China Relations Hit New Lows Amid Pandemic", *Comparative Connections*, Jan-Apr 2020, available at http://cc.pacforum.org/2020/05/us-china-relations-hit-new-lows-amid-pandemic/
105. Bao Huaying, "China's Daunting Post-COVID Challenges", *The Diplomat*, 8 May 2020, available at https://thediplomat.com/2020/05/chinas-daunting-post-covid-challenges/

Chapter 3: India's Response

1. Nitin Pai, "Why is China so keen to alienate half a billion young Indians with no memories of the war?", *This Week in Asia*, 25 July 2017, available at https://www.scmp.com/week-asia/geopolitics/article/2104017/why-china-so-keen-alienate-half-billion-young-indians-no
2. Frank O'Donnell and Alexander K. Bollfrass, op.cit.
3. Jingdong Yuan, "Sino–Indian Economic Ties since 1988: Progress, Problems, and Prospects for Future Development", *Journal of Current Chinese Affairs*, 1 December 2016, available at https://journals.sagepub.com/doi/full/10.1177/186810261604500302
4. Brigadier (Dr.) Rajeev Bhutani, "Sino-Indian Equation: Competition + Cooperation-Confrontation", op.cit., p.46.
5. "India's trade deficit with China reduces to USD 48.66 bn in FY20", *The Economic Times*, 02 July 2020, available at https://economictimes.indiatimes.com/news/economy/foreign-trade/indias-trade-deficit-with-china-reduces-to-usd-48-66-bn-in-fy20/articleshow/76750117.cms
6. Giancarlo Elia Valori, op.cit.
7. Shishir Gupta, "China moves troops near Lipulekh Pass", Sunday *Hindustan Times*, New Delhi, 02 August 2020, p.4.
8. "Bishop Ussher Dates the World: 4004 BC", available at https://www.lockhaven.edu/~dsimanek/ussher.htm
9. Sugata Srinivasaraju, "Year of the Guru", Outlook, 27 July 2009, available at outlookindia.com/magazine/story/year-of-the-guru/250522

10. Ichadwick, "Chanakya: The Indian Machiavelli", *The Municipal Machiavelli*, 16 May 2013, available at ianchadwick.com/machiavelli/chanakya-the-indian-machiavelli/
11. Dr. Rajeev, "Inter-State Relations in Kautilyan Arthashastra", *Journal of Advances and Scholarly Researches in Allied Education*, Vol. II, Issue II, October 2011, ISSN 2230-7540, available at http://ignited.in/File_upload/16795_50741156.pdf; and "Kautilya's Concept of Raja Mandala (Mandala Doctrine) and Shadguna in Foreign Policy", available at https://www.gktoday.in/gk/kautilyas-concept-of-raja-mandala-and-shadguna-in-foreign-policy/
12. Prof. Sachidananda Mohanty, op.cit.
13. "Non-Alignment Movement struggles for relevancy in post-Cold war world", *DW.com*, available at https://www.dw.com/en/non-aligned-movement-struggles-for-relevancy-in-post-cold-war-world/a-4475706
14. Nirupama Rao, "Transcript of Foreign Secretary Smt. Nirupama Rao's speech at the French Institute of International Relations (IFRI), Paris", 05 May 2011, available at http:// www.mea.gov.in/mystart.php?id=530117612
15. Sarang Shidore, "Higher Order", *India Today*, 15 December 2016, available at https:// / www.indiatoday.in/magazine/books/story/20161226-india-us-south-asia-foreign-policy-830047-2016-12-15
16. Rakesh Krishnan Simha, "1971 War: How Russian sank Nixon's gun boat diplomacy", *Russia Beyond*, 20 December 2011 available at https://www.rbth.com/articles/2011/12/20/1971_war_how_russia_sank_nixons_gunboat_diplomacy_14041; and Rakesh Krishna Simha, "Gunboat diplomacy: Revisiting the Enterprise incident", Russia Beyond, 14 December 2016, available at https://www.rbth.com/blogs/stranger_than_fiction/2016/12/14/gunboatdiplomacy-revisiting-the-enterprise-incident_657434
17. "Invest in a country you can trust, Modi tells US", *Hindustan Times*, New Delhi, Thursday, 23 July 2020, pp. 1-4.
18. "Will India join U.S. counter to China's BRI?", *The New Indian Express*, 25 February 2020, available at https://www.newindianexpress.com/opinions/editorials/2020/feb/25/will-india-join-us-counter-to-chinas-bri-2108084.html
19. Rahul Singh, "Logistics support pact with US helps naval ties", *Hindustan Times*, 26 December 2018, available at https://www.hindustantimes.com/india-news/logistic-support-pact-with-us-naval-ties/story-saqNwKfsM2hBrBhwC5YJ5O.html
20. Anna Fifield, "China's next challenge: Coronavirus breaks the links in the world's supply chain", *The Washington Post*, 11 March 2020, available at https://www.washingtonpost.com/world/asia_pacific/chinas-next-challenge-coronavirus-breaks-the-links-in-the-worlds-supply-chain/2020/03/11/175f391e-6270-11ea-8a8e-5c5336b32760_story.html
21. Huileng Tan, "There will be a 'massive' shuffling of supply chains globally after coronavirus shutdowns", *CNBC*, 20 March 2020, available at https://www.cnbc.com/2020/03/20/coronavirus-shocks-will-lead-to-massive-global-supply-chain-shuffle.html
22. "Secretary Michael R. Pompeo, At a Press Availability: Remarks to the Press", 29 April 2020, available at https://www.state.gov/secretary-michael-r-pompeo-at-a-press-availability-4/

23. "Economy showing green shoots: PM", *Hindustan Times*, 10 July 2020, available at https://www.hindustantimes.com/india-news/economy-showing-green-shoots-pm/story-PKlmwfg4pSNEWJ3UKEdYJO.html
24. "China hikes defence budget to USD 179 billion, nearly three times that of India", *The Indian Express*, 22 May 2020, available at https://indianexpress.com/article/world/china-defence-budget-three-times-of-india-6422500/
25. Shaurya Karanbir Gurung, "India third largest military spender in world, after US and China", *The Economic Times*, 27 April 2020, available at https://economictimes.indiatimes.com/news/defence/global-military-spending-saw-largest-increase-in-decade-in-2019-china-india-in-top-3-study/articleshow/75404166.cms?from=mdr
26. "Comparing China and India by Economy", *Statistics Times*, 28 August 2019, available at http://statisticstimes.com/economy/china-vs-india-economy.php
27. Sushant Singh, "Explained: What happened to the Mountain Strike Corps?", *Indian Express*, 19 June 2020, available at https://indianexpress.com/article/explained/explained-what-happened-to-the-mountain-strike-corps-6465221/
28. M.K.Venu, "Rafale Twist: Why Did France Refuse to Give India a Sovereign Guarantee?", *The Wire*, 14 November 2018, available at https://thewire.in/government/india-france-rafale-fighter-jets-deal
29. "Deal for 114 fighters critical for IAF to retain edge against China", *The Week*, 26 June 2020, available at https://www.theweek.in/news/india/2020/06/26/deal-for-114-fighters-critical-for-iaf-to-retain-edge-against-china.html
30. Shaurya Karanbir Gurung, "Navy requests government for additional funds, cuts 200-ship requirement", *The Economic Times*, 3 December 2019, available at https://economictimes.indiatimes.com/news/defence/navy-requests-government-for-additional-funds-cuts-200-ship-requirement/articleshow/72353735.cms
31. "The urgency of defence reforms", Editorial, *Hindustan Times*, New Delhi, Sunday, 05 July 2020.
32. Joseph S. Nye, Jr., "Soft Power: The Means to Success in World Politics", *Foreign Affairs, Capsule Review* May/June 2004 Issue available at https://www.foreignaffairs.com/reviews/capsule-review/2004-05-01/soft-power-means-success-world-politics
33. Brigadier (Dr.) Rajeev Bhutani, "Sino-Indian Equation: Competition + Cooperation-Confrontation", op.cit., pp. 152-158. (See for detailed analysis of India's relations with Nepal).
34. "Vasudhaiva Kutumbakam - The Whole World is one family", available at vedicambassador.wordpress.com/2012/09/29/vasudhaiv-kutumbakam-the-whole-world-is-one-family.
35. Bernard Marr, "The Top 10 Technology Trends of The 4th Industrial Revolution", *Forbes*, 4 May 2020, available at https://www.forbes.com/sites/bernardmarr/2020/05/04/here-are-the-top-10-technology-trends-of-the-4th-industrial-revolution/#6bc0ecda1fbe
36. Alex Lockie, "Trump said Xi Jinping abandoned a signature economic initiative because he told him it was insulting", Business Insider India, 10 June 2019, available at https://www.businessinsider.in/trump-said-xi-jinping-abandoned-a-signature-economic-initiative-because-he-told-him-it-was-insulting/articleshow/69730068.cms

37. Daniel Gros, "This is not a trade war, it is a struggle for technological and geo-strategic dominance", *Cesifo Forum*, Vol. 20. No. 1, Spring 2019, p.25., available at https://www.ifo.de/DocDL/CESifo-Forum-2019-1-march.pdf
38. *Hindustan Times*, New Delhi, Thursday, 23 July 2020, op.cit.
39. Brigadier (Dr.) Rajeev Bhutani, "Sino-Indian Equation: Competition + Cooperation-Confrontation", op.cit., pp. 147-148.
40. Ankit Panda, "US, India, Australia, Japan 'Quad' Holds Senior Officials Meeting in Bangkok", *The Diplomat*, 05 November 2019, available at https://thediplomat.com/2019/11/us-india-australia-japan-quad-holds-senior-officials-meeting-in-bangkok/
41. Anirban Bhaumik, "US plans to train fighter pilots of India, Japan, Oz in Guam amid China's growing belligerence in Indo-Pacific", *Deccan Herald*, 26 June 2020, available at https://www.deccanherald.com/national/us-plans-to-train-fighter-pilots-of-india-japan-oz-in-guam-amid-china-s-growing-belligerence-in-indo-pacific-853865.html
42. "D10: Britain proposes new alliance of 10 democracies including India, South Korea, Australia and G7 nations to break China's monopoly on 5G technology", Op India, 29 May 2020, available at https://www.opindia.com/2020/05/d10-britain-alliance-india-south-korea-australia-g7-china-monopoly-5g-huawei/
43. Abhishek Singhvi, "A blueprint to counter CCP and Xi", *Hindustan Times*, New Delhi, Tuesday, 11 August 2020.
44. Dipanjan Roy Chaudhury, "Rethink India's one-China Policy", *The Economic Times*, 03 July 2020, available at https://economictimes.indiatimes.com/news/defence/rethink-indias-one-china-policy/articleshow/76762670.cms?from=mdr
45. "India's unreciprocated 'One China Policy' needs to be reviewed, says EFSAS", *India Leaks*, 13 November 2019, available at https://www.indialeaks.com/indias-unreciprocated-one-china-policy-needs-to-be-reviewed-says-efsas
46. S D Pradhan, "PCA Ruling on the Chinese claims of Sovereignty in South China Sea", *The Times of India*, 7 June 2020, available at https://timesofindia.indiatimes.com/blogs/ChanakyaCode/pca-ruling-on-the-chinese-claims-of-sovereignty-in-south-china-sea/
47. Lt Gen P G Kamath, "If China Does Not restore Status Quo: What Next?", LinkedIn.
48. Rajat Pandit, "Rush defence supplies, India to tell Russia amid crisis", *The Times of India*, 23 June 2020, available at https://timesofindia.indiatimes.com/india/rush-defence-supplies-india-to-tell-russia-amid-crisis/articleshow/76520949.cms
49. Akshay Narang, "'This is our land,' China now claims Russia's Vladivostok as part of its territory", *TFI Post*, 4 July 2020, available at https://tfipost.com/2020/07/this-is-our-land-china-now-claims-russias-vladivostok-as-part-of-its-territory/
50. "'Will boost security,' US Secretary Pompeo welcomes India's ban on Chinese apps", *Livemint*, 01 July 2020, available at https://www.livemint.com/news/india/-will-boost-security-us-secretary-pompeo-welcomes-india-s-ban-on-chinese-apps-11593621405411.html
51. "Speech By Chairman of the Delegation of the People's Republic of China, Deng Xiaoping, At the Special Session of the U.N. General Assembly", 10 April 1974, op.cit.

Chapter 4: The Novel Coronavirus

1. Mark Wheelis, "Biological Warfare at the 1346 Siege of Caffa", Centers for Disease Control and Prevention, Vol. 8, No. 9, September 2002 available at https://wwwnc.cdc.gov/eid/article/8/9/01-0536_article; and Ole J. Benedictow, "The Black Death: The Greatest Catastrophe Ever", *History Today*, Vol. 55 Issue 3 March 2005, available at https://www.historytoday.com/archive/black-death-greatest-catastrophe-ever
2. "Spanish Flu", History.com Editors, 12 October 2010, updated on 27 March 2020 https://www.history.com/topics/world-war-i/1918-flu-pandemic
3. Ibid.
4. "Frequently Asked Questions about Estimated Flu Burden", Centers for Disease Control and Prevention, 05 November 2018, available at https://www.cdc.gov/flu/about/burden/faq.htm
5. Sanchita Sharma, "Covid not the last pandemic, world has to build resilience", *Hindustan Times*, 21 April 2020, available at https://epaper.hindustantimes.com/Home/MShareArticle?Orgld=8a273f8a&imageview=0
6. "COVID-19 compared to other epidemic coronavirus diseases and the flu", *World Journal of Clinical Infectious Diseases* (*WJCID*), 15 May 2020, available at https://www.wjgnet.com/2220-3176/full/v10/i1/1.htm
7. Sanchita Sharma, "Coronavirus outbreak: India is infection free, but risk continues to remain high", *Hindustan Times*, 23 February 2020, available at https://www.hindustantimes.com/india-news/coronavirus-outbreak-india-is-infection-free-but-risk-continues-to-remain-high/story-QX2Xvbgu7WWDOTBfZZkBdM.html
8. Shuai Xia et al., "Inhibition of SARS-CoV-2 (previously 2019-nCoV) infection by a highly potent pan-coronavirus fusion inhibitor targeting its spike protein that harbors a high capacity to mediate membrane fusion", Nature-Cell Research, 30 March 2020, available at https://www.nature.com/articles/s41422-020-0305-x
9. Sanchita Sharma, "Enzyme makes men vulnerable to coronavirus disease", *Hindustan Times*, 12 May 2020, available at https://www.hindustantimes.com/india-news/enzyme-makes-men-vulnerable-to-disease/story-mTSvRnonr8KcunYZ69Qw1O.html
10. Sanchita Sharma, "Coronavirus outbreak: India is infection free, but risk continues to remain high", *Hindustan Times*, 23 February 2020, available at https://www.hindustantimes.com/india-news/coronavirus-outbreak-india-is-infection-free-but-risk-continues-to-remain-high/story-QX2Xvbgu7WWDOTBfZZkBdM.html
11. WHO. Coronavirus disease 2019 (COVID-19) situation report-32 (21 February 2020) available at https://www.who.int/docs/default-source/coronaviruse/situation-reports/20200221-sitrep-32-covid-19.pdf?sfvrsn=4802d089_2
12. Laurel Wamsley and Selena Simmons-Duffin, "The Science Behind A 14-Day Quarantine After Possible COVID-19 Exposure", *NPR*, 01 April 2020, available at https://www.npr.org/sections/health-shots/2020/04/01/824903684/the-science-behind-a-14-day-quarantine-after-possible-covid-19-exposure
13. Hiroshi Nishiura et al., "Serial interval of novel coronavirus (COVID-19) infections", International Journal of Infectious Diseases, Vol. 93, April 2020, pp. 284-286, available at https://www.sciencedirect.com/science/article/pii/

S1201971220301193

14. Shamika Ravi, "Covid: Fight uncertainty with data", *Hindustan Times*, New Delhi, Monday, 25 May 2020.
15. "Explained: What is the term R0, used to measure coronavirus transmission?", *The Indian Express*, 10 April 2020, available at https://indianexpress.com/article/explained/coronavirus-r0-reproduction-number-explained-6354339/
16. Ibid.
17. Giulio Viceconte and Nicola Petrosillo, "COVID-19 R0: Magic number or conundrum?", Infectious Disease Report, 24 February 2020, (citing the WHO report at n.7.) available at https://www.ncbi.nlm.nih.gov/pmc/articles/PMC7073717/
18. Ying Liu, "The reproductive number of COVID-19 is higher compared to SARS coronavirus", *Journal of Travel Medicine*, Vol. 27, Issue 2, March 2020, taaa021, 13 February 2020, available at https://academic.oup.com/jtm/article/27/2/taaa021/5735319
19. "How fast is the virus reproducing in India? Here is what the readings for the crucial R0 number say", Times Now Digital, 20 May 2020, available at https://www.timesnownews.com/times-facts/article/how-fast-is-the-virus-reproducing-in-india-here-is-what-the-readings-for-the-crucial-r0-number-say/594677; and Mohana Basu, "India's R value for Covid-19 drops back to 1.11, after three-month high last week", The Print, 13 July 2020, available at https://theprint.in/health/indias-r-value-for-covid-19-drops-back-to-1-11-after-three-month-high-last-week/459874/ (R and R0 (basic reproduction number) are an estimate of the number of people one patient can infect. R0 is calculated at the beginning of the epidemic when the entire population is assumed to be susceptible to the disease. The 'R' changes with time, and takes into account that some individuals are protected from the disease—either because they have developed immunity or because of social distancing and other measures).
20. Dominic Gilbert, "How does coronavirus compare to flu, Sars, and other diseases?", *The Telegraph*, 25 March 2020, available at https://www.telegraph.co.uk/news/0/coronavirus-vs-sars-mers-flu-how-deaths-compare-covid-19/
21. Thomas R. Frieden and Christopher T. Lee, "Identifying and Interrupting Superspreading Events—Implications for Control of Severe Acute Respiratory Syndrome Coronavirus 2", *Emerging Infectious Diseases (EID) Journal*, Vol. 26, No. 6, June 2020, available at https://wwwnc.cdc.gov/eid/article/26/6/20-0495_article
22. Josephine Ma, "Coronavirus: China's first confirmed Covid-19 case traced back to November 17", *South China Morning Post*, 13 March 2020, available at https://www.scmp.com/news/china/society/article/3074991/coronavirus-chinas-first-confirmed-covid-19-case-traced-back
23. "Here's how China misled the world on coronavirus", *The Times of India*, 27 March 2020, available at https://timesofindia.indiatimes.com/world/us/heres-how-china-misled-the-world-on-coronavirus/articleshow/74843543.cms
24. Manish Tewari, "Does China have a case to answer on Covid-19?", Deccan Chronicle, 26 April 2020, available at https://www.deccanchronicle.com/amp/opinion/columnists/260420/does-china-have-a-case-to-answer-on-covid-19.html?utm_source=latestPromotion&utm_medium=end&utm_campaign=latest

25. "Mission summary: WHO Field Visit to Wuhan, China 20-21 January 2020", *WHO*, 22 January 2020, available at https://www.who.int/china/news/detail/22-01-2020-field-visit-wuhan-china-jan-2020
26. "Outbreak is now a pandemic, declares WHO as global cases surpass 119,000", *Hindustan Times*, New Delhi, 12 March 2020.
27. "UN launches COVID-19 plan that could 'defeat the virus and build a better world", *UN News*, 31 March 2020, available at https://news.un.org/en/story/2020/03/1060702
28. Graham Readfearn, "How did coronavirus start and where did it come from? Was it really Wuhan's animal market? *The Guardian*, 28 April 2020, available at https://www.theguardian.com/world/2020/apr/28/how-did-the-coronavirus-start-where-did-it-come-from-how-did-it-spread-humans-was-it-really-bats-pangolins-wuhan-animal-market
29. David Cyranoski, "Inside the Chinese lab poised to study world's most dangerous pathogens", *Nature*, 22 February 2017, available at https://www.nature.com/news/inside-the-chinese-lab-poised-to-study-world-s-most-dangerous-pathogens-1.21487
30. "Biosafety Level 4 Laboratory, Wuhan Institute of Virology, China", *Pharma Industry Review*, 13 March 2020, available at https://pharma-industry-review.com/biosafety-level-4-laboratory-wuhan-institute-of-virology-china
31. Brian Mcgleenon, "Was this coronavirus PATIENT ZERO? Scientist describes gruesome bat attack at Chinese lab", *Express*, 16 February 2020, available at https://www.express.co.uk/news/world/1243000/coronavirus-latest-lab-leak-infected-bat-attack-outbreak-patient-zero-bioweapon
32. "Does China have a case to answer for coronavirus outbreak?", *Asian Age*, 26 April 2020, available at https://m.dailyhunt.in/news/nepal/english/asian+age-epaper-asianage/does+china+have+a+case+to+answer+for+coronavirus+out break-newsid-n180795870
33. "Biosafety Level 4 Laboratory, Wuhan Institute of Virology, China", *Pharma Industry Review*, 13 March 2020, op.cit.
34. Manish Tewari, op.cit.
35. Steven Lee Myers, "China Spins Tale That the U.S. Army Started the Coronavirus Epidemic", *New York Times*, 13 March 2020, available at https://www.nytimes.com/2020/03/13/world/asia/coronavirus-china-conspiracy-theory.html
36. "The United States President Donald Trump's letter to Dr. Tedros Adhanom Ghebreyesus, Director General WHO", dated 18 May 2020, available at https://www.whitehouse.gov/wp-content/uploads/2020/05/Tedros-Letter.pdf
37. "US President Donald Trump Cuts Ties, Terminates WHO Funding Permanently", *India.com*, 30 May 2020, available at https://www.india.com/news/world/us-president-donald-trump-cuts-ties-terminates-who-funding-permanently-4043575/
38. S Gurumurthy, "Tablighi Jamaat - its other, evil side", *The New Indian Express*, 02 April 2020, available at https://www.newindianexpress.com/opinions/columns/s-gurumurthy/2020/apr/02/coronavirus-tablighi-jamaat—its-other-evil-side-2124563.html
39. Brahma Chellaney, "The perils of political and religious extremism", *Hindustan Times*, 06 April 2020, available at https://www.hindustantimes.com/columns/

the-perils-of-political-and-religious-extremism-writes-brahma-chellaney/story-iKfc9Rhj69sTPAeI1XEUUM.html

40. Neetu Chandra Sharma, "Coronavirus: Nizamuddin's Tablighi Jamaat has doubled cases in India", *Livemint*, 05 April 2020, available at https://www.livemint.com/news/india/coronavirus-nizamuddin-s-tablighi-jamaat-has-doubled-cases-in-india-11586088692350.html
41. Akash Bisht and Sadiq Naqvi, "How Tablighi Jamaat event became India's worst coronavirus vector", Aljazeera, 07 April 2020, available at https://www.aljazeera.com/news/2020/04/tablighi-jamaat-event-india-worst-coronavirus-vector-200407052957511.html
42. Brahma Chellaney, op.cit.

Chapter 5: The Multitudinous Effects of the COVID-19 Pandemic

1. Thomas L. Friedman, "The World is Flat: The Globalized World in the Twenty-First Century", Penguin Books, England, 2006, pp.9-10.
2. "World Economic Outlook, April 2020: The Great Lockdown", *International Monetary Fund*, 14 April 2020, available at https://www.imf.org/en/Publications/WEO/Issues/2020/04/14/World-Economic-Outlook-April-2020-The-Great-Lockdown-49306
3. Shubham Singh, "COVID-19: Creating a New World Order", *Kootneeti*, 06 April 2020, available at https://thekootneeti.in/2020/04/06/covid-19-creating-a-new-world-order/
4. "World Economic Outlook, April 2020: The Great Lockdown, op.cit., pp.vii-ix ; and "World Economic Outlook Update, June 2020", op.cit.
5. "Barclays slashes India growth in calendar 2020 to 0%, sharply revises lockdown losses", *The Hindu* Business Line, 14 April 2020, available at https://www.thehindubusiness line.com/economy/barclays-slashes-india-growth-in-calendar-2020-to-0-sharply-revises-lockdown-losses/article31340890.ece ; and Puneet Wadhwa, "Barclays sticks to GDP projection of 0% in 2020; says lockdown 3 priced in", *Business Standard*, 01 May 2020, available at https://www.business-standard.com/article/economy-policy/barclays-sticks-to-gdp-projection-of-0-in-2020-says-lockdown-3-priced-in-120050101405_1.html
6. "India Inc stands by lockdown extension call; seeks stimulus package to rebuild economy", *The Economic Times*, 14 April 2020, available at http://ficci.in/ficci-in-news-page.asp?nid=21381
7. Rajeev Jayaswal, "Industry bodies call on govt for stimulus of up to Rs. 16L cr", *Hindustan Times*, 15 April 2020, available at https://epaper.hindustantimes.com/Home/MShareArticle?OrgId=de124048&imageview=0
8. Erica Werner, Mike DeBonis and Paul Kane, "Senate approves $2.2 trillion coronavirus bill aimed at slowing economic free fall", *The Washington Post*, 26 March 2020, available at https://www.washingtonpost.com/business/2020/03/25/trump-senate-coronavirus-economic-stimulus-2-trillion/
9. "India's Rs 20 lakh crore Covid relief package one among the largest in the world", *The Economic Times*, 15 May 2020, available at https://economictimes.indiatimes.com/news/economy/finance/latest-stimulus-package-among-largest-in-the-world/articleshow/75701976.cms?from=mdr

10. Gaurie Dwivedi, "The new economic world order post Covid-19", *Sunday Guardian Live*, 4 April 2020, available at https://www.sundayguardianlive.com/business/new-economic-world-order-post-covid-19
11. Sohini Das, "Covid-19 impact: Hydroxychloroquine's share in pharma exports minuscule", *Business Standard*, 09 April 2020, available at https://www.business-standard.com/article/companies/covid-19-impact-hydroxychloroquine-s-share-in-pharma-exports-minuscule-120040700063_1.html
12. Geeta Mohan, "India sending Hydroxychloroquine to 55 countries, will not procure PPES from China", *India Today*, 17 April 2020, available at https://www.indiatoday.in/india/story/india-sending-hydroxychloroquine-to-55-countries-will-not-procure-ppes-from-china-1667822-2020-04-17
13. Wilson Dizard, "We must invent a new world order now to stop Covid-19", *TRT World*, 27 March 2020, TRT World, available at https://www.trtworld.com/perspectives/we-must-invent-a-new-world-order-now-to-stop-covid-19-34907
14. Henry A. Kissinger, "The Coronavirus Pandemic Will Forever Alter the World Order", *Wall Street Journal*, 03 April 2020, https://www.wsj.com/articles/the-coronavirus-pandemic-will-forever-alter-the-world-order-11585953005
15. Secretary-General's Remarks to the Security Council on the COVID-19 Pandemic, United Nations, April 9, 2020. https://www.un.org/sg/en/content/sg/statement/2020-04-09/secretary-generals-remarks-the-security-council-thecovid-19-pandemic-delivered (as cited in "Global Economic Effects of COVID-19", US Congressional Research Service, 01 May 2020, p.3., available at https://fas.org/sgp/crs/row/R46270.pdf)
16. M K Narayanan, "The spectre of a post-COVID-19 world", *The Hindu*, 04 April 2020, https://www.thehindu.com/opinion/lead/the-spectre-of-a-post-covid-19-world/article31252172.ece
17. Janna Anderson and Lee Rainie, "Improvements ahead: How humans and AI might evolve together in the next decade", Pew Research Center, Internet & Technology, 10 December 2018, available at https://www.pewresearch.org/internet/2018/12/10/improvements-ahead-how-humans-and-ai-might-evolve-together-in-the-next-decade/
18. Bahar Dutt, "Turn the coronavirus crisis into an opportunity", *Hindustan Times*, New Delhi, Thursday, 12 March 2020.

Chapter 6: Emerging New World Order (Post-COVID-19)

1. Mark Leonard, "What does China think?", London, Great Britain, FOURTHESTATE, 2008, pp.85-86.
2. Brigadier (Dr.) Rajeev Bhutani, "Geopolitics to Geo-economics to the New Era of Geo-technology", *Centre for Joint Warfare*, p.17.
3. Parag Khanna and Karan Khemka, "The coronavirus butterfly effect: Six predictions for a new world order", *Fast Company*, 14 April 2020, available at https://www.fastcompany.com/90488665/the-coronavirus-butterfly-effect-six-predictions-for-a-new-world-order
4. Talha Kose, " Scenarios for post-COVID-19 global order include possible rise of China, expanded US manufacturing", *Dailysabah.com*, 01 April 2020, available at https://www.dailysabah.com/opinion/columns/scenarios-for-post-covid-19-

global-order-include-possible-rise-of-china-expanded-us-manufacturing

5. Happymon Jacob, "COVID-19 and the crumbling world order", *The Hindu*, 13 April 2020,available at https://www.thehindu.com/opinion/op-ed/covid-19-and-the-crumbling-world-order/article31324259.ece
6. Zhang Jun, "China backs UN role in anti-virus fight", *China Daily*, 18 April 2020, available at https://global.chinadaily.com.cn/a/202004/18/WS5e9a4feca3105d50a3 d171b6.html
7. Happymon Jacob, op.cit.
8. "Italy signs deals worth 2.5 billion euros with China", *Reuters*, 23 March 2019, available at https://www.reuters.com/article/us-italy-china-deals-factbox-idUSKCN1R40KN
9. Alexander Chipman Koty, "Why China's COVID-19 Stimulus Will Look Different Than in the Past", *China Briefing*, 06 April 2020, available at https://www.china-briefing.com/news/chinas-stimulus-measures-after-covid-19-different-from-2008-financial-crisis/
10. Sutirtho Patranobis, "Chinese economy takes massive Covid-19 hit, shrinks first time in decades", *Hindustan Times*, 17 April 2020, available at https://www.hindustantimes.com/world-news/chinese-economy-takes-massive-covid-19-hit-shrinks-first-time-in-decades/story-7aXs8AyEjr0sgu3IOkjZIL.html
11. M. Ramesh, "Post-Covid-19 world will be 'very different' for China", *The Hindu*, 02 April 2020, available at https://www.thehindubusinessline.com/news/world/post-covid-19-world-will-be-very-different-for-china/article31224016.ece
12. Ibid.
13. Ibid.
14. "China Economic Update – July 2020", *The World Bank*, July 2020, available at https://www.worldbank.org/en/country/china/publication/china-economic-update-july-2020
15. Tao Zhang, "Speech on the Global and Asia Economic Outlook", *International Monetary Fund*, 10 July 2020, available at https://www.imf.org/en/News/Articles/2020/07/10/sp071020-speech-on-the-global-and-asia-economic-outlook
16. Satyajit Das, "View: $3 trillion can't buy China out of virus trouble", *The Economic Times*, 11 February 2020, available at https://economictimes.indiatimes.com/news/international/world-news/view-3-trillion-cant-buy-china-out-of-virus-trouble/articleshow/74077788.cms
17. M. Ramesh, op.cit.
18. Brigadier (Dr.) Rajeev Bhutani, "SINO-INDIAN EQUATION: Competition + Cooperation - Confrontation", Pentagon Press LLP, New Delhi, 2019, p.87.
19. M. Ramesh, op.cit.
20. Gaurie Dwivedi, "The new economic world order post Covid-19", *Sunday Guardian Live*, 4 April 2020, op.cit.
21. Alexander Chipman Koty, op.cit.
22. "How governments worldwide support people amid COVID-19", Payspace Magazine, 17 April 2020, available at https://payspacemagazine.com/coronavirus/how-governments-worldwide-support-people-amid-covid-19/
23. Ibid; and Alexander Chipman Koty, op.cit.
24. M. Ramesh, op.cit.

25. "United States (USA) GDP – Gross Domestic Product", available at https://countryeconomy.com/gdp/usa
26. Henry A. Kissinger, *"The Coronavirus Pandemic Will Forever Alter the World Order"*, *Wall Street Journal*, 03 April 2020, op.cit.
27. Shubham Singh, "COVID-19: Creating a New World Order", *Kootneeti*, 06 April 2020, op.cit.
28. "Number of new coronavirus (COVID-19) deaths in Europe since February 2020 (as of August 16, 2020), by date of report", *Statista*, 17 August 2020, available at https://www.statista.com/statistics/1102288/coronavirus-deaths-development-europe/
29. Daniel Woker, "Europe hasn't fallen for China – if anything, it's the opposite", *The Interpreter*, 23 April 2020, available at https://www.lowyinstitute.org/the-interpreter/debate/coronavirus-pandemic
30. Lisa Louis, "Hit hard, Could Covid lead Europe to rethink economic policy?", *The Interpreter*, 21 April 2020, available at https://www.lowyinstitute.org/the-interpreter/debate/coronavirus-pandemic
31. Nishtha Yadav, "Will India's FDI Policy Change Impact Chinese Investments Post-COVD-19?", *India Briefing*, 24 April 2020, available at https://www.india-briefing.com/news/will-indias-fdi-policy-change-impact-chinese-investments-post-covid-19-20256.html/
32. Katsuji Nakazawa, "Xi fears Japan-led manufacturing exodus from China", *Nikkei Asian Review*, 16 April 2020, available at https://asia.nikkei.com/Editor-s-Picks/China-up-close/Xi-fears-Japan-led-manufacturing-exodus-from-China
33. Gaurie Dwivedi, op.cit.
34. Alison Rourke and agencies, "Trump warns China over Covid-19 outbreak as Europe approaches 100,000 deaths", *The Guardian*, 19 April 2020, available at https://www.theguardian.com/world/2020/apr/19/trump-warns-china-over-covid-19-outbreak-as-europe-approaches-100000-deaths
35. Sarah Pruitt, "What is NATO's Article 5?", *History.com*, 31 August 2018, available at https://www.history.com/news/nato-article-5-meaning-history-world-war-2

Chapter 7: Challenges and Opportunities for India

1. Vijay Gokhale, "Rethinking Globalisation: COVID and the International Order", *Strategic News Global*, 08 February 2020, available at https://stratnewsglobal.com/rethinking-globalisation-covid-and-the-international-order/
2. Harivansh, "India has played an exemplary role in tackling the Covid-19 crisis", *The Indian Express*, 24 April 2020, available at https://indianexpress.com/article/opinion/columns/coronavirus-lockdown-india-tackling-covid-19-crisis-healthcare-workers-harivansh-narendra-modi-6376372/
3. Narendra Modi, "Lockdown in India will be extended till 3rd May: PM Modi", 24 April 2020, available at https://www.narendramodi.in/text-of-pm-s-address-to-the-nation-549264
4. "India crosses 26k cases with biggest 1-day spike", *Hindustan Times*, 26 April 2020, available at https://epaper.hindustantimes.com/Home/ShareArticle?Orgld=6180e1f7&imageview=0 ; and Jamie Mullick, "India posts its second million in just 21 days", *Hindustan Times*, 07 August 2020, available at https://epaper.

hindustantimes.com/Home/ShareArticle?Orgld=78e768d552& imageview=0

5. M K Narayanan, "The spectre of a post-COVID-19 world", *The Hindu*, 04 April 2020, op.cit.
6. "40-day lockdown to inflict USD 320 billion loss on Indian economy: Report", *New Indian Express*, 3 May 2020, available at https://www.newindianexpress.com/business/2020/may/03/40-day-lockdown-to-inflict-usd-320-billion-loss-on-indian-economy-report-2138664.html
7. Nishtha Saluja, "Covid-19 serves opportunity for increasing India's exports, should be seen as 'blessing in disguise': Nitin Gadkari", *Economic Times*, 13 April 2020, available at https://economictimes.indiatimes.com/news/economy/policy/covid-19-serves-opportunity-for-increasing-indias-exports-should-be-seen-as-blessing-in-disguise-nitin-gadkari/articleshow/75125791.cms?from=mdr
8. "Trade War: Why manufacturers are not rushing into India, Indonesia", *The Economic Times*, 07 October 2019, available at https://economictimes.indiatimes.com/news/economy/indicators/trade-war-why-manufacturers-are-not-rushing-into-india-indonesia/articleshow/71474941.cms?from=mdr
9. Lakshmi Puri, "Covid-19: Economic opportunities and challenges | Opinion", *Hindustan Times*, 06 April 2020, available at https://www.hindustantimes.com/analysis/covid-19-economic-opportunities-and-challenges-opinion/story-OCqr08BR5pLPjJIMxH7ZjK.html
10. "Remittances To India Likely To Decline By 23% In 2020 Due To Covid-19: World Bank", *Bloomberg /Quint*, 23 April 2020, available at https://www.bloombergquint.com/business/remittances-to-india-likely-to-decline-by-23-in-2020-due-to-covid-19-world-bank
11. Sunetra Choudhury and Chetan Chauhan, "Need to focus on economy in battle against Covid: PM", *Hindustan Times*, 28 April 2020, available at https://www.hindustan times.com/india-news/need-to-focus-on-economy-in-battle-against-covid-pm/story-zwPL7jySKD14nXmejffw2K.html
12. "Manufacturing Sector in India", August 2019, https://www.ibef.org/industry/manufacturing-sector-india.aspx
13. Jyotindra Dubey, "Share of manufacturing in India's GDP falling despite 'Make in India'", *CNBC TV 18*, 24 July 2018, available at https://www.cnbctv18.com/economy/share-of-manufacturing-in-indias-gdp-falling-despite-make-in-india-360521.htm
14. Sanjeev K. Ahuja, "What is forcing Korean companies to quit China, and skip India?", *Asian Community News*, 27 April 2020, available at https://www.asiancommunity news.com/what-is-forcing-korean-companies-to-quit-china-and-skip-india/
15. "Trade War: Why manufacturers are not rushing into India, Indonesia", *The Economic Times*, 07 October 2019, op.cit.
16. Tanya Thomas and Deborshi Chaki, "Make in India has failed to create enough jobs: Naik", *Hindustan Times*, New Delhi, Monday, 19 August 2019.
17. Yogima Sharma, "Modi govt eyes a comprehensive makeover for Skill India mission", *The Economic Times*, 30 January 2019, available at https://economictimes.indiatimes.com/news/economy/policy/government-looks-to-hone-skill-india-mission/articleshow/67748895.cms?from=mdr

18. Brigadier (Dr.) Rajeev Bhutani, "Sustained Double-Digit Growth for India's Economy: Economist's vs. Generalist's View", *Centre For Joint Warfare Studies*, New Delhi, October 2019, pp. 32-33.
19. Subash S, "Covid-19, an Opportunity for Indian industry", *The Hindu Business Line*, 21 March 2020, available at https://www.thehindubusinessline.com/opinion/covid-19-an-opportunity-for-indian-industry/article31121373.ece#
20. Yogima Seth Sharma, "India jumps to 63rd position in World Bank's Ease of Doing Business 2020 report", *The Economic Times*, 24 October 2019, available at https://economictimes.indiatimes.com/news/economy/indicators/india-jumps-to-63rd-position-in-world-banks-doing-business-2020-report/articleshow/71731589.cms?from=mdr
21. "Doing Business 2019 - Fact Sheet: East Asia and Pacific", *World Bank Group*, available at https://www.doingbusiness.org/content/dam/doingBusiness/media/Fact-Sheets/DB19/FactSheet_DoingBusiness2019_EAP_Eng.pdf
22. Sanjeev K. Ahuja, op.cit.
23. Deepshikha Sikarwar, "Corporate tax rate cuts: New contract manufacturing units eligible for 15 per cent tax benefit", *The Economic Times*, 30 September 2019, available at https://m.economictimes.com/news/economy/policy/corporate-tax-rate-cuts-new-contract-manufacturing-units-eligible-for-15-per-cent-tax-benefit/articleshow/71367211.cms
24. "How governments worldwide support people amid COVID-19", *Payspace Magazine*, 17 April 2020, op.cit.
25. Rajeev Jayaswal, "Fiscal Cost of Package Rs.1.5L-cr to Rs.4L-cr", *Hindustan Times*, 17 May 2020, available at https://epaper.hindustantimes.com/Home/MShareArticle?Orgld=17568d83d17&imageview=0
26. "Studied measures by other nations, says Sitharaman", *Hindustan Times*, 24 May 2020, available at https://epaper.hindustantimes.com/Home/MShareArticle?Orgld=2450a67ccf8&imageview=0
27. Prableen Bajpai, "The 5 Largest Economies In The World And Their Growth In 2020", *Nasdaq*, 22 January 2020, available at https://www.nasdaq.com/articles/the-5-largest-economies-in-the-world-and-their-growth-in-2020-2020-01-22
28. "GDP per capita of India", 09 September 2019, available at http://statisticstimes.com/economy/gdp-capita-of-india.php
29. "Self-reliance India's biggest lesson from Covid, says PM", *Hindustan Times*, 25 April 2020, available at https://www.hindustantimes.com/india-news/self-reliance-india-s-biggest-lesson-from-covid-says-pm/story-MRmhLClsDjbkmma9CyFt2O.html
30. Mohd Mustaquim, "How do economists foresee India's rural economy?", *Rural Marketing*, 25 September 2018, available at https://ruralmarketing.in/industry/policy/how-do-economists-foresee-indias-rural-economy
31. Brigadier (Dr.) Rajeev Bhutani, *Rise of China: 2030 and Its Strategic Implications*, Pentagon Press, New Delhi, 2015, p.60.
32. Angus Maddison, "Chinese Economic Performance in the Long Run, Second Edition, Revised and Updated: 960 – 2030 AD", op.cit., p.35.
33. Zia Haq, "Govt plans major agri reforms post-corona", *Hindustan Times*, 03 May 2020, available at https://epaper.hindustantimes.com/Home/MShareArticle?Orgld= eabd5c14&imageview=0

34. John Farndon, "China Rises, How China's Astonishing Growth Will Change the World", *Thames Wharf Studios*, Rainville Road, London: Virgin Books Ltd, 2007, p. 81.
35. Richa Verma, "India Unclear How Many Villages It Has, And Why That Matters", *India Spend*, 03 August 2017,available at https://archive.indiaspend.com/cover-story/india-unclear-how-many-villages-it-has-and-why-that-matters-56076
36. Sanchita Sharma, "Covid vaccine development sees unparalleled progress", *Hindustan Times*, 08 May 2020, available at https://epaper.hindustantimes.com/Home/ShareArticle?OrgId=274a2daf&imageview=0
37. Ewen Callaway, "The Race for Coronavirus Vaccines", *Nature*, Vol. 580, No. 30 April 2020, available at https://media.nature.com/original/magazine-assets/d41586-020-01221-y/d41586-020-01221-y.pdf
38. Tiziana Celine, "COVID-19 Update: Pfizer's Coronavirus Vaccine Could Be Ready in the Autumn – Reports", *Tech Times*, 29 April 2020, available at https://www.techtimes. com/articles/249209/20200429/covid-19-update-coronavirus-vaccine-could-be-ready-in-the-autumn-says-pfizer.htm
39. Dave Roos, "How a New Vaccine Was Developed in Record Time in the 1960s", *History Stories*, 22 June 2020, available at https://www.history.com/news/mumps-vaccine-world-war-ii
40. R Sukumar, "Covid-19: What you need to know today", *Hindustan Times*, New Delhi, Saturday, 04 July 2020, p.2.
41. Himani Chandna, "How India can be a world leader in making Covid vaccine and keeping it cheap too", *The Print*, 06 May 2020, available at https://theprint.in/india/how-india-can-be-a-world-leader-in-making-covid-vaccine-and-keeping-it-cheap-too/414701/
42. R Sukumar, "Covid-19: What you need to know today", *Hindustan Times*, 08 May 2020, available at https://epaper.hindustantimes.com/Home/MShareArticle?Orgld= 4b6b6912&imageview=0
43. "India, a world leader in manufacturing vaccines, has a critical role to play in battle against coronavirus", *Times Now Digital*, 06 May 2020, available at https://www.timesnownews.com/india/article/india-a-world-leader-in-manufacturing-vaccines-has-a-critical-role-to-play-in-battle-against-coronavirus/588024
44. "Coronavirus Pandemic: Serum Institute plans to produce up to 6 crore doses of potential COVID-19 vaccine", *Jagran English*, 30 April 2020, available at https://english.jagran.com/lifestyle/coronavirus-pandemic-serum-institute-plans-to-produce-up-to-6-crore-doses-of-potential-covid19-vaccine-10011321
45. Himani Chandna, op.cit.
46. Times Now Digital, 06 May 2020, op.cit.
47. Rythma Kaul, "ICMR will develop indigenous vaccine - MAKE IN INDIA: Research body gives virus strain to Bharat Biotech", *Hindustan Times*, 10 May 2020, available at https://epaper.hindustantimes.com/Home/MShareArticle?Orgld=70c3b7c0 &imageview=0 ; and "Covid-19: ICMR joins hands with Bharat Biotech to develop indigenous coronavirus vaccine", *The Indian Express*, 10 May 2020, available at https://indianexpress.com/article/india/coronavirus-vaccine-india-covid-19-icmr-6402206/
48. Sanchita Sharma, "Bharat Biotech ties up with US varsity for Covid vaccine",

Hindustan Times, 21 May 2020, available at https://www.hindustantimes.com/india-news/bharat-biotech-ties-up-with-us-varsity-for-covid-vaccine/story-dyJPOzW2G2r Xcwsa9XV3tL.html

49. Rhythma Kaul, "Govt kick-starts talks to explore vaccine deal", *Hindustan Times*, 18 August 2020, available at https://epaper.hindustantimes.com/Home/MShareArticle?Orgld=18845adade6&imageview=0
50. Saubhadra Chatterji and Rhythma Kaul, "India eyes global front runners in vaccine plan", *Hindustan Times*, 17 August 2020, available at https://epaper.hindustan times.com/Home/MShareArticle?Orgld=17872f13a1f&image view=0
51. Rhythma Kaul, op.cit.
52. Amitabh Kant, "Enable Make in India to become the new normal, writes Amitabh Kant", *Hindustan Times*, 04 May 2020, available at https://www.hindustan times.com/analysis/enable-make-in-india-to-become-the-new-normal-writes-amitabh-kant/story-mfpm0Qc4hZCxGUNba655XO.html
53. Shruti Srivastava, "India to Boost Drug Ingredient Output to Pare China Reliance", *Bloomberg Quint*, 13 April 2020, available at https://www.bloombergquint.com/global-economics/india-to-boost-drug-ingredient-output-to-pare-china-s-dominance
54. Deepika Khurana and Dr. Sobuhi Iqbal, "Why India depends heavily on China for drug raw materials?", *Health Analytics Asia*, 3 January 2020, available at https://www.ha-asia.com/why-india-still-depends-on-apis-imported-from-china/
55. Malini Goyal, "How China beats India hollow in Trade and dominates Indian homes, markets and economy", *The Economic Times*, 16 July 2017, available at https://economictimes.indiatimes.com/news/economy/foreign-trade/china-dominates-indian-homes-markets-andeconomy-as-trade-deficit-widens/articleshow/59611452.cms
56. Dr K K Aggarwal, "An Opportunity for India", *India Legal*, 14 March 2020, available at https://www.indialegallive.com/top-news-of-the-day/news/an-opportunity-for-india-2-92384
57. Deepika Khurana and Dr. Sobuhi Iqbal, op.cit.
58. "India should reduce dependence on China for APIs, says industry insider", *European Pharmaceutical Review*, 13 March 2020, available at https://www.european pharmaceuticalreview.com/news/115163/india-should-reduce-dependence-on-china-for-apis-says-industry-insider/
59. Dr K K Aggarwal, op.cit.
60. Deepika Khurana and Dr. Sobuhi Iqbal, op.cit.
61. Shruti Srivastava, op.cit.
62. Ibid.
63. "India needs to build a manufacturing base for PPE and ventilators, says Amitabh Kant", *The Economic Times*, 01 April 2020, available at https://economictimes.indiatimes.com/industry/healthcare/biotech/healthcare/india-needs-to-build-a-manufacturing-base-for-ppe-and-ventilators-says-amitabh-kant/articleshow/74938964.cms?from=mdr
64. Shwweta Punj, "India Inc joins coronavirus war | *India Today* Insight", *India Today*, 03 April 2020, available at https://www.indiatoday.in/web-exclusive/story/india-inc-joins-coronavirus-war-1663076-2020-04-03

65. Sudhi Ranjan Sen, "Modi govt wants defence firms to make medical equipment to fight coronavirus", *The Print*, 17 April 2020, available at https://theprint.in/india/modi-govt-wants-defence-firms-to-make-medical-equipment-to-fight-coronavirus/403462/
66. Surojit Gupta, "Covid-19: 'Make in India' push for ventilators, PPEs", *Times of India*, 05 April 2020, available at https://timesofindia.indiatimes.com/india/covid-19-make-in-india-push-for-ventilators-ppes/articleshow/74988501.cms
67. Shwweta Punj, op.cit.
68. Aman Rawat, "Ventilators, Masks & PPE Suits: Here's How DRDO Is Taking On Covid-19", *Inc42*, 04 April 2020, available at https://inc42.com/buzz/ventilators-masks-ppe-suits-heres-how-drdo-is-taking-on-covid-19/
69. Mayank Singh, "To help fight COVID-19, Indian Navy's innovation will allow Oxygen cylinder to support multiple patients", *The New Indian Express*, 31 March 2020, available at https://www.newindianexpress.com/nation/2020/mar/31/to-help-fight-covid-19-indian-navy-innovates-oxygen-cylinder-to-support-multiple-patients-2123616.html
70. Shwweta Punj, op.cit.
71. "'Mission Self-Reliant India': COVID-19 crisis opportunity, says PM Modi as he announces Rs 20 lakh crore package", *DNA*, 12 May 2020, available at https://www.dnaindia.com/india/report-mission-self-reliant-india-covid-19-crisis-opportunity-says-pm-modi-as-he-announces-rs-20-lakh-crore-package-2824591
72. C P Gurnani, "Covid 19 is writing a New World Order" *Economic Times*, 25 March 2020, available at https://economictimes.indiatimes.com/blogs/et-commentary/covid-19-is-writing-a-new-world-order/
73. "Make in India", India Brand Equity Foundation (IBEF), available at https://www.ibef.org/economy/make-in-india
74. "Make in India: The Vision, New Processes, Sectors, Infrastructure and Mindset", available at https://www.makeinindia.com/article/-/v/make-in-india-reason-vision-for-the-initiative
75. "Trade War: Why manufacturers are not rushing into India, Indonesia", *The Economic Times*, 07 October 2019, op.cit.
76. Ruchi Sachan and Aditya Bordalai, "Boosting India's manufacturing prowess post COVID-19 crisis", *North East Now*, 29 April 2020, available at https://nenow.in/opinion/boosting-indias-manufacturing-prowess-post-covid-19-crisis.html
77. Ibid.
78. Harsh V Shringla, "How India has responded to the global pandemic", *Hindustan Times*, 08 July 2020, available at https://epaper.hindustantimes.com/Home/MShareArticle?Orgld=8733bc0f2a&imageview=0
79. "Team of scientists begin work on ways to revive Indian economy after Covid crisis", *Hindustan Times*, 21 April 2020, available at https://www.hindustantimes.com/india-news/team-of-scientists-begin-work-on-ways-to-revive-indian-economy-after-covid-crisis/story-Z7yTOq1RI8kRwQWp0vSaQK.html
80. Rajeev Jayaswal, "Once lockdown ends, govt plans Make in India boost", *Hindustan Times*, 28 April 2020, available at https://www.hindustantimes.com/india-news/once-lockdown-ends-govt-plans-make-in-india-boost/story-5CPKUtHTeQau4sK8GPg8zN.html

81. Ibid.
82. Zia Haq, Saubhadra Chatterji and Smriti Kak Ramachandran, "Some states put freeze on labour laws to get business going", *Hindustan Times*, 09 May 2020, available at https://www.hindustantimes.com/india-news/some-states-freeze-labour-laws/story-6JMELEPdIugsHt8YjQT5vN.html
83. Zia Haq, "States' labour law changes under central govt scanner", *Hindustan Times*, 01 June 2020, available at https://epaper.hindustantimes.com/Home/MShareArticle?OrgId=16b0e39467&imageview=0
84. Zia Haq, Saubhadra Chatterji and Smriti Kak Ramachandran, op.cit.
85. Sreemoy Talukdar, "COVID-19 crisis puts China's monopoly of global supply chains in focus, but presumptions of India benefitting are misguided, here's why", *First Post*, 04 May 2020, available at https://www.firstpost.com/health/covid-19-crisis-puts-chinas-global-monopoly-in-sharp-focus-but-presumptions-of-india-benefitting-are-misguided-heres-why-8327971.html
86. Manisha Mirchandani, "Reducing Global Supply Chain Reliance on China Won't Be Easy", *Brink News*, 22 April 2020, available at https://www.brinknews.com/coronavirus-global-supply-chain-reliance-china-manufacturers-economic-recession-risk/
87. Ibid.
88. "The impact of Covid-19 on global supply chains", *Transport Economic News*, 24 April 2020, available at https://oxfordbusinessgroup.com/news/impact-covid-19-global-supply-chains
89. "COVID-19 pandemic: USIBC", *Economic Times*, 14 April 2020, available at https://economictimes.indiatimes.com/news/economy/finance/india-has-opportunity-to-build-a-more-resilient-and-diverse-economy-after-covid-19-pandemic-usibc/articleshow/75139553.cms
90. Deepto Roy, "Covid-19 exposes Indian industries supply chain vulnerabilities", *The Hindu Business Line*, 01 April 2020, available at https://www.thehindubusinessline.com/opinion/covid-19-exposes-indian-industrys-supply-chain-vulnerabilities/article31224928.ece
91. Shariq Khan, "A $163 billion industry struggles to reduce its dependency on Chinese imports", *Economic Times*, 06 April 2020, available at https://economictimes.indiatimes.com/small-biz/sme-sector/a-163-billion-industry-struggles-to-reduce-its-dependency-on-chinese-imports/articleshow/74942617.cms?from=mdr
92. Shariq Khan and Neha Dewan, "Trade in the time of Coronavirus: Sectors overdependent on Chinese imports face a grim reality", *Economic Times*, 27 February 2020, available at https://economictimes.indiatimes.com/small-biz/sme-sector/trade-in-the-time-of-coronavirus-sectors-overdependent-on-chinese-imports-face-a-grim-reality/articleshow/74312184.cms
93. Deepto Roy, op.cit.
94. Kaushika Madhavan, "Opinion | Reset your supply chains", *Livemint*, 24 April 2020, available at https://www.livemint.com/opinion/online-views/opinion-india-has-fared-better-than-others-against-coronavirus-11587718662417.html
95. Ibid.
96. Anchita Ghosh, "How tech firms are helping build robust local supply chains amid Covid-19", *Business Standard*, 19 April 2020, available at https://

www.business-standard.com/article/technology/how-tech-firms-are-helping-build-robust-local-supply-chains-amid-covid-19-120041900767_1.html

97. Soumyarendra Barik, "Government invites applications for solutions for kirana stores to take and deliver orders online", *Medianama*, 24 April 2020, available at https://www.medianama.com/2020/04/223-dpiit-kirana-stores-online-delivery/
98. Brigadier (Dr.) Rajeev Bhutani, *Rise of China: 2030 and Its Strategic Implications*, op.cit., pp. 78-79.
99. Dennis C. Blair and Keith Alexander, China's Intellectual Property Theft Must Stop, *The New York Times*, 15 August 2017, available at https://www.nytimes.com/2017/08/15/opinion/china-us-intellectual-property-trump.html
100. Jane Cai and Keegan Elmer, Is the US right to cry foul about forced technology transfer to do business in China – and what is Beijing's position?, *South China Morning Post*, 10 January 2019, available at https://www.scmp.com/news/china/diplomacy/article/2181528/us-right-cry-foul-about-forced-technology-transfer-do-business
101. "Railways To Invest Rs 9,800 Crore In Mumbai-Ahmedabad Bullet Train Project, Construction Begins In 2018", *India Times*, 15 February 2016, available at https://www.indiatimes.com/news/india/railways-to-invest-rs-9-800-crore-in-mumbai-ahmedabad-bullet-train-project-construction-begins-in-2018_-250734.html
102. Borge Brende, "India's opportunity and role in shaping the Fourth Industrial Revolution", 10 April 2018, available at https://www.narendramodi.in/reflections/india-s-opportunity-and- role-in-shaping-the-fourth-industrial-revolution-42/
103. Roberto Bocca, "As coronavirus shocks the energy sector and economy, is now the time for a new energy order?", *World Economic Forum*, 26 April 2020, available at https://www.weforum.org/agenda/2020/04/energy-oil-gas-electricity-sustainability-economy-covid19-coronavirus-pandemic-market-stability/
104. Mayank Aggarwal, "The Covid-19 pandemic is an opportunity for India to pursue clean energy more aggressively", *Quartz India*, 20 April 2020, available at https://qz.com/india/1841174/coronavirus-is-indias-chance-to-pursue-clean-energy-aggressively/
105. Ibid.
106. Bhasker Tripathy, "How India can make its economic recovery clean, sustainable post Covid-19", *Business Standard*, 09 May 2020, available at https://www.business-standard.com/article/economy-policy/how-india-can-make-its-economic-recovery-clean-sustainable-post-covid-19-120050901116_1.html
107. "How embracing renewable energy can help India achieve its target of becoming a $5 trillion economy by 2024-25", *Economic Times*, 18 May 2020, available at https://economictimes.indiatimes.com/small-biz/productline/power-generation/how-embracing-renewable-energy-can-help-india-achieve-its-target-of-becoming-a-5-trillion-economy-by-2024-25/articleshow/74668710.cms
108. Bhasker Tripathy, op.cit.
109. "How embracing renewable energy can help India achieve its target of becoming a $5 trillion economy by 2024-25", *Economic Times*, 18 May 2020, op.cit.
110. "Today United Nations is less credible than its history," says MEA S Jaishankar", *HW English*, 15 February 2020, available at https://hwnews.in/international/

today-united-nations-is-less-credible-than-its-history-says-mea-s-jaishankar/125721

111. Indrani Bagchi, "The current world disorder: For the post-coronavirus world, we will need to reinvent multilateralism", *The Times of India*, 09 April 2020, available at https://timesofindia.indiatimes.com/blogs/Globespotting/the-current-world-disorder-for-the-post-coronavirus-world-we-will-need-to-reinvent-multilateralism/
112. Courtney J. Fung and Shing-Hon Lam *The Washington Post*, "China leads four of the 15 U.N. specialized agencies and is aiming for a fifth", *Eagle.com*, 03 March 2020, available at https://www.theeagle.com/opinion/columnists/china-leads-four-of-the-u-n-specialized-agencies-and/article_d0272d67-6f93-53d1-a0b0-0312d4c056a3.html
113. Kimberly Dozier, "China Wins: Why Trump's WHO Funding Cut is a Gift to Beijing", *MSN News*, 16 April 2020, available at https://www.msn.com/en-in/news/opinion/china-wins-why-trumps-who-funding-cut-is-a-gift-to-beijing/ar-BB12IdVG
114. "India will play greater role in new world order post coronavirus: Ram Madhav", *Livemint*, 03 May 2020, available at https://www.livemint.com/news/india/india-will-play-greater-role-in-new-world-order-post-coronavirus-ram-madhav-11588443183993.html
115. Mohamed Zeeshan, "Can India Organize Post-COVID–19 Global Action?", *The Diplomat*, 07 April 2020, available at https://thediplomat.com/2020/04/can-india-organize-post-covid-19-global-action/
116. "PM pitches for new crisis management protocol at G-20 video conference on coronavirus", *The Economic Times*, 26 March 2020, available at https://economictimes. indiatimes.com/news/politics-and-nation/pm-pitches-for-new-crisis-management-protocol-at-g-20-video-conference-on-coronavirus/articleshow/74835492.cms
117. Ram Madhav, "Covid-19 and the contours of a new world order | Analysis", *Hindustan Times*, 14 April 2020, available at https://www.hindustantimes.com/analysis/covid-19-and-the-contours-of-a-new-world-order-analysis/story-DUqursm0t8sunJl1gaBJmO.html

Chapter 8: Self-Reliant India

1. "Full text of Prime Minister Narendra Modi's speech on May 12, 2020", *Free Press Journal*, 13 May 2020, available at https://www.freepressjournal.in/india/full-text-of-prime-minister-narendra-modis-speech-on-may-12-2020
2. Ibid.
3. "PM gives a clarion call for Atmanirbhar Bharat", PIB, Delhi, 12 May 2020, available at https://pib.gov.in/PressReleasePage.aspx?PRID=1623391
4. Sridhar Kundu, "At least 23 million migrants are returning to India's villages. Can the rural economy keep up?" *Indiaspend.com*, 25 May 2020, available at https://scroll.in/article/962804/at-least-23-million-migrants-are-returning-to-indias-villages-can-the-rural-economy-keep-up
5. Abraham Thomas, "Migrant workers must be sent home in 15 days, says Supreme Court", *Hindustan Times*, 10 June 2020, available at https://www.hindustan

times.com/india-news/migrant-workers-must-be-sent-home-in-15-days-says-supreme-court/story-YQsRZroVIJFzUdw2GaTgCL.html

6. Abhishek Behl, "Labour crisis forces industries to woo migrants with better pay", *Hindustan Times*, New Delhi / Gurugram, Tuesday, 09 June 2020, p.3.; and Srinivasa Rao Apparasu, Urvashi Dev Rawal and Aneesha Sareen Kumar, "Firms make efforts to bring back migrants, restart work", *Hindustan Times*, New Delhi / Gurugram, Thursday, 11 June 2020, p.4.
7. Mark Tully, "Create Opportunities for Migrants Back Home", *Hindustan Times*, 06 June 2020, available at https://www.hindustantimes.com/columns/create-opportunities-for-migrants-back-home/story-uJgKvlXueiQaGb9PD25UuM.html
8. "UP govt. decided to provide employment to skilled and training to unskilled migrants: Navneet Sehgal", Uttar Pradesh, 07 June 2020, available at https://www.skill reporter.com/2020/06/regional/uttar-pradesh/up-govt-decided-to-provide-employment-to-skilled-and-training-to-unskilled-migrants-navneet-sehgal/
9. "Marshall Plan", *History.com editors*, 16 December 2009 (updated 5 June 2020), available at https://www.history.com/topics/world-war-ii/marshall-plan-1
10. "Boom & Bust cycles, the New Deal, and the financial crisis of 2008", available at https://www.hyperhistory.com/online_n2/connections_n2/bust1.html
11. "SAGARMALA – Building Gateways of Growth", Ministry of Shipping, Government of India, National Perspective Plan, April 2016, p.7. available at http://sagarmala.gov.in/sites/default/files/5457695312te1.pdf
12. Meera Siva, "All you wanted to know about Sagarmala", *The Hindu*, 24 May 2016, available at https://www.thehindubusinessline.com/opinion/columns/all-you-wanted-to-know-aboutsagarmala/article8640858.ece
13. M K Rasgotra and Vishnu Kirpalani, "India can recover from the recession. Here is a plan | Analysis", *Hindustan Times*, 28 May 2020, available at https://www.hindustan times.com/analysis/india-can-recover-from-the-recession-here-is-a-plan/story-0nMRX6OS97wHDoNJllRziK.html
14. "Industrial Corridors", Press Information Bureau, Government of India, Ministry of Commerce & Industry, 20 November 2019, available at https://pib.gov.in/Pressreleaseshare.aspx?PRID=1592382
15. Samuel Sherraden, "Putting China's Low Household Consumption in Perspective", New America Foundation's World Economic Roundtable, 15 March 2011, pp.1-3., available at http://roundtable.newamerica.net/blogposts/2011/
16. Ravi Agrawal and Kathryn Salam, "South Asia Used to Be the World's Fastest Growing Region. Now It's Facing an Economic Slowdown", *Foreign Policy*, 15 October 2019, available at https://foreignpolicy.com/2019/10/15/south-asia-used-to-be-the-worlds-fastest-growing-region-now-its-facing-an-economic-slowdown-world-bank-report-india-gdp-consumption-narendra-modi-kashmir-internet-blackout-pakistan-imran-khan/
17. Roshan Kishore, "Boosting demand key for economic revival", *Hindustan Times*, 08 June 2020, available at https://www.hindustantimes.com/india-news/boosting-demand-key-for-economic-revival/story-HVPcub0YRt5drpDDuQWGQN.html
18. Niranjan Rajadhyaksha, "Opinion | The covid shock could alter people's financial

priorities", *Livemint*, 05 May 2020, available at https://www.livemint.com/opinion/columns/the-covid-shock-could-alter-people-s-financial-priorities-11588695737275. html

19. Roshan Kishore, op.cit.
20. Karthik Muralidharan, "Universal income may aid India's economic recovery", *Hindustan Times*, 09 June 2020, available at https://epaper.hindustantimes.com/Home/MShareArticle?Orgld=961048b4b9&imageview=0
21. "Government actively considering universal basic income, NHRC tells U.N.", *The Hindu*, 11 June 2020, available at https://www.thehindu.com/news/national/govt-actively-considering-universal-basic-income-nhrc-tells-un/article31805107.ece
22. Brigadier (Dr.) Rajeev Bhutani, *Rise of China: 2030 and Its Strategic Implications*, Pentagon Press, New Delhi, 2015, p.106.
23. Loren Brandt et.al. (2008), "China's Great Transformation", China's Great Transformation, Cambridge: Cambridge University Press, p.13.
24. Thomas G. Rawski, et.al., (2008), "China's Industrial Development", China's Great Transformation, Cambridge: Cambridge University Press, p.593.
25. "Global crude steel output increases by 4.6% in 2018", World Steel Association, 25 January 2019, available at https://www.worldsteel.org/media-centre/press-releases/2019/Global-crude-steel-output-increases-by-4.6—in-2018.html
26. Joseph Kahn and Mark Landler, "China Grabs West's Smoke-Spewing Factories", *New York Times*, 21 December 2007, available at https://www.nytimes.com/2007/12/21/world/asia/21transfer.html
27. Mark Suzman, "India is key to the global battle against Covid-19", *Hindustan Times*, New Delhi/Gurugram, Wednesday, 17 June 2020, p.10.
28. Ritu Kumar, "It is time to tap potential of handicrafts and textiles", *Hindustan Times*, New Delhi/Gurugram, Tuesday, 16 June 2020, p.10.
29. Vishal Chawla, "Why has India lagged behind in Semiconductor Chip Manufacturing?", *Analytics India Magazine*, 21 August 2019, available at https://analyticsindiamag.com/india-semiconductor-chip-manufacturing/
30. "USCC Report: China's Program for S&T Modernization 2011", op. cit., pp. 63-64; and "China's 21st Century", *Business Herald*, 21 March 2009 giving details of Project 909.
31. "Does size matter? Understanding Wafer Size", *anysilicon*, 23 October 2012, available at https://anysilicon.com/does-size-matter-understanding-wafer-size/
32. Zen Soo and Meng Jing, "How China is still paying the price for squandering its chance to build a home-grown semiconductor industry", *South China Morning Post*, 28 August 2019, available at https://www.scmp.com/tech/big-tech/article/3024687/how-china-still-paying-price-squandering-its-chance-build-home-grown
33. Dr. Milind Thomas Themalil, "Semiconductor Chip Designing Strategic Necessity for India", *Data Quest India*, 7 April 2020, available at https://www.dqindia.com/semiconductor-chip-designing-strategic-necessity-india/
34. "Full text of Prime Minister Narendra Modi's speech on May 12, 2020", *Free Press Journal*, 13 May 2020, op.cit.
35. "LG Electronics", available at https://en.wikipedia.org/wiki/LG_Electronics
36. "Red Bull", available at https://en.wikipedia.org/wiki/Red_Bull

37. "Full text of Prime Minister Narendra Modi's speech on May 12, 2020", *Free Press Journal*, 13 May 2020, op.cit.
38. Iliana Magra, "Europe Suffers Heat Wave of Dangerous, Record-High Temperatures", *The New York Times*, 24 July 2019, available at https://www.nytimes.com/2019/07/24/world/europe/record-temperatures-heatwave.html
39. Sudha Ramachandran, "The Indian Foreign Service: Worthy of an Emerging Power?", *The Diplomat*, 12 July 2013, available at https://thediplomat.com/2013/07/the-indian-foreign-service-worthy-of-an-emerging-power/

Chapter 9: Conclusion

1. Rajeev Jayaswal, "Fiscal Cost of Package Rs.1.5L-cr to Rs.4L-cr", *Hindustan Times*, 17 May 2020, op.cit.
2. N K Ganguly, "Covid-19: The search for a vaccine", *Hindustan Times*, 15 May 2020, available at https://epaper.hindustantimes.com/Home/MShareArticle?Orgld=83ae 98c6&imageview=0
3. Jamie Mullick, "India posts its second million in just 21 days", *Hindustan Times*, New Delhi, Friday, 07 August 2020; and Rhythma Kaul, "Daily tests up to 700k, 1 million target in sight", *Hindustan Times*, New Delhi, Monday, 10 August 2020. (Antigen tests were rolled out on 14 June 2020. An antigen is a protein (in this case present on the virus) that induces an immune response in the human body in the form of production of antibodies against a disease, and detecting its presence through an antigen-based test determines a present infection. An antigen test, also known as a rapid test, has become popular with many governments as it offers tests within an hour as opposed to the RT-PCR tests whose results reach the subject after 24 to 48 hours. Since the former can possibly lead to false negatives, several cases can slide under the radar. But it can be used in small areas of hot spots to test every resident and quickly isolate as many patients as possible. In contrast, the real-time reverse transcription polymerase chain reaction (rRT-PCR) test is considered the gold standard to diagnose COVID-19. It is used for the detection of nucleic acid from SARS-CoV-2 in throat swabs taken from suspected patients and detects the genetic signature of the virus. In case of antigen tests, ICMR guidelines say, all symptomatic negative cases have to be confirmed through an rRT-PCR test to rule out a false negative.)
4. Rhythma Kaul, "At 650k, India closes in on 1mn daily tests target", *Hindustan Times*, New Delhi/Gurugram, Saturday, 01 August 2020, pp. 1-18.
5. "PM pitches NCR model for 10 hardest hit states", *Hindustan Times*, 12 August 2020, available at https://epaper.hindustantimes.com/Home/ShareArticle?Orgld=128c9055 baa&imageview=0
6. Rhythma Kaul, "India tests a million people in one day", *Hindustan Times*, 23 August 2020, available at https://epaper.hindustantimes.com/Home/MShareArticle?Orgld=2385652f000&imageview=0
7. "Coronavirus Update Live", *Worldometer*, 01 September 2020, available at https://www.worldometers.info/coronavirus/ (accessed on 01 September 2020).
8. Jamie Mullick, "Coronavirus: Has 3rd curve flattening begun?", *Hindustan Times*, 12 August 2020, available at https://www.hindustantimes.com/india-news/has-3rd-curve-flattening-begun/story-WSTrirfCGSQ5eCmKIqK5XO.html

9. R Sukumar, "Covid-19: What you need to know today", *Hindustan Times*, 11 July 2020, available at https://epaper.hindustantimes.com/Home/ShareArticle?Orgld =1179cc7a 72e&imageview=0
10. R Sukumar, "Covid-19: What you need to know today", *Hindustan Times*, New Delhi, Tuesday, 18 July 2020.
11. Apoorva Mandavilli, "You May Have Antibodies After Coronavirus Infection. But Not for Long.", *The New York Times*, 18 June 2020, available at https://www.nytimes.com/2020/06/18/health/coronavirus-antibodies.html
12. R Sukumar, "Covid-19: What you need to know today", *Hindustan Times*, 20 June 2020, available at https://www.hindustantimes.com/india-news/covid-19-what-you-need-to-know-today/story-NuDekdyvSdzlMh1eFNY8xJ.html
13. "Coronavirus: When will the second wave of infections hit?", *dw.com*, 14 May 2020, available at https://www.dw.com/en/coronavirus-when-will-the-second-wave-of-infections-hit/a-53435135
14. Sunetra Choudhury, "Covid deaths low, green shoots in economy: Modi", *Hindustan Times*, New Delhi/Gurugram, Wednesday, 17 June 2020, p.1.
15. "English rendering of PM's opening remarks during Interaction with Chief Ministers on Covid-19", *PIB*, Delhi, 16 June 2020, available at https://pib.gov.in/PressRelease Page.aspx?PRID=1631905
16. Samrat Sharma, "Modi's five 'I's to make India self-reliant economy; tells industry to 'trust me', govt is supporting you", *Financial Express*, 2 June 2020, available at https://www.financialexpress.com/economy/modis-five-is-to-make-india-self-reliant-economy-tells-industry-to-trust-me-govt-is-supporting-you/1978615/
17. Vivek Raghuvanshi, "India announces ban on 101 imported arms. Who benefits, and who loses out?", *Defense News*, 13 August, 2020, available at https://www.defense news.com/global/asia-pacific/2020/08/13/india-announces-ban-on-101-imported-arms-who-benefits-and-who-loses-out/

ANNEXURE

SAGARMALA: National Perspective Plan

415 Projects; US$123 billion (2015–2025)

KEY OBJECTIVES

1. PORT MODERNISATION & NEW PORT DEVELOPMENT
189 Projects; US $ 21 Billion
(Devp. 6 new ports)
2. PORT CONNECTIVITY ENHANCEMENT
170 Projects; US $ 35 Billion
(111 Inland Waterways)
3. PORT LINKED INDUSTRIALISATION
(14 CEZs ALIGNED TO INDUSTRIAL CORRIDORS)
33 Projects; US $ 65 Billion
Boost exports from $ 465 Billion (2014-15)
to $ 900 Billion (2020)
4. COASTAL COMMUNITY DEVELOPMENT
23 Projects; US $ 648 Million
(Skill Devp., Cold chain Devp. etc.)

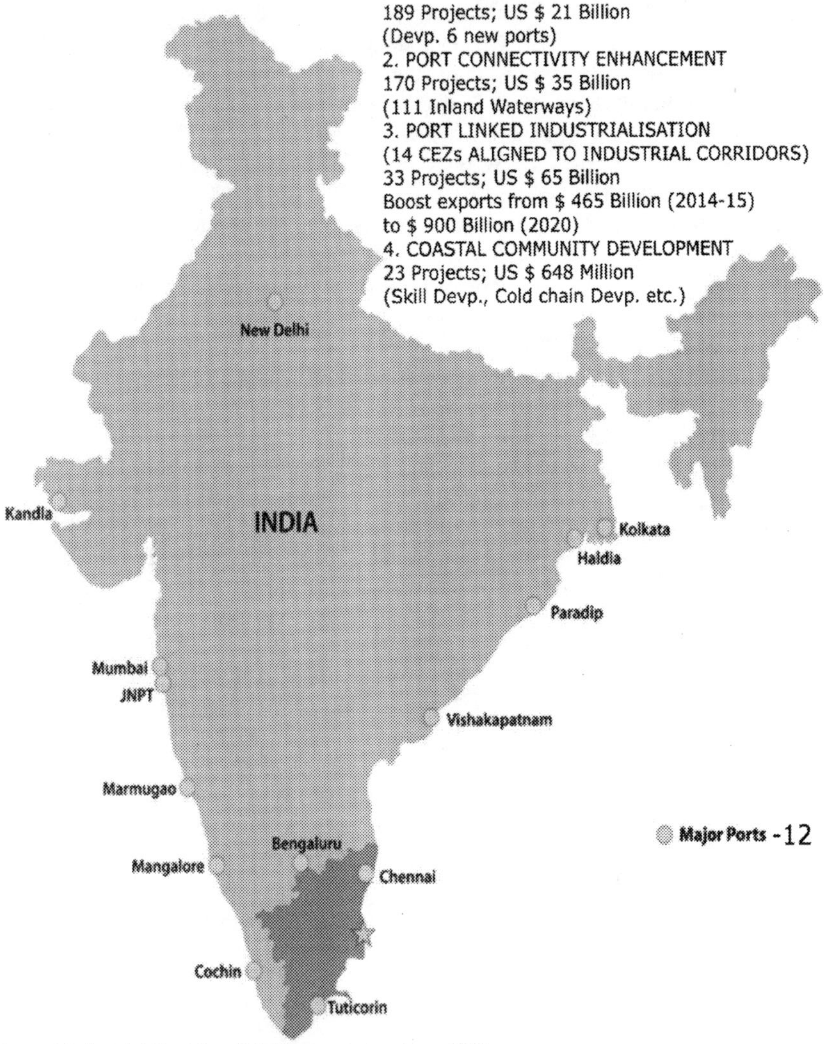

Planned Industrial Corridors (IC)/Economic Corridors (EC):
Delhi - Mumbai IC (DMIC) - 1504 km
Bengaluru - Mumbai EC (BMEC) - 1,000 km
Chennai - Bengaluru IC (CBIC) - 560 km
Vizag - Chennai IC [Ph 1 of East Coast EC (ECEC)] - 800 km
Amritsar-Kolkata IC (AKIC) - 1,839 km

Index